PROFESSIONAL COMMUNICATION AND REMEDIAL ENGLISH

PROFESSIONAL COMMUNICATION AND REMEDIAL ENGLISH

By

Prof. Sadhana Gupta

Principal

Govt. Degree College for Women

Udhampur

(J & K)

UNIVERSITY SCIENCE PRESS

(An Imprint of Laxmi Publications Pvt. Ltd.)

BANGALORE • CHENNAI • COCHIN • GUWAHATI • HYDERABAD
JALANDHAR • KOLKATA • LUCKNOW • MUMBAI • RANCHI

NEW DELHI • BOSTON, USA

Published by :
UNIVERSITY SCIENCE PRESS
(An Imprint of Laxmi Publications Pvt. Ltd.)
113, Golden House, Daryaganj,
New Delhi-110002

Phone : 011-43 53 25 00
Fax : 011-43 53 25 28

www.laxmipublications.com
info@laxmipublications.com

Price : **₹ 195.00** *Only.*

First Edition : 2013

OFFICES

Bangalore	080-26 75 69 30	**Chennai**	044-24 34 47 26
Cochin	0484-237 70 04, 405 13 03	**Guwahati**	0361-251 36 69
Hyderabad	040-24 65 23 33	**Jalandhar**	0181-222 12 72
Kolkata	033-22 27 43 84	**Lucknow**	0522-220 99 16
Mumbai	022-24 91 54 15, 24 92 78 69	**Ranchi**	0651-220 44 64

UPC–9676–195–PROF COMM REM ENGLISH-GUP

C—5594/012/09

Typeset at : ABRO Enterprises, Delhi.

Printed at : Giri Raj Offset Press, Delhi

Dedicated to
My Late Father
Dr. Satyapal Gupta
Who lived the whole life for others
(My humble tributes to the great soul)

Contents

Foreword

It gives me immense pleasure to write this Foreword to Mrs. Sadhana Gupta's book on "Professional Communication". I am confident that this book will be very useful not only to the students but also for the faculty members and the personnel involved in Corporate Communications.

In the today's age of globalized economies, multinational companies and liberal governments, the importance of Corporate Communications cannot be overemphasized. Proper communication not only helps to fulfill the purpose for which it is made, but also helps build the positive corporate image as well as the brand identity. The present book has made an attempt to instill the sense of corporate communication in its readers in a very simplified manner making this book amenable even to the students who are not very adept in the English Language. The topics and sub-topics have been arranged in proper sequence, making easy the process of step-by-step learning. The examples narrated in the book are very practical and cover wide range of ideas and thoughts. The vocabulary used is also simple, which enhances its receptivity and assimilation.

With her long teaching experience, Mrs. Sadhana Gupta has been amply successful to present a book that is very simple and yet very useful. I hope that the complete gamut of readers, ranging from students of professional courses to the professionals themselves, will be adequately benefited by the book.

D.P. Singh
Vice Chancellor
Banaras Hindu University
Varanasi-221005

Preface

The first edition of "communication skills and functional grammar", having been sold out demonstrated amply the usefulness of that book and the interest shown by the readers gave confidence to write this book on" Professional communication and Remedial English" which has series of connections with the earlier book. With the inflow of large number of multinational companies and Government policy of liberalization, the Professional communication is bound to gain importance. Taking this opportunity, an attempt has been made to make this book plain and simple with maximum distinctive coverage possible.

With the changing circumstances and the corporates attempting to recognize brand identities, the corporate communication is gaining value worldwide. It is hard to assume a corporate life in which there is absolutely no communication. Professional communication works as a chain between an organization and its public. It helps to brighten corporate presence, its existence and reputation, preserve long term image and brand identity. Good corporate style demands an effective process for communication and gives birth to transparency and accountability.

Whereas, the primary goal of Professional communication does not change *i.e.,* it communicates information to all concerned but there are other dimensions to it. It highlights positive corporate image. It is not only restricted to marketing or human resources or public relation departments but the emphasis is on all the staff members from top to bottom *i.e.,* from mail room to board room. After all it affects the profitability.

The subject matter is very vast and calls for written and oral conversation and cannot be represented in a small book like the present one but efforts have been made not to neglect the broad features. In a book of this type written in the midst of growing technology, errors and omissions are inevitable for which the author craves the indulgence of her readers. The author will acknowledge her work to be fully repaid if this book serves, even in small part, the objective in which it has been written.

—Author

Acknowledgement

I wish to express my sincere gratitude to my Gurudev Param Pujya Sh. Chandra Swami Ji (Sadhana Kendra Ashram, Domet, Dehradun) who gave me spiritual courage to take up the task of writing "Professional Communication and Remedial English" and made me capable of completing this project. My sincere thanks to my beloved mother, Smt. Raj Gupta for the inspiration, encouragement and blessings which she showered abundantly. I wish to avail myself of this opportunity to express a sense of gratitude and love to my husband Mr. B.B. Gupta and my beloved children Alok and Divya for their guidance, manual, intellectual and emotional support, strength and for everything. Last but not least my special thanks to Lakshmi Publication for its kind co-operation.

—Author

Unit I
Basics of Technical Communication

Chapter 1

TECHNICAL COMMUNICATION—INTRODUCTION

"Communication Works for those who Work at it." —**John Powell**

INTRODUCTION

Communication is the process of understanding and being understood through gesture, language, thoughts and expressions. The importance of good communication lies in how well we have been understood and not on how well we say. The word communication is derived from the Latin word *'Communicare'* which means to impart to share.

Communication is the process of exchanging information and ideas. The information is transmitted through a common system of symbols, signs, behaviour, speech, writing or signals. Human communication refers to the social interaction of sharing information for the purpose of understanding and social connection. Communication happens at many levels, in many different ways and for all beings. Whenever communication takes place, an information is conveyed. The information may be shaped in number of ways. A message is conveyed through the use of medias which can be a written text, a picture, a speech, a gesture or a computer or even expressions. The message thus conveyed takes some form which reveals the order, amount and kind of information presented to audience. The shaping of information according to the requirement is "TECHNICAL COMMUNICATION".

TECHNICAL COMMUNICATION

My neighbour bought a microwave oven last year. The oven stopped working in a week's time. The grilling adjustment was not performed by her due to misunderstanding of the manufacture's instructions. This is an example of poor communication. According to the Oxford English Dictionary "Communicate is to succeed in conveying information".

We have a product or service, it may be a tool, device, software, anything that is used. Somehow we have to get the information on how to use the product or how to put the details into practice. Professional communicators are the bridge builders between the product and the user. We live in a world where majority of our functions depend on technology. Whether we are using household appliances, doing business negotiations, operating our banks, working on computers or going for shopping, we are affected by technologies. The modern workplace depends on technology so much that Technical Communication is also called as Business, Professional or Work Place Communication. Communication is an essential ingredient for the success and quality of any product, service or business. It involves scientific and technical knowledge of the subject and an understanding of how we communicate.

Definition of Technical Communication

"Technical communication is the process of conveying technical information through writing, speech and other mediums to a specific audience about a specific domain. Technical domain can be of any kind including the soft and hard sciences, high technology including computer and software, consumer electronics and business processes and practices. Information is usable if the intended audience can perform an action or make a decision based on it."

—(From Wikipedia, the free encyclopedia)

❑❑❑

Chapter 2

FEATURES OF TECHNICAL COMMUNICATION

"To effectively communicate, we must realize that we are all different in the way we perceive the world and use this understanding as a guide to our communication with others."

—Anthony Robbins

FEATURES OF TECHNICAL COMMUNICATION

1. Technical communication is tailored to the specific needs of the audience. It is created, drafted, tested and revised according to their needs.
2. Technical communication focuses on the subject, not the writer or the speaker. It is the product of a writer or speaker who has a systematic understanding of the scientific and technical subjects and effectively transmits his information.
3. Technical communication supplies the right information at the right time at the right level of detail. The information development is a process in which the communicator refines the information so that it is conveyed in a right manner to the receiver. This way a message is created which matches a given purpose, audience and medium.
4. Technical communication involves many people working together. It is not the domain of a single communicator. The information is needed to perform a task, answer a question, solve a problem or make a decision because information is to be used for a definite need and purpose.
5. Technical communication conveys one meaning only, it allows only one interpretation.

6. Technical communication is denotative, descriptive, multidimensional, dynamic and interactive. It is not passive since technical communicator is expected to actively engage himself in gathering and developing information for better understanding of the subject.
7. Technical communication is required in e-mails, business and official letters, reports, proposals, brochures, news letters, resume's, websites, user manuals, technical descriptions, journals, seminars etc.

CHARACTERISTICS OF EFFECTIVE TECHNICAL COMMUNICATION

1. **Clarity**. Understandable.
2. **Professional appearance**. Format, design and print of the document.
3. **Accuracy**. Factual, correct, unbiased.
4. **Conciseness**. Without any wordiness, repetition or details.
5. **Correctness**. Conventions of grammar, punctuation, spelling and usage.
6. **Accessibility.** Headings, indexes, table of contents.
7. **Comprehensive**. All necessary information included.
8. **Appropriate**. Related to the topic.

POINTS TO REMEMBER

1. Technical communication focuses on the subject.
2. Need is definite. It consists of reporting specialised information.
3. It is for the practical use.
4. It conveys one meaning only.
5. It is at the technical level.
6. It is understood by the specific audience.
7. It involves the systematic understanding of the subject.
8. Information will stay fresh if it is valuable, valid and credible.
9. Know your audience and base your information on their specific needs, preferences, environment and background.
10. Understand the macro and micro-structure of the content.
11. Wherever possible, use active voice because it creates a direct and concise message.

❑❑❑

Chapter **3**

TECHNICAL WRITING

"Think like a wise man, but communicate in the language of people."

—W.B. Yeats

TECHNICAL WRITING

The most commonly used form of technical communication is technical writing. Technical writing includes project proposals, memos, manuals, user's guides, technical reports, journals, articles, business and official letters, minutes of the meeting, notices, agendas etc.

Good technical writing presents information in a clear manner so that it is clearly understood by the intended audience. Effective communication requires quality, content, language, proper format. Good technical writing should be concise, precise and in a language the user understands. Follow the following principles, while indulging in technical writing so that the communication is clear, to the point and easier to understand.

1. Use Simple Vocabulary

Use simple words, avoid inflated diction. While a large vocabulary is useful, try to avoid inflated diction if a simpler phrase works equally well.

AVOID	USE
Cognizant of	aware of, knows
Facilitate	help
Impact on	affect
Implement	carry out
Of considerable magnitude	big, large
On account of the fact	because

Subsequent to	after
Terminate	end
Utilize	use

2. Reduce Explitive Constructions

Explitive constructions are phrases such as it is, there is, there are. Try to avoid using them since these constructions merely obscure the main subject and action of a sentence.

AVOID	USE
It is inevitable that the oil prices will rise.	Oil prices will inevitably rise.
There are likely to be many members participating in this project.	Many members are likely to participate in this project.

3. Avoid Needless Jargons

Communicate in a way which everyone can easily understand. Professional communicators need not use management jargons to create an effect. Needless jargons baffle the audience and create confusion.

Compare:

A	B
Blue-sky thinking may not have a practical application yet, but it is still important to consider all the possibilities.	Revenues are the total of all sales.

NOTE: *Keep in mind that everyone does not understand phrases instantly.*

4. Reduce Unnecessary Prepositional Phrases

Sometimes prepositional phrases are not really necessary, so avoid using too many of them.

AVOID	USE
It is a matter of gravest possible importance to the health of anyone with a history of problem with disease of the heart that he or she should avoid the sort of foods with a high percentage of saturated fats.	Anyone with a history of heart disease should avoid saturated fats.

5. Avoid The Over use of Trite Expressions or Cliches

They may create an expression of laziness or lack of careful thought. They can even become a barrier to communication or people may miss the important point. Quite a lot of cliche'd expressions are just fillers without any real meaning. We should avoid the following phrases.

- as a matter of fact
- as you already know
- at loose ends
- at acid test
- first and foremost
- in my opinion
- it is a small world
- it is interesting to note that
- it may be said that
- last but not the least
- of all things
- needless to say

6. Avoid Nominalization

Avoid the use of words that have been formed into nouns by adding suffixes.

AVOID	USE
The procedures need to be evaluated.	We need to evaluate the procedures.
An evaluation of the procedures need to be done.	We need to evaluate the procedures.
The establishment of a different approach on the part of the committee has become a necessity.	The committee has to approach it differently.

POINTS TO REMEMBER

- Avoid trite expressions cliche's and jargons.
- Use words to express and not impress.
- Prefer active voice to passive voice.
- Reduce prepositional phrases, nominalizations and expletive constructions.
- Accentuate the positive when delivering negative messages.

❑❑❑

Chapter **4**

TECHNICAL VOCABULARY

"Be sincere, be brief, be seated."

—F. D. Roosevelt

TECHNICAL VOCABULARY

Using technical vocabulary is a difficult task, but an important one because without an extensive vocabulary we will be unable to use the structures and functions we may have learned for comprehensible communication. Technical vocabulary comes into existence by many different word-forming processes.

1. **Many technical words have Greek or Latin base forms. Some words are taken entirely from these languages.**

   Greek — Larynx

   Latin — Focus, cortex, quantum

2. **Suffixes and prefixes from classical languages are used to form new words.**

   Greek → aer – air

   Greek → nautikos – sailor

   would make AERONAUTICS

   Greek → bios – life

   Greek → logos – knowledge

   would make BIOLOGY

   Greek → photo – light

   Greek → syn – together

   Greek → thesis – a placing

   would make PHOTOSYNTHESIS

   Greek → pyr – fire

   Greek → metron – measure

   would make PYROMETER

3. **Taking words in ordinary use and giving them specific technical meaning. Example:**

   Physics — Current, energy, particle, power.

   Chemistry — Element, reaction, salt, solution.

   Biology — Cell, evolution.

   Computer and IT — Drive, monitor, mouse, programme.

4. **Deriving from names of scientists. Example:**

   ampere – (unit of electric current)

   newton – (unit of force)

   ohm – (unit of electrical resistance)

   volt – (unit of electromotive force)

   watt – (unit of power)

5. **Forming Acronyms:**

   AIDS – (Acquired Immune Deficiency Syndrome)

   RAM – (Random Access Memory)

   LASER – (Light Amplication by Stimulated Emission of Radiation)

   CAT – (Common Admission Test)

AFFIXES COMMONLY USED IN TECHNICAL COMMUNICATION

Prefixes

- a – atom, achromatic
- an – anaesthesia, anaerobic
- anti – antibiotic, antiseptic
- dia – diameter
- epi – epicentre
- micro – microscopic
- poly – polymeter
- trans – transmit
- ultra – ultra-violet, ultra-sound

Suffixes

- ics – physics, electronics
- meter – thermometer, spectrometer
- scope – microscope, telescope
- logy – zoology, geology
- mer – polymer

❑❑❑

Chapter **5**

General and Technical Communication

"Genuine poetry can communicate before it is understood."

—T. S. Eliot

DISTINCTION BETWEEN TECHNICAL COMMUNICATION AND GENERAL COMMUNICATION

"Self expression must pass into communication for its fulfillment." **—P. S. Buck**

Technical communication conveys specific information about a technical subject to specific audience for a specific purpose. It deals with a topic analytically and objectively.

General communication is a subjective response to personal experience. It may use both formal or informal styles of communication.

It conveys general information intended for general audience so the style and content of communication may vary according to the subject and the audience.

Example

General Communication

The wind was blowing fiercely and the air outside was growing chilled.

Technical Communication

Onshore winds travelling at 45 km. per hour brought temperature down to 15 degree celsius.

1. Technical communication is informative, instructional or persuasive while general communication is entertaining, provocative and captivating.

2. Technical communication needs to be clear, precise, and straight forward, leaving no room for misinterpretations but general communication can be artistic, figurative, symbolic, ambiguous, even vague sometimes.
3. Technical communication must be objective whereas general communication is subjective with the thoughts, opinions and attitudes of the writer.
4. Technical communicators use specialised vocabulary depending on the topic as well as on the intended audience but general communicators may use a general vocabulary understood by a general audience.
5. Technical communication is factual while general communication may be fictional and imaginative.
6. Technical communication must achieve job goals since it is intended for specific purpose whereas general communication is not required to achieve job goals.
7. Technical communication creates legal liability for the writer/speaker and the organisation. General communication does not create any legal liability since it can be interpreted in many ways.
8. Technical communicators use simple, concise and clear style of writing while general writing may be artistic, figurative, symbolic, ambiguous and sometimes vague too.
9. Technical writing is straightforward. It follows accepted standards for grammar and format and general communication is not bound to follow grammatical rules or restrict to any format. It can break the rules.

GENERAL COMMUNICATION	TECHNICAL COMMUNICATION
– Personal, subjective	– Impersonal, objective
– Ambiguous	– Conveys one meaning only
– Allows different interpretation	– Allows one interpretation
– Creative	– Scientific
– Fictional and imaginative	– Factual
– Entertaining, provocative captivating	– Informative, Instructive, persuasive
– General	– Specific
– Metaphoric, symbolic	– Straight forward
– Informal	– Formal
– Arbitrary	– Sequential, systematic
– Ambiguous, vague	– Simple, concise, clear
– Evocative	– Specialised
– Figurative, artistic	– Academic
– Not always structured	– Organised and structured

❑❑❑

Chapter **6**

LANGUAGE AS A TOOL OF COMMUNICATION

"Words are, of course, the most powerful drug used by mankind."

—Rudyard Kipling

LANGUAGE AS A TOOL OF COMMUNICATION

In writing and speaking people insert their thoughts and feelings in words. Words accomplish the transfer by containing thoughts and feelings and conveying them to others. In listening or reading, people extract thoughts and feelings once again from words. Communication can best be summarised as transmission of message from Sender to Receiver in an understandable manner.

The importance of effective communication is immeasurable in the world of business and in personal life. Poor communication reduces quality, weakens productivity, leads to anger and lack of trust among individuals in an organisation. Language is an important instrument which helps in achieving effective communication skill.

"Language is the dress of thought." **—Samuel Johnson**

Desire to communicate motivates people to learn language—both the first language and the second language. There is no such thing as a language teacher, there are only language learners because language cannot be taught, it is only acquired. Refinement can be achieved by learning about words, sentences, patterns, intonational patterns, non-verbal cues etc. Interaction with others helps us achieve confidence in the use of a language. Language development is a long-term process that is interdependant with word experience, home and community language environment, attitude and opportunities to use and practice language.

Keys to effective communication rest in developing and using various language skills such as developing ideas, formulating a strategy, locating and developing sufficient support materials and organizing material in an understandable manner. Once these skills are learned, they must be used frequently, developing such skills is a time-consuming process, but a necessary process. Effective communication requires a sincere level of committment. Ability to communicate well—to read, to write, to listen and to speak—may be achieved through experience and hard work. These skills are essential instruments, because further learning is based on them. Communication skill is one of the essential conditions for career growth. Employs consistently rank ability to communicate as number one characteristic when considering candidates for employment.

IMPORTANCE OF LEARNING ENGLISH LANGUAGE

English is probably world's most important language not just because of the number of people who speak it, but also because of its significance in international, social, cultural and political activities. English continues to be the world's standard language and sustains its global popularity. English is the vehicle for international communication as it allows people to share and contribute to current and future-local and global-communities and cultures. In today's business world, English is no longer viewed as a foreign language. It is the global means of communication. Officially English now has a special status in more than seventy-five countries with a total population of more than two billion speakers.

MODES OF COMMUNICATION OF A LANGUAGE

Communication is an aspect of life that cannot be avoided. It is always there with us in formal or informal manner. The two main modes of communication are Verbal and Non-verbal.

Non-verbal Communication

Non-verbal Communication is defined as creating meaning with body language, eye contact, gestures, tone of voice, mannerism, signs, signals, touch etc. In other words, Non-verbal communication transmits your message without the use of verbal words. Verbal communication means using words to produce meaning. Both Verbal and Non-verbal means of communication are used by every person. Non-verbal signals are continuous and spontaneous and to some extent natural while verbal signals are planned.

For communication to occur, there must be a two-way interchange of feelings, expressions, motives. One way communication is highly ineffective and unproductive. Since there is no way to find out whether the message has been received in the same way as it was intended. To make sure that the communication is not one-way, feedback process should be initiated. Feedback process encourages sharing of information.

Verbal Communication is Goal-oriented

It is driven by sender's effort to impart some news and secure a particular effect. It is normally the concern of both the parties to achieve success in communication.

Following capabilities in your communication may help you achieve desired results.

1. **Observation:** Accurately observing what is going on in your verbal communication with others will increase your ability to improve outcome.
2. **Socialising:** It will help you to understand and connect with others. Positive outlook maintains constructive and open relationships. It helps us in resolving conflicts and difference of opinion.
3. **Self Analysis:** Know your strengths and weaknesses. When you are aware of your true-self, you can achieve good outcomes.
4. **Keep Yourself Updated:** Knowledge creates confidence besides broadening your outlook. If you know something, you will be more confident in your communication. Lack of confidence arises out of lack of knowledge.
5. **Balancing:** Say assertively what you have to say but also listen openly to what others say. Invite others to express their opinion. Balancing can help create more constructive communication.

❑❑❑

Chapter 7

THE COMMUNICATION PROCESS

"Take advantage of every opportunity to practice your communication skills so that when important occasions arise, you will have the gift, the style, the sharpness, the clarity and the emotions to affect other people."

—Jim Rohn

PROCESS OF COMMUNICATION

Communication is a dynamic process involving a speaker who sends a message, the channels through which the message is sent and the feedback sent by the receiver to the sender. It is through the communication process that the sharing of a common meaning between the SENDER and the RECEIVER takes place. Knowledge about the communication process helps the communicator to choose a proper medium and guard against the errors so that the right message is received and proper feedback is sent back.

The process starts with a SENDER who has a MESSAGE for a RECEIVER. Two or more people are involved in this process. The sender has the responsibility for the message. His message travels to the receiver through one or more channels chosen by the sender. The channels may be Verbal or Non-verbal, Direct or Indirect. They may involve only one of the senses for example hearing or they may involve all the five senses, for example, hearing, seeing, touch, smell and taste. Non-verbal communication primarily relies on seeing rather than hearing. After sending the information sender becomes a Receiver and Receiver becomes a sender through the process of feedback. Feedback is the Receiver's response to the message sent by the sender. The channels for feedback may be quite different from the channels adopted by the sender of the message. A puzzled look may be the feedback to what the sender considered a perfectly clear oral presentation or instruction. Effect on the receiver completes the communication process.

So we know that the communication process is made up of seven components.

1. Sender
2. Message
3. Encoding
4. Medium of Transmission
5. Receiver
6. Decoding
7. Feedback

The communication process begins with the sender who encodes the message, selects a medium or channel and sends it to the Receiver but the process does not end with the Receiver receiving or decoding it. The process gets completed after the sender gets the feedback from the Receiver. The Receiver follows the same path while giving feedback, making communication a circular process.

The following model will clarify the communication process.

The Communication Process

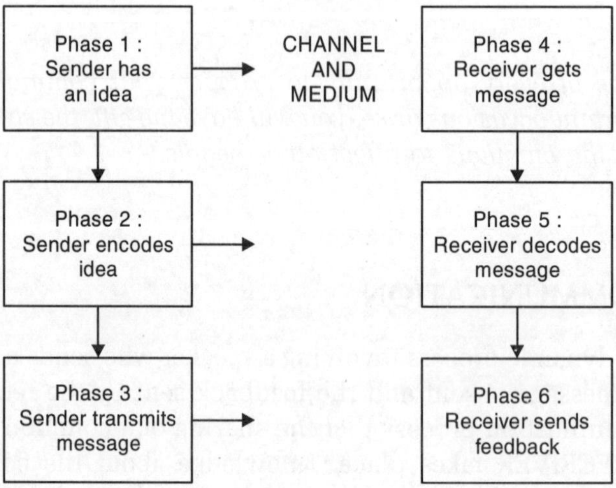

The above model of communication process shows that communication is a transactional *i.e.*, a two way process that can be broken into six phases. The channel or medium of communication is added to complete the process. So we know that communication process is made up of seven components. The communication process is repeated until both the parties have finished expressing themselves.

❑❑❑

Chapter **8**

INTERPERSONAL COMMUNICATION

"People are different from each other—no amount of getting after them is going to change them, nor is there any reason to change them, because the differences are probably good."

—David Keirsey, Ph.D.

"Please Understand Me ||"

Communication is a complex process that requires constant attention so that intended messages are sent and received without being misunderstood.

The team leader announces "There will be a meeting at sharp 8 o'clock tomorrow". To his dismay only fifty per cent of the team members attend the meeting. The message was not sent properly as there was a confusion about the time 8 o'clock in the morning or in the evening. If one listens or speaks well, then there is little or no scope for misunderstanding. The ability to communicate is the primary factor that distinguishes human beings from animals. And it is the ability to communicate well that distinguishes one individual from another.

Interpersonal communication is the ability to relate to people in written as well as verbal communication. It is a personal interaction which can happen between individuals or members of a group. Effective Interpersonal communication is not only saying or writing the correct words. It depends on a variety of interpersonal skills including listening, asserting, influencing, persuading, empathizing etc. It is affected by our emotional state, the situation and style of communication.

Interpersonal communication is defined as communication that occurs between people who know each other. We engage in interpersonal communication in order to express ourselves and receive the same from others. The communication can take place directly or indirectly through telephone, e-mail, letters or meetings. The channels used in conveying the message may be Direct or Indirect.

Direct channels are under the direct control of the sender. Verbal and Non-verbal channels come under this category. The sender can select the channel according to the situation, need and audience. Indirect channels are not under his control. They include kinesics as body language, expression, involuntary movements. Which are automatic, natural and uncontrolled. They also send across a message and the message may be negative or positive. The sender can not help it.

PRINCIPLES OF INTERPERSONAL COMMUNICATION

1. **Irreversible.** The words once uttered cannot be taken back. Both verbal and Non-verbal communication creates a lasting effect in the mind of the receiver.
2. **Complicated.** Interpersonal communication is complicated because a message can be understood in many ways. It is difficult for others to read your mind. The message received by them may be exactly the opposite of what you wanted to send making communication a complicated process.
3. **Inescapable.** No one can escape communication. Willing or not willing you have to communicate. Even if you do not use words, you communicate with gestures, expressions, involuntary body movements. You just can not escape communication.
4. **Contextual.** Communication always happens in some context, be it a psychological, situational, relational, cultural, environmental, social or emotional context. Communication cannot take place in isolation.

INTERPERSONAL NEEDS

We engage in Interpersonal commuication because we need to express ourselves to others, we need to establish our identity and we need to build a context of understanding.

William Schutz has identified three such needs:

"**Inclusion**—need to establish identity with others.

Control—need to exercise leadership and prove one's abilities. Groups provide outlets for this need. Some individuals do not want to be leaders. For them groups provide necessary control over aspects of their lives.

Affection—need to develop relationship with people. Groups are an excellent way to make friends and establish relationship."

TYPES OF INTERPERSONAL COMMUNICATION

1. Dyadic

Happens between two people through letters, e-mail, telephonic conversation or even face to face. Your past experience of interaction with an individual or information about his behaviour from different sources will determine the way you communicate with him. For example, your past experience of interaction was not pleasant or a friend of yours gives you the information about the arrogant attitude of your boss, you go and meet him with a pre-determined notion. Belief system also has an effect on dyadic communication. A belief that things can be got done by assertive attitude will impose assertiveness on you.

2. Small Group Communication

"Some of your most important communication will take place in one group or another. It is estimated that over eleven million meetings are held each day and that atleast forty per cent of your work life will be spent attending group meetings and conferences. A recent survey showed that the typical executive spends about 700 hours per year interacting in groups. This is the equivalent of two of every five days on the job. Thus, knowing how to relate to others in a group setting is not only vital if you are to attain personal success but also if you are to attain professional success."

(Gamble and Gamble, "Communication Horks" p.267)

Small Group Communication takes place between three to thirteen members to work on a project or to solve a problem.

Characteristics of Small Groups

1. Unity in diversification
2. Secular attitude
3. Patient behaviour
4. Cultural exchange
5. Professionalism
6. Discipline
7. Incentives
8. Team spirit
9. Division of work according to the capability
10. Comic relief
11. Commitment

Benefits of Small Groups

1. Size is small so personal interaction may take place; conditions will be workable.
2. Small group meetings may take place without prior planning.
3. Recognition of capability is easier which will benefit the working system. The results will be faster and better.
4. Cohesiveness and commitment will create the effectiveness.
5. Team spirit for a common goal caters self-less attitude among members.
6. Small groups work towards emotional and psychological growth of its members.

Things to consider while forming Small Groups

- Encourage members to raise objects and concerns.
- Refrain the members from making their choices regarding the work allotment at the beginning of group activities.
- Encourage unbiased attitude in the group.
- Allow the group to be evaluated independently by a separate group with a different leader.
- Allow members to get feedback on their decisions from their own constituents.
- Take the help of the experts if there are problems in decision making regarding important issues.

– Allow critical review of the decisions from the members before approval is given.
– Always discuss the issues in meetings so that members participate with open arguments.
– Assign work according to the capability of the members.

3. Public Speaking

Public speaking is the process of speaking to a group of people in a structured, deliberate manner intended to inform, influence or entertain the listeners.

Basic Elements of Public Speaking

– Who is the speaker.
– To whom the speaker is addressing.
– What is topic of address.
– What channels and mediums are used by him.
– Feedback.

The purpose of public speaking may vary. It may be just the transmission of information or it may be intended to motivate the people or public speaking may just be a medium in narrating a story. Public speaking can be used to motivate, influence, persuade, inform, translate, preach or entertain.

Types

1. *Public Speech Writing.* The speaker knows before hand his topic, the audience and the venue. He can make the prior arrangements, prepare his speech, can write it down and deliver it by taking the help from his notes.
2. *Proposals and Presentation.* Proposals and presentation are often done with business purposes where the goal is specific and the audience are limited.
3. *Impromptu Speech.* An impromptu speech is rather difficult form of public speaking assignment. The speaker does not get enough time to prepare the topic. He may be asked to deliver an extempore.

Things to keep in mind while delivering a public speech.

– Do enough homework on the topic to be delivered if it is not extempore.
– Understand your audience and prepare accordingly.
– Keep your language and expression simple so that it is understood by your audience.
– Use humour in between to make the atmosphere light and comic.
– Captivate the audience by relating some anecdotes or small stories.
– Include gestures but avoid the overuse of gestures.
– If possible, use Audio-visual aids to catch the attention of your audience.
– Encourage feedback.
– Be loud enough but do not shout.
– Maintain eye-contact.
– Do not simply read from the paper.

□□□

Chapter 9

GROUP COMMUNICATION

"Seek first to understand, then to be understood."

—Stephen Covery

A group is made up of few individuals who acknowledge each other to be a part of the group and outsiders also acknowledge them as a part of the same group. Once a group is set up, users in the group can communicate with each other securely and confidently. Too large a group inhibits the group members' ability to communicate. Since group communication is dynamic, members in the group may change over time *i.e.,* new members may join the group and existing members may leave the group. This gives an opportunity to the members to interact with different people. Groups are formed with a common purpose for decision making, targets or solving some problems. A group is formed in four stages.

1. Forming

In the forming stage, members attempt to become oriented to the task as well as to each other. Discussion centres around defining the task, its scope, handling the task and distributing the duties.

2. Storming

As denoted by the word, storming stage is charaterized by conflict. As the group members attempt to organize for the task, the conflict arises. Members are expected to be adoptable and they adjust to the environment. They have to change their ideas, beliefs, attitudes, habits to suit the group organisation. Members should try to develop problem-solving mentality and not fault-finding mentality.

3. Norming

When members start interacting with each other, the level of trust is also built. They start acknowledging the efforts, contributions and assistance of other members. They develop a sense of group belonging and start feeling a part of the group. They value other's viewpoints and feel that they can achieve their goals in team and not single handedly.

4. Performing

Performing stage is marked by interdependence in personal as well as work relationship. Members have grown to be task oriented. They rise above self-issues and the focus is on the performance. In this stage, people can work independently, in sub-groups, or as a total unit with equal facility. The adaptability is at the highest level, as a result the members become highly productive as well as considerate towards others.

BENEFITS OF GROUP COMMUNICATION TO ORGANISATION

- Increases productivity.
- Increases quality.
- Builds up morale of the members.
- Better problem solving conditions.
- Increases creativity.
- Better decisions are made.

BENEFITS OF GROUP COMMUNICATION TO INDIVIDUALS

- Less stress in work.
- Responsibility is shared.
- Rewards and recognitions are shared.
- Members can influence each other.
- Members experience a sense of accomplishment.

❑❑❑

Chapter **10**

MASS COMMUNICATION

"Independent media can go to where the silence is and break the sound barrier doing what the corporate networks refuse to."

Mass communication is a delivery of message to target audience by a person or group of persons utilizing print, audio or visual medium. We can define Mass communication as a process by which a complex organisation transmits messages to a mass audience with the help of mass media. Mass media is a means of public communication reaching a large audience. The message delivered through mass media has the potential to reach anonymous audience and the market at once. The mass communication is capable of reaching a large number of audience whom the sender does not know personally.

DIFFERENT TYPES OF MASS MEDIA

Television, Radio, Cinema, Internet or World Wide Web, Newspaper, Magazine, Journal, other print media like pamphlets, brochures, posters and outdoor media like bill-board, signs, flying bill-board, sky writing and blimps.

CHARACTERISTICS OF MASS COMMUNICATION

- "It comprises technical and institutional methods of production."
- Mass communication provides and emphasizes selected information.
- It caters to large heterogeneous and scattered audience.
- It is controlled and regulated by certain norms.
- "Mass communication is public oriented. Feedback is minimal. Noise may be semantic, environmental or mechanical."
- The information is presented through various channels and the public can generally choose to read, listen, view or disregard the material offered.

- Mass communication has an anonymous appeal, perhaps with only a general and not particular knowledge of the target audience.
- Mass communication relies on sophisticated technology.

STRENGTHS OF MASS COMMUNICATION

- The message is sent atonce to a large audience, covering large number of people from heterogeneous and scattered groups.
- It is a convenient and credible source of communication.
- Mass communication can increase the perceived credibility and worth of your project.
- There is an option to choose from the varied channels.
- It is a convenient source of reaching the masses.

WEAKNESSES OF MASS COMMUNICATION

- There is no guarantee that the intended message will reach the target audience.
- Mass communication is generally one-way process.
- Information conveyed is limited and may not support the main message.
- There is a possibility of the distortion of message.
- Audience are generally passive. There is little or no feedback on the information that had been given to the audience.
- Mass communication may be biased because the communicator has an opportunity to display only that information which suits him.

IMPORTANCE OF MASS COMMUNICATION

- Mass communication creates **Awareness** about policies and programmes of development.
- Mass communication **Entertains** the masses by providing enjoyment and relaxation and relief from stress and worries.
- Social and cultural values are transmitted which can help in **Sustaining the Society.**
- **Education** is another important function of Mass Communication. It removes ignorance and superstition by changing the negative attitude of the people and motivating them into purposeful action.
- The media provides people with information regarding important facts about the world, "Survellience of the Environment" or an information about some difficulties such as weather forecast, traffic problems, natural calamities.

- Mass Communication helps both people and the nation to visualize their position in the global framework and compete accordingly.

PROCESS OF MASS COMMUNICATION

The process of Mass communication is consisted of six components.

1. Sender
2. Content
3. Encoding
4. Channel/Medium
5. Receiver
6. Decoding

There is little or no feedback on the information that had been given to the receiver. Sender may be a newspaper reporter who has a content or a newspaper story to compose. The content has to be given a form of words which is encoding. Newspaper serves as a channel or medium for the sender to send his message to the audience. Finally the receiver decodes the content of the message into meaning.

❑❑❑

Chapter 11

ORGANISATIONAL COMMUNICATION

"We must be able to communicate with each other in a moment's notice."

—Dennis P. Slatton

Managers spent maximum of their time in an organisation communicating with each other. The communication may be in the form of meetings, seminars, face to face discussions, reports, memos, orders, notices etc. Communication is an integral part of any organisation, involving the transformation of information from one party to the other. If there is no communication, there would not be any activity in an organisation.

Myres and Myres define organizational communication as "the central binding force that permits coordination among people and thus allows for organized behaviour". Effective communication can be seen as the building stone or life source of organizations. The basic function of communication is to influence the behaviour of the receiver by informing, directing, socializing, regulating and persuading. An organization cannot stand without imparting the basic functions of communication.

FUNCTIONS OF ORGANISATIONAL COMMUNICATION

Neher (1997) identifies the primary functions of organisational communication as:

- Compliance-gaining
- Leading
- Motivating
- Influencing
- Sense-making
- Problem-solving
- Decision-making
- Conflict management
- Negotiating
- Bargaining.

"Neher (1997) and Rogers and Rogers (1976) emphasize the social functions of organizational communication as a whole rather than focusing on the functions of specific communication exchanges. Thus they combine the functions of **informing, directing and**

regulating into the broader category of behavioral compliance. They also give greater emphasis to the role of communication in managing threats to organizational order and control identifying problem-solving and conflict management, negotiation and bargaining as key functions of organizational communication."

(Kathryn A. Baker)

Myers and Myers (1982) identify three primary functions of organisational communication:

- Coordination and regulation of production activities.
- Socialization.
- Innovation.

"Their approach focuses on the functional goals of organizational communication rather than on the near term outcome of particular acts of communication such as to make a decision, to persuade or to resolve a conflict. The more specific functions of communication such as decision making, informing, persuading, negotiating, problem-solving are mixed into the three primary functions of organizational communication."

❑❑❑

Chapter 12

DOWNWARD COMMUNICATION

"The two words 'Information' and 'Communication' are often used interchangeably, but they signify quite different things. Information is giving out, communication is getting things."

—Sydney J. Harris

THE FLOW OF BUSINESS COMMUNICATION

Any act of giving or receiving information about a person's needs, desires, perceptions, knowledge or affective states from one to another is Communication. Communication may take up any form from being intentional or unintentional, adopting conventional or unconventional signals, take linguistic or non-linguistic forms, and may occur through spoken or other modes. One may also choose to be simple by quoting communication as the exchange of ideas, opinions and information through written or spoken words, symbols or actions.

Any kind of Communication used to promote a product, service or organization with an objective of profit maximization is Business Communication. The purpose of this chapter is to make you familiarize with the primary bifurcations in the internal Business Communication.

DOWNWARD COMMUNICATION

"Information flowing from the top of the organization in a hierarchical manner with a purpose of letting the members understand the mission and various valued policies of the organization."

INTRODUCTION

Downward communication flow involves the information which is transferred from the supervisor to the subordinate in a particular organization. Information from the top to middle level and from middle to the lower level forms the premise of the study. When the information follows in this particular pattern it becomes really important to chose the most appropriate method of communication.

The information in an organization can be communicated either in the form of Oral or Written manner. Opting for the correct subcategory among the above mentioned methodologies is an integrative part of Downward Communication. One needs to understand that the information from the top authority to its subordinates has to be coherent as more than often it is directed towards a whole set of operating members involved. Not with an aim of acceptance, the downward message adapts a written media as it has the capability of transmitting the basic objectives and goals of the message to the target audience in a more effective way.

With the organizations adapting various advanced means of communication, the world has experienced the birth of a number of information carrying models. These would include a varied range of written ideas – handouts, bulletins, letters, posters, folders etc. Although the importance of written communication has been highlighted, we cannot simply ignore the revolution caused in the new oral communications field with – grapevine, face to face conversation, house journals etc.

Master the talent of understanding the three W's in Downward Communication is a prerequisite for an efficient manager. A manager should be able to know What (content), When (Optimum Time) & Where (Target Direction) is the information going to flow. A perfect decision would involve the perfect timing, scope and means of the downward information flow. The aim of this chapter is to familiarize one with various ways of downward communication, the purpose and finally the merits and demerits encountered with this particular way of communication.

CARRIERS OF DOWNWARD COMMUNICATION

The communication with the basic motive to pass information from the top to the bottom end tends to be a little formal. It becomes extremely important to choose the right carrier of the information as there are various people who are on the receiving end. There are ample options available among the written as well as oral communication; a few important of them have been elaborated here:

1. **Bulletin Board:** One of the easiest ways to pass on the required information to the target section of people is by displaying it on a clearly visible Notice Board. These generally are statements approved by the concerned high authority with their due sign and date.

2. **Written Orders:** A command or some sort of instruction from a superior to one of the subordinates on completion of some assigned activity. The flow of information is generally from one to one, but can also be flexible depending on the situation.

3. **Posters:** The degree of visibility of a few areas in the campuses is always more than the other, and the best way to utilize these spaces is to capture them by sticking relevant posters. One should understand that the Posters need to be attractive and precise.

4. **Letters:** One of the most prevalent and widespread way of communicating with an individual or a group of subordinates has been through letters. Starting with the letter of

joining to the letter of appreciation and finally till the letter of resignation, termination or retirement, all of them are the most efficient ways to pass on the message. Again these are ideally intended towards individuals, but are equally effective if directed to a group of people.

5. E-Mail: Organizations have to change with the changing world. Almost all the important flow of information has perfectly adapted a path of the latest technology. The success of e-mails accounts to its low cost, and also to the fact that the information can be delivered easily to the uncountable desired segment of people.

6. In-house journals: The channel generally utilized by bigger firms to pass on the primary information about company's policies, rules and regulations, profit and loss statements, vision and mission statements, targets, changes incorporated recently etc. The journals can be published monthly, quarterly or yearly as per the desired requirements.

7. Addressing the Public: Circumstances when the company wants some message to be delivered to a set of people, it would call for a gathering where one of the higher authorities addresses the lower lot and passes on the relevant information. This is one of the most useful ways of oral communication, provided the focus is on whether the message has been correctly inferred by all.

8. Grapevine: There are times when a senior would want to pass on some information without wasting on the time. One of the effective channels sufficing the need is an informal way of passing on the desired information.

There may be various media channels available to pass on the information from the top to the bottom end, but it basically depends on the need of the organization to choose on the specific channel. The needs of middle level management may vary in various organizations and also among different teams, hence the channel which delivers the information in the most effective and efficient way should be adopted.

WHY DOWNWARD COMMUNICATION?

The existence of the Downward Communication depends on the following five objectives suggested by Katz and Khan.

- "To provide specific task directives or instructions on how to do the job;
- To provide information to produce an understanding of the task and its relationship to the other organizational tasks;
- To provide information about organizational policies, procedures and practices;
- To provide feedback on performance to the subordinates;
- To provide philosophical information regarding the organization's mission or orientation towards its goals."

MERITS

1. Clear information on the objectives and policies to be adopted is passed on to the desired subordinate;
2. System helps to improve the quality of the response;
3. Concerned parties have prevalent evidences intact with them;
4. Object at the receiving end can do the needful after carefully reading the information; he can also keep the same for his future use;
5. Any form of communication channel can be adopted: Oral or Written;
6. Cost involvement in the flow of information can be minimized with the right media channel.

DEMERITS

1. A clear focus on the written communication delays the flow of information at times;
2. In order to avoid the delays there are chances that the seniors would pass on the message to the subordinates directly, thereby encouraging communication gap;
3. Segment of people at the receiving end are not considered before passing the information;
4. Feedback mechanism is not generally incorporated in this kind of communication system;
5. Downward Communication system stands on the assumption that the structure of the organization is flexible to incorporate the flow of information.

Downward Communication being a formal set of channel, a great focus should be levied on the kind and amount of information flow and the suitable time for the same. Except this, improving the prevailing relationship between the receiver and the source, would undoubtedly help the communication and eventually increase the acceptance of the task at the receiving end.

❑❑❑

Chapter **13**

UPWARD COMMUNICATION

"Information flowing from the bottom of the organization to the top management with a purpose of encouraging a two-way convenient flow so as to break the prolonged barrier."

INTRODUCTION

Flow of information, consisting of employees' concerns, comments on working atmosphere, reactions towards other members, advice to the senior team, understanding of the various policies and practices, from a subordinate to an executive member of an organization defines an Upward Flow of Communication. As opposed to the Downward Communication, the flow of Upward Communication is from the low levels of a hierarchy to the upper levels. The information flow from middle management to upper management and from lower management to upper management is also constituted in the process.

In the era of extreme competition duelling all around, each and every industry would want to progress at a pace greater than the other. To achieve this success, an organization should focus on achieving the defined goals and objectives in the allotted time, and also provide means to motivate the employees at regular intervals. It is true to state that in practice the top management generally does not intend to implement the ideal Upward Communication, but the importance of the same makes it a common exercise in any successful industry.

Companies which tend to implement this particular communication methodology portray a sense of concern for all the employees at any level, this gets converted to a feeling of belonging for the lower staff towards the company, and finally helps the upper management keep a track of the progress and achievements of an individual. If this particular communication happens in a coherent fashion, it can prove to be as fruitful as the downward communication.

Upward Communication can further take the modes of written as well as oral communication channels including personal letters, face to face communication, informal communications, social groups, complaints and suggestions etc. The media channels may be similar to the previous communication but the motive, messages and addressing would completely depend on the situation in hand. This part of the chapter would try and focus on the various media channels to deliver the required information, the rules of Upward Communication, a few merits and demerits of this particular methodology.

CARRIERS OF UPWARD COMMUNICATION

Both the primary communication methods (Downward and Upward) are clear examples of formal communication. In case of Upward Communication, when the person at the receiving end is one of the senior executives, the source needs to be a lot more serious while choosing channel to deliver the message. The choice of the media used basically depends on the message, the intended recipient and the duration of the flow. A few of the prevalent channels have been discussed here—

1. **Suggestions:** One of the easiest ways to bridge the gap between a senior and a subordinate is to open the channels of communication between them. These can ideally be initiated by allowing your juniors to provide their work related relevant suggestions on various issues. A free two way communication is the stepping stone to success for a particular organization.

2. **Complaints:** An organization which encourages its employees to find the loop holes in the process is the one which is heading towards a path of maturity. A lower level employee is generally aware of the bad practices in the lower levels of the organization. To eradicate this, a company encourages various complaints from its employees to be regularly deposited in the Complaint Box. A follow up on these complaints needs to be done to see the difference.

3. **Survey:** Management in many organizations follows a policy of distributing questionnaires to its employees asking them about their grievances and gives them a chance to express their feelings without any fear. In most of the cases all these surveys are confidential and the responses are shared by a few senior officials.

4. **Open Door Policy:** A closed door attitude towards subordinates does not allow a free two way relationship between an employee and employer. The concept generally followed in a small organization, where the seniors have an open door attitude towards their subordinates is one of the most encouraging features of an Upward Communication.

5. **Exit Interviews:** Most of the medium scale as well as big organization have a process in place to conduct an Exit Interview of the employee who has decided to quit the job. With the help of this interaction the employee is enquired about his feeling on the various practices followed, the improvement vents and other concerning issues. More than often an employee at this time is not reluctant in providing a correct feedback and hence a true picture is depicted about the work culture in the company.

It is true that the time utilized in responding to a problem mainly depends on the media used to carry the information, but it is not right to compare the media's efficiency to the time taken to receive a response. The duty of any media is to deliver the information from one place to another, and there may be other loop holes in the system, which are restricting the quick approach.

RULES OF UPWARD COMMUNICATION

The need of Upward Communication becomes more crucial with the latest trend in the organization of relying on the teams to manage themselves independently. To be a perfectionist in the field, an organization needs to follow a few proposed rules of this communication:

1. Senior Management needs to be regularly informed about the latest updates;
2. Considerable time should be given to the Senior Management to respond to actions;
3. Only the major issues need to be brought to the notice of higher authorities;
4. Reports submitted to the heads should be transparent in every sense;
5. Realized problems should be accompanied with the analysis and options to solve before putting it in front of the decision maker;
6. Source of the information should be ready with the minute details on the issues to be resolved before passing it to the receiver.

DUTIES OF THE SUPERVISOR

As mentioned, the Upward Communication is an ideal example of a two way process where the information flow has to be bidirectional. In order to make this a success, there are a few duties which need to be performed by the higher level members:

1. The need and interest of hearing messages from the subordinates should be made clear to them;
2. Encourage the subordinates by rewarding them on following the Upward Communication in a serious manner;
3. Gain the trust and respect of his subordinates;
4. Positive as well as the negative uses made of the messages should be discussed with the subordinates;
5. Evaluate the level of Upward Communication followed in the organization, and improvise on the same with time.

MERITS

1. Initiates the much needed process of two way communication;
2. With this mechanism the option of obtaining a genuine feedback is realized;
3. Accurate track of individual's performance is kept and updated;

4. Flat organization realizes the importance of Upward Communication noticing the huge count of the issues to be discussed with the Senior Management.

RELUCTANCE IN PRACTICING UPWARD COMMUNICATION

1. Subordinates are hesitant in sending the information to the senior level thinking of the negative consequences;
2. Subordinates develop distrust with the supervisor who is task focused or unsympathetic;
3. At times the importance of the job is not realized by the lower level team members.

The nature and the relationship of the senior level with the lower level teams is the main judging factor in the success of the Upward Communication. The cordial the relationship, the better are the chances of the company to excel in the fields of competition. It is true to state that the importance of both the communication techniques discussed is almost the same, but Upward Communication is an extra step taken with a purpose of establishing an ideal organization.

❑❑❑

Chapter 14

HORIZONTAL COMMUNICATION

"An exchange of Information between different departments or functional units with the primary motto of organization's benefit by increasing the level of coordination in the activities."

INTRODUCTION

Referred to as sideways communication, lateral communication or crosswise communication, Horizontal Communication is different from the other two discussed in the chapter by not being counted into the category of formal communication channels. This is one of the informal ways of communication followed among similar levels of a hierarchy in an organization. Interactions among various functional departments and other such teams headed by one authority, is the core essence of Horizontal information flow.

Communication between the members at the same level in a company is one of the most crucial aspects in the successful accomplishment of the work. This particular communication focuses on a trend of the flow of ideas and opinions between the parties involved. Hence by not losing a track of the information flow, an informal nature of communication incorporates ways of sharing the wonderful and profit generating knowledge.

The three levers which help an organization flourish in a steep manner are—the understanding between various teams, coordination between sub-divisions and an efficient team work in all the departments. All of these can be achieved with a proper formal communication in its place, but to improve it further to a level of excellence the company needs to adapt a free and frank approach among its employees. This encourages the sub-heads to coordinate in an improved manner with maximum understanding and high quality team work.

Horizontal Communication can be correctly perceived to involve mainly oral methods of communication, but a successful use of written media channels can also be as fruitful as the previous. One may have ample bunch of offerings ranging from lectures, conference, telephonic conversations to notes, reports, posters etc., but it is the decision on the channel selection which decides the rate of success. This part of the chapter would elaborate on a few media channels, the primary objectives and functions associated to this communication technique.

CARRIERS OF HORIZONTAL COMMUNICATION

By being defined as an informal way of communication, the boundary to choose the media from the available list is not limited. It is generally easier for a subordinate to convey the message to another subordinate. The trouble generally comes when a channel needs to be selected to encourage an information flow from one to all or all to all. If one member of a team wants to convey his message to the other team members, this is an example of one to one communication. If a few members of one department want to provide information to the members of another department, this is an example of all to all communication. The source should weigh the situation correctly and choose from the most suitable options of channels available:

1. Labour Union Issues: The publications issued by the Labour unions are a great way to express the feelings of the employees to the senior management. To come up to a common understanding of the issues faced by a number of employees in varied departments, the best way is to organize meetings of the teams involved in the decision making. This is a wonderful way of depicting the execution of Horizontal Communication.

2. House Organs: Similar to the publishing of a Magazine, House Organs is a channel which speaks to the large section of employees in a cost effective manner. If one employee wants his thoughts to be heard by other employees in the similar level and under the same senior he can opt for publishing them in House Organs.

3. Conference, Meetings etc.: These are the examples of the most famous channels for this purpose. The primary difference between both Conference and Meeting is the number of people participating in them. Meetings are generally targeted towards a smaller segment rather than a Conference which is inclined for a larger group. The decision results in a conference or the minutes of a meeting are the channel judging parameters in either case.

4. Telephonic Conversation: In the generation where the scarcest resource is the availability of time, a channel which provides the least utilization of it is most preferred. The frequency of telephonic conversations completely depends on the teams, but they may vary from weekly reports to daily updates to hourly findings.

5. Instructions: This is an ideal example of one to one communication, where one subordinate passes on instructions to another subordinate reporting to the same supervisor. These generally happen between interdepartment heads, with the constraint of time not given due priority.

The motives of Horizontal Communication are to solve the problem, accomplish tasks, improve teamwork, build goodwill and boost the efficiency of employees. All the members of an organization should think of these purposes and then opt for a channel which is in line with the mentioned factors.

OBJECTIVES OF HORIZONTAL COMMUNICATION

With time the Horizontal Communication aims at achieving the mentioned objectives:

1. Initiate and encourage the peer coordination;
2. Provides tremendous emotional and social help by making the employees realize that people in the same boat face the same issues;
3. Information flow is perfect without the barrier of difference between Senior Management and Lower Level employees;
4. Speeds up the information flow and increases the level of understanding between members of the organization.

Approximately 50% to 80% time of the Business Managers is contributed towards communicating with their supervisors, peers or juniors. If an organization wants all its employees to equally contribute towards the achievement of its Mission, a well-developed communication skill needs to be followed with idealistic approach. In the chapter we realized how an open communication enhances the knowledge and satisfaction level of the employees.

❑❑❑

Chapter 15

IMPORTANCE OF ORGANIZATIONAL COMMUNICATION

"Communication leads to community, that is to understanding intimacy and mutual valuing."

—Rallo May

IMPARTING TECHNICAL INFORMATION

Organizational communication serves as a bridge between the different members of an organization by imparting information. The information is required both ways–from sender to receiver and vice versa. If the manager does not impart information to his juniors about the technicalities of the work to be done, he will not achieve results. Similarly he is required to inform his seniors about his performance. When the employers are well informed about the various aspects of the work, they get expected results. To get good appraisal, the employees in turn should apprise their seniors about the work they have done otherwise, they will not get the due benefits.

The information may be collected from outside as well as inside the organisation. Internal information may include the qualification and skill of the employees, production of sales data, Absentee statement, Performance data, Budget statement, Accounts etc. The external information includes knowledge about the market sources from outside, policies of the government, survey of the public, future prospects of the company etc. Information of whatever kind, must be concise, accurate, up-to-date and reliable to avoid misunderstanding of any kind.

IMPARTING EDUCATION AND TRAINING

Communication plays a vital role in imparting education—both formal and informal. Information for the purpose of education can be given through lectures, class notes, seminars, study-tours, T.V., newspapers, press, journals, Internet, Websites, e-mail etc.

Take the example of modernisation of agriculture or family planning or personal hygiene or eradication of epidemics like polio, bird-flu etc. The public in rural areas is educated through television, radio, advertisement, personal interaction. Mass media helps in providing education for family-planning, hygiene, road-safety, child abuse, child-labour, foeticide, different addictions, pollution control etc. Inside an organisation the employees are informed about the rules and procedures of the company. They are given formal training in which communication plays its role.

ISSUING ORDERS AND INSTRUCTIONS

Orders and Instructions may be sent orally or in written way. They may be in the form of notices, circulars, telephone, manuals, e-mail, handbooks or oral. Annual reports can also be prepared to issue instructions, rules and procedures. Orders and instructions are authority based and the employees cannot ignore them.

COUNSELLING

Majority of the problems in an organization can be resolved through psychological counselling. Effective communication can help in this direction. Employees can be counselled to perform better. The team leader can be counselled not to be dominating. Counselling may produce cordial relationship among the different levels of employees in an organization. Counselling also increases the creativity, brings out the hidden potentials and brings the positive change in the behaviour of the employees.

PERSUADING

Persuation is the art of influencing the attitudes, opinions and actions of the people. Politicians persuade people to vote. A salesman persuades the customers to buy the product. The companies persuade the public to take their product, through advertisements. Companies spend millions of rupees on advertisement to persuade the public. Persuation is very important when the company decides to bring some changes in the administration or in its rules and procedures. Persuation should be convincing and cordial.

PROVIDING ADVICE

An employee may be very good in his work but if he is not friendly with his colleagues, juniors or seniors the advice may help him to develop friendly attitude. The advice must be friendly and not dictatorial. It should be for the betterment and not to show superiority.

RECEIVING SUGGESTIONS

An employee should be receptive. Suggestions may come from any quarter, from juniors or seniors. Useful suggestions should be implemented and the sender should be rewarded. The betterment of the organisation is always above your personal ego. Suggestion boxes should be installed at the workplace to encourage the employees to suggest openly. The management must welcome the suggestions and act against complaints.

MOTIVATING

The employees may be motivated to perform better by getting due recognition for their work. Timely due appraisal from the management motivates others to perform better. Organization is like a family. If manager gives his hundred per cent for its growth and the management treats its employees like family members, the motivation to do better, increases.

Due rewards for work, cordial relationship between management and the employee, sympathetic ear towards the problems of the workers, timely and deserved appraisal motivate the employees to do better for the organization in which they work.

IMPROVING DISCIPLINE

Discipline is an integral part of the growth of any organization. Discipline may be taught by issuing warnings and notices.

❑❑❑

Chapter **16**

BARRIERS TO COMMUNICATION

"Wise men talk because they have something to say, fools because they have to say something."

—Plato

Proper communication is an art which is natural as well as acquired. Interference in the communication process is called **Noise** which can be caused by a variety of communication barriers. These barriers are inevitable which cannot be completely avoided but both Sender and Receiver can work at improvement. The barriers may be external or internal. They may relate to the sender or the receiver or the circumstances. Knowing the common barriers to communication is the first step to minimize their impact.

Each person has a unique mental map that represents his **Perception of Reality**. Senders use selective perception to choose the details that seem important to them. Receivers can distort details that do not fit into their perception patterns. Language is an arbitrary code that depends on shared definitions. There is a limit to how completely any two people share the same meaning for a word.

A Restrictive Environment can be a formal communication network that limits the flow of information, so communication becomes fragmented.

Physical Distractions such as bad connections, poor accoustics, or illegible writing can block an otherwise effective message.

Emotional Distractions can also get into the way of your message.

Deceptive Communicators may exaggerate positive or hide negative information.

People constantly receive messages via e-mail, express couriers, fax machines, voice mail, websites, regular mail, papers, cell phones.

Information Overload caused by the sheer number of messages can be distracting, making it hard to discriminate between useful and useless information.

There may be the following barriers to organizational barriers.

1. Muddled Messages

Muddled messages are a barrier to communication because receiver will not be able to get the intended message from the sender if the message is muddled. Compare these two messages "You are invited to attend the seminar at about 2.00 in the afternoon" and "You are invited to attend the seminar at 2.00 in the afternoon." Only one word difference makes the first sentence muddled and second clear. Muddled messages may happen because of many reasons. Sender may be confused in his thoughts. He may be at a loss of appropriate words or he carelessly uses the language without knowing that one word here or there may change the entire meaning of the message.

2. Weak Delivery

It does not matter how important or impressive the subject of your communication is, if your delivery of the message is poor. If you deliver your message without any 'push', you will not get the desired results. It is important not to get confused between delivery and presentation. Good presentation may lack a suitable structure, still it can be impressive. I know of a friend who is not a powerful orator, but still she creates a strong impact on the audience because of her strong delivery of message.

3. Improper Channel

Variety of channels help the receiver understand the nature and importance of a message. A teacher may write "Good Morning" on the blackboard as she enters into the classroom. Writing "Good Morning" on the blackboard is not as effective as a warm oral greeting. In choice of a medium, the sender must consider the knowledge, skill and ability of the receiver. Writing "Good morning" for a deaf and dumb class is a better medium than oral greeting.

4. Language Problem

Language is the most important medium of communication. Language is an arbitrary code that depends on shared definitions, but there is a limit to how completely any of us share the same meaning for a given word. To overcome the language barriers, use the most specific and accurate words possible. Always try to use the vocabulary and expressions your audience will understand.

5. Listening vs Hearing

If audience do not pay attention to what you deliver, you lose the objective of your communication. People are likely to drift off when they are forced to listen to information that is monotonous or difficult to understand, or too technical, or too philosophical. To make your audience listen carefully, you must view the situation through the eyes of the receiver. Add lightness to your communication, clarify meaning by asking non-threatening questions. Humour appeals to everybody. Plan comic element in your communication.

6. Incorrect Filtering

Filtering is screening your message before it is passed on to someone else. There are many filters between the sender and the receiver in an organizational communication-secretaries,

Assistants, Receptionists, Answering machines etc. Try to establish more than one channel. If possible, try to have direct approach by eliminating the role of intermediaries.

7. Varied attitudes and Perceptions

You see a situation according to your own way of thinking. Your attitudes and thoughts are unique and they may not match with other people. Why force your opinion on others? Others may have different perceptions. As senders we choose the details important to us. As receivers we try to fit new details into our existing pattern. If a detail does not fit into our pre-determined notion, the message may take a distorted shape.

8. Lack of Feedback

Communication is a two-way process but without feedback, it remains one way. Both sender and receiver can play an active role in using feedback to make communication a two way. Feedback should be helpful rather than hurting. Immediate feedback is more useful than waiting for the 'right' moment.

9. Varied Backgrounds

Age, education, gender, social status, economic position, cultural background, temperament, health, popularity, religion, personal beliefs, beauty, even the mood swings—all separate one human being from another and make understanding difficult. Imposing one's personal background, beliefs or culture onto others is a great barrier to communication.

10. Distracting Environment

Physical disturbance like too many people talking in the room, police and ambulance sirens creating noise, ringing mobile phones will not make communication audible. Slow Internet connections, if you are using the one, unfavourable climatic conditions in the room, etc., may hamper the flow of communication.

11. Varied Emotional Behaviour

Every message has a content meaning and a relationship meaning. The relationship meaning suggests the nature of interaction between the sender and the receiver. You may have to deal with the people when they are upset. Be sensitive towards the feelings that may arise in yourself and others as you communicate, negative emotional outcomes during the process of communication may distort the message.

❑❑❑

Chapter 17

EXERCISE AND ASSIGNMENT

EXERCISE 1

A. Answer the Following Questions

1. Define technical communication.
2. What do you understand by the process of communication?
3. How can you minimize the communication gap between sender and the receiver?
4. Discuss the functions of technical communication?
5. What do you understand by communication? Discuss the importance of feedback in the communication process.
6. Discuss the different barriers to communication.
7. What can management of an organisation do to improve the efficiency of the employees?
8. What is the importance of technical communication?
9. What do you understand by Interpersonal communication? How is it different to organizational communication?
10. What are the different parts of Interpersonal communication? Explain.

B. Assignment

1. Your company has produced a new model of cellphone. Write a technical manual for the cellphone.
2. As a manager of an organisation, what role can you play for its growth?

C. Correct the Following Statements

1. Technical communication conveys general information about a technical subject.
2. Use of jargons and cliches make technical writing effective.

3. Non-verbal signals are always planned.
4. Communication process is constituted of five components.
5. Communication is a one-way process.
6. Technical communication is the process of conveying technical information through writing.
7. Technical communication may be interpreted in many ways.
8. Use of too many prepositional phrases create an impact on the reader.

D. Fill in the Blanks with Appropriate Words

1. The message travels to the sender through the .... chose by the ....
2. Effective communication brings the .... results.
3. .... is the global means of communication.
4. Non-verbal signals are .... and verbal signals are ....
5. Self analysis means knowing your ....
6. Use of .... create confusion.
7. Prefer .... voice to .... voice.
8. Communicate in a .... manner even if you are conveying negative messages.
9. Technical communication is understood by the .... audience.
10. Information will last longer if it is ....
11. Technical communication is used in ....
12. General communication may be fictional whereas technical communication ....

E. Say True or False

1. The employees of an organization should be dominated at work.
2. The performance of an employee depends on his efficiency of work and not his relationship with his juniors.
3. Communication is a creative process.
4. It is always better to maintain a distance between seniors and juniors.
5. Effective communication happens only with the saying or writing of words.
6. Group communication decreases productivity, quality and creativity.
7. The barriers to communication are inevitable but can be avoided with efforts.
8. Muddle messages clarify the doubts and remove misunderstanding.
9. Downward communication is the communication which travels from superior to subordinate.
10. Horizontal communication facilitates the task of coordination among peers.
11. Successful management should have variety of communication skills to function effectively.
12. Work would not be affected in the organization in the absence of communication.

EXERCISE 2

A. Answer the Following Questions:

1. What points should be kept in mind in technical writing?
2. Point out the differences between technical communication and general communication.
3. Discuss the significance of English language in technical domain.
4. How can communication skill help in the growth of an organization?
5. Discuss the features of technical communication.
6. What do you understand by the flow of communication? How many formal channels of communication are there in an organization? Explain.
7. Discuss the significance of 'Grapevine' in an organization.
8. What are the different stages of communication?
9. How many levels of communication are there? Discuss.
10. Discuss the advantages and disadvantages of group communication.
11. What do you understand by Mass Communication? Discuss the importance of mass communication.
12. How can you overcome the barriers to communication?

B. Assignment

1. You are a technical advisor to the Prime-Minister of India. You are required to send a report on the terrorist events which took place in Mumbai on 26th November 2008 giving the sequences of blast, failures on the part of Intelligence, involvement of the foreign hand, approximate number of lives lost and injured, commendable works of the security forces.
2. You are the CMD of a company. Inform your staff about their revised salary structure as forced by the recent downturn in the global market explaining them the reasons and assuring them that this is a short term adjustment in the benefit of the members and organization.
3. You are one of the junior employees of a company. Write a letter to your project manager stating the problems you are facing with your team leader for example his lack of knowledge in technical field, his biased attitude and his non-cooperative behaviour.

C. Say True or False

1. Listening is an important aspect of any communication.
2. Communication is a creative process.
3. The main purpose of technical communication is to make technologies appear more attractive to the consumer.
4. Technical communication is intended to convey specific information to a specific audience for a specific purpose.

5. Technical writing generally deals with human emotions and sentiments.
6. You can achieve accuracy and precision if you use jargons, trite expressions, Cliche's.
7. The most effective style is the one that accurately encodes the message into appropriate language.
8. General communication can be both formal and informal.
9. Wordiness can be avoided by substituting one word for several words or phrases.
10. A technical writer needs imagery to express his ideas.

D. Answer the Following Questions by Choosing the Best Alternative

1. *Communication barriers are generally created by:*
   (*a*) Physical distraction (*b*) Psychological distraction
   (*c*) Emotional disturbance (*d*) Improper encoding
   (*e*) All of these.
2. *Horizontal communication may be carried out in:*
   (*a*) Seminars (*b*) Meetings
   (*c*) Informal gatherings (*d*) Conferences.
3. *Indirect channels of communication may include:*
   (*a*) Kinesics (*b*) Language
   (*c*) Verbal communication (*d*) None of these.
4. *Group communication increases:*
   (*a*) Disturbance (*b*) Noise
   (*c*) Problems (*d*) Quality.
5. *The process of Mass Communication, consists of:*
   (*a*) Seven components (*b*) Six components
   (*c*) Five components (*d*) None of these
6. *The barriers to communication may relate to:*
   (*a*) The sender (*b*) The receiver
   (*c*) The circumstances (*d*) All of these.
7. *The process of mass communication has little or no:*
   (*a*) Feedback (*b*) Decoding
   (*c*) Encoding (*d*) Content.
8. *Lack of communication skill often results in:*
   (*a*) Depression (*b*) Shyness
   (*c*) Negativity (*d*) Stress
   (*e*) All of these.
9. *In a dynamic group:*
   (*a*) Members are permanent (*b*) New members may join
   (*c*) Existing members do not leave (*d*) None of these.

10. *Storming stage of the group is characterized by*
(*a*) Problem solving mentality (*b*) Fault-finding mentality
(*c*) conflict (*d*) None of these.

11. *Technical communication is:*
(*a*) Transmission of general information to specific audience
(*b*) Transmission of specific information to specific audience
(*c*) Transmission of specific information to general audience
(*d*) None of these.

12. *Technical writing must have:*
(*a*) Jargons, Cliche's (*b*) Prepositional phrases
(*c*) Nominalizations (*d*) Accuracy and clarity.

13. *The techniques used in technical writing include:*
(*a*) Explanation (*b*) Imagination
(*c*) Exposition (*d*) Comparison and contrast.

14. *Process of communication is incomplete if there is no:*
(*a*) Feedback (*b*) Listening process
(*c*) Attention (*d*) Medium of communication
(*e*) All of these.

15. *Technical communication may be required in:*
(*a*) Day-to-day conversation (*b*) E-mails, journals and seminars
(*c*) Novel writing (*d*) Poetry writing.

E. Fill in the Blanks with Appropriate Words:

1. The grapevine is not always .... and can be helpful for an ....

2. Decoding in written communication refers to .... and .... a written message.

3. Communication is an .... process.

4. Upward channel involves communication from .... to ....

5. The main objective of horizontal communication is to promote .... coordination.

6. .... communication is less formal and structured then both .... and .... communication.

7. Technical communication makes .... interaction possible.

8. Dyadic is a type of .... communication which happens ....

9. Organization communication serves as a .... between different .... of an ....

10. Interference in the communication process is called ....

❑❑❑

Unit II
Constituents of Technical Written Communication

Chapter 1
ENRICHING TOOLS OF COMMUNICATION

"The words you choose to say something are just as important as the decision to speak."

—Anonymous

VOCABULARY EXTENSION METHODS

1. Use flash cards. Write the target words or phrases on the cards which can be put in your wallet or pocket. While reviewing the words, separate the words into two piles, those you have learned and those you have not. Keep going through the words you have not learned until you are confident about them.

Flash card technology is the inexpensive and quickest way to learn words by repetition. You can pick out the card any time anywhere.

2. Visualize and Vocalize. Meditate on the image that the word represents or suggests as you say it along.

3. Learn complete sentences. It is often easier to learn a complete sentence than individual words. By learning sentences, you get an example of the word being used. Moreover, you learn all the words contained in a sentence and not only one individual word. Pick a sentence which illustrates a point for you, look up the words and memorize it.

4. Organize your vocabulary list. Organize the words into an order that makes sense to you. It is always easier to learn words by category. So group words by category for example, phobias, forms of government etc.

5. Rhyming and other mnemonic devices. They help in adding the word to the memory so it will not be forgotten. Rhyme the words with words you know. Relate the new word to something you already know.

6. Do new activities. Try something completely out of your routine activity. New activities will increase the vocabulary as well as add interest to life.

7. Read. Reading helps in increasing your vocabulary even when you may not be aware of it. Don't interrupt your reading by looking up every new word in the dictionary. It is always better to guess the meaning of the new word you come across. You may speak loudly the new word, you might recognize the word when you hear it or you can also examine the structure of the word. Look for familiar word parts and see if you can tell the meaning of the stem or you recognize the root of the word or prefixes or suffixes are familiar to you. Then check the dictionary. You may be right in your guess. Write out the definition of new word in your own words. It is not essential to check the dictionary immediately. You can note down new words and when you have finished your reading you can consult the dictionary.

WORD FORMATION

The Root of the Word. The basic part of any word is the root. Many words in the English language are derived from Greek and Latin roots. When we know the roots, it will be easy for us to group the meaning of any new word that comes across, bearing the same root.

Some Common Greek and Latin Roots

Root	*Meaning*	*Words*
aster (G)	star	astronomy, astrology
audi (L)	to hear	audible, auditorium
bene (L)	good, well	benefit, benevolent
bio (G)	life	biology, autobiography
dic, dict (L)	to speak	diction, dictate
fer (L)	to carry	reference, transfer
fix (L)	to fasten	prefix, suffix, fixation
geo (G)	earth	geology, geography
graph (G)	to write	graphic, photography
just (L)	law	justice, justify
logue (G)	thought, word	monologue, catalogue
luc (L)	light	lucid, translucent
manu (L)	hand	manuscript, manual
meter (G)	measure	barometer, meterology, centimeter
oper (L)	work	operate, co-operate,
path (G)	feeling	sympathetic, empathy
phil (G)	love	philosophy, philanthropy
phy (G)	body	physical, physiology,
script (L)	to write	manuscript, transcript
tele (G)	far off	teleprinter, telex, telephone
ter (L)	earth	territory, terrestrial,
vac (L)	empty	vacuum, vacant
verb (L)	word	verbal, proverbs,
vis (L)	to see	vision, supervision, television

Some Word Forms

Noun	*Adjective*	*Verb*
Accuser	accusing	accuse
Addition	added	add
Administrator	administrative	administrate
Advertisement	advertised	advertise
Assassination	assassinated	assassinate
Baker	baked	bake
Belief	believable	believe
Calculation	calculated	calculate
Cheerfulness	cheerful	cheer
Civilization	civil	civilize
Competition	competitive	compete
Dealer/Deal	dealt	deal
Designer/Design	designed	design
Destruction	destructive	destroy
Development	developed	develop
Drama	dramatic	dramatize
Drunkard	drunk	drink
Education	educational	educate
Embezzlement	embezzled	embezzle
Employment	employed	employ
Entertainment	entertaining	entertain
Enthusiasm	enthusiastic	enthuse
Exaggeration	exaggerated	exaggerate
Examiner/Examination	examined	examine
Exporter	exported	export
Fight/Fighting	fought	fight
Finance	financial	finance
Forgery	forged	forge
Foundation	founded	found
Gambling	gambled	gamble
Guidance	guided	guide
Hospitalization	hospitalized	hospitalize
Humanist	humanitarian	humanize
Idealist	idealistic	idealize
Illustration	illustrative	illustrate
Immigrant	immigrated	immigrate
Immortality	immortal	immortalize

Noun	Adjective	Verb
Importer	imported	import
Inspector	inspected	inspect
Invention	inventive	invent
Justice	justifiable	justify
Learner	learned	learn
Liberation	liberal	liberalize
Management/Manager	manageable	manage
Migrant	migratory	migrate
Modification	modificatory	modify
Nationalism	nationalistic	nationalize
Negotiation	negotiable	negotiate
Offense	offensive	offend
Office	official	officiate
Organization	organizational	organize
Owner	owned	own
Participation	participated	participate
Perfection	perfect	perfect
Perpetuation	perpetual	perpetuated
Purification	pure	purify
Quitting	quit	quit
Reception	receptive	receive
Relative	related	relate
Representation	representative	represent
Sales	sold	sell
Service	serviceable	serve
Slave	slavish	enslave
Socialist	sociable	socialize
Speaker	spoken	speak
Student	studious	study
Sympathy	sympathetic	sympathize
Talk	talkative	talk
Teacher	taught	teach
Theory	theoretical	theorize
Thinking	thought	think
Usefulness	useful	use
Utility	utilized	utilize
Violation	violated	violate
Volunteer	volunteered	volunteer
Winner	won	win

PREFIXES AND SUFFIXES

An English word can be divided into three parts: a prefix, a stem and a suffix.

Prefix. Pre means 'before', so prefix is added at the beginning of a stem or base word. Prefix is added to the stem to add or change the meaning of the word, for example, prefix semi (meaning half) is added to the word annual making it semi-annual and changing the meaning of the word yearly to half yearly.

1. Prefixes Showing Quantity/Size

Prefixes	*Meaning*	*Word*
Semi, hemi	half	Semiliquid, hemisphere
Uni, mono	one	monologue, unity
bi, di	two	bilingual, dilemma
cent	hundred	Century, centimeter
kilo	thousand	kilogram
micro-	very small	microscopic
mega	large	megabyte

2. Prefixes of Location

Prefixes	*Meaning*	*Word*
Inter	between, among	Inter dependant, Interactive
Super	over	Supersonic
trans	across	transmit
ex	out	exclude
extra	beyond	extraordinary
peri	around	periphery
sub	under	subway

3. Prefixes of Time and Order

Prefixes	*Meaning*	*Word*
ante	before	antecedent
pre	before	prefix, precedent
prime	first	primer, primary
post	after	posthumous, post-script
retro	backward	retroactive

4. Negative Prefixes

Prefixes	*Meaning*	*Word*
In		Incomplete
Im	not	Impossible
Il		Illiterate
Ir		Irrelevant
Non	not	Non-transferrable
Mis	bad	mismanagement
Mal		maltreatment
dis	opposite	disagree
anti	against	anticlockwise
de	reduce	deactivate
Under	too little	Underestimate

5. Positive Prefixes

Prefixes	*Meaning*	*Word*
re	do again	re-establish, relocate
over	too much	overconfident

SUFFIXES

Suffix. A suffix is attached to the end of the stem. Suffix changes the tense of the verb, for example 'ed' added to the verb 'Learn' + ed 'Learned', changes it from the present to the past. Suffix also changes the word from one part of speech to another. For example, —'ly' added to the adjective changes the word to adverbs —'Smart' is an adjective, but smart + ly = 'smartly' is an adverb. So suffix modifies the meaning of a word.

1. Noun Suffixes

Suffix	*Word*
—ence	Reference, dependence, interference
—ance	Attendance, acceptance, performance
—or	Conductor, operator, stimulator
—er	Driver, computer, silencer
—ment	Employment, advertisement, sentiment
—list	Specialist,
—ism	Hinduism, formalism
—ship	Friendship, relationship
—ency	Frequency

—tion/sion	Demonstration, alteration, admission
—ness	Cleanliness, kindness
—hood	Childhood
—dom	Kingdom

Note: Adverb suffixes usually take 'ly'

2. Verb Suffixes

Suffix	*Word*
en	Moisten, freshen
fy	Specify, clarify
ize	Fantasize, pressurize
ate	Delegate, propogate, graduate

3. Adjective Suffixes

Suffix	*Word*
able	Refundable, presentable
ible	Incredible, edible, legible
al	Structural, categorical
tial	Partial, sequential
tic	Fantastic,
ly	Partly, friendly, timely
ful	Beautiful, shameful
ous	Spacious, cautious
tive	Interrogative, comparative
less	Penniless, selfless
ish	Selfish, snobbish
ulent	Virulent

IDIOMS, PROVERBS AND PHRASES

I. Idioms

1. **A bad apple.** Someone who has a bad effect on a whole group.
2. **Apple of someone's eye.** Be loved very much by someone.
3. **Beat around the bush.** Delay talking about something.
4. **Butterflies in the stomach.** Very nervous or excited.
5. **Cannot make head or tail.** Cannot understand at all.
6. **Catch someone's eye.** Attract someone.

7. **Cold feet.** Very nervous.
8. **Cook someone's goose.** Get someone in trouble.
9. **Cool as a cucumber.** Very calm and relaxed even in a difficult situation.
10. **Couch potato.** One who remains inactive and idle.
11. **Don't let the grass grow under your feet.** Act now without any delay.
12. **Drive someone up the wall.** Annoy or irritate someone very much.
13. **Easy as pie.** Very easy.
14. **Eat one's words.** Admit that what you said was wrong.
15. **Feel like a fish out of water.** To feel uncomfortable in an unfamiliar situation.
16. **Be fishy.** Seem not to be true.
17. **Food for thought.** Ideas that make you think carefully.
18. **Get over something.** To feel better again.
19. **Get up on the wrong side of the bed.** Feel a little angry and annoyed.
20. **Give someone a hand.** To help someone.
21. **Be glued to something.** Watching something attentively.
22. **Go nuts.** Become very angry.
23. **Grab a bite.** Eat food quickly.
24. **Hat trick.** A series of three wins.
25. **Hit the books.** Study very hard.
26. **Hit the nail on the head.** Be exactly right about something.
27. **Hold one's horses.** Be patient and careful.
28. **In a pickle.** In a difficult situation.
29. **In the same boat.** In the same situation.
30. **It is easier said than done.** Easier to suggest but hard to do.
31. **In hot water.** In trouble.
32. **Keep an eye.** To watch.
33. **Keep one's bed.** Stay in bed because of sickness or other cause.
34. **Like taking candy from a baby.** Very easy to do.
35. **Low key.** On a small scale.
36. **Make ends meets.** Earn enough money to live.
37. **Not hold water.** Does not seem reasonable or correct.
38. **On the tip of someone's tongue.** Cannot remember something although you think you know it.
39. **Once in a blue moon.** Rarely.
40. **Out of the blue.** Suddenly and unexpectedly.
41. **Out of the frying pan and into the fire.** Moving from bad to worse situation.
42. **Over the hill.** Too old to do something.
43. **Pull someone's leg.** Tease someone.
44. **Put all your eggs into one basket.** Depend totally on one course of action.
45. **Put yourself in someone's shoes.** Try to understand someone's situation.

46. **Race against the clock/time.** Do something very fast to finish it before a deadline.
47. **Rain cats and dogs.** Rain heavily.
48. **Read between the lines.** To understand the real meaning of words.
49. **Rings a bell.** Reminds you of something.
50. **See the light.** Understand or believe something that you didn't before.
51. **Shake like a leaf.** Nervous or frightened.
52. **So far so good.** Things have been going well until now.
53. **Speak of the devil.** When someone you have been talking about comes in unexpectedly.
54. **Take it easy.** Don't worry.
55. **Tip of the iceberg.** Suggesting or showing a much larger problem.
56. **Be tongue tied.** Unable to speak because of some reasons.
57. **Turn over a new leaf.** Start to do something again in a better way, forgetting past errors.
58. **Turn your back on.** Refuse to help others.
59. **Twenty-four seven (24/7).** Twenty-four hours a day, seven days a week.
60. **Under pressure.** Work in a way that frustrates you.
61. **Up and running.** Working well.
62. **Up in the air.** Not decided yet.
63. **Wear one's heart on one's sleeve.** Show emotions or feelings openly.
64. **When it rains, it pours.** Bad things happen at the same time.
65. **When pigs fly.** Something a person said will never happen.

II. Proverbs

1. **Beauty is in the eyes of a beholder.** People have different opinions about what is beautiful/good.
2. **Best advice is found on the pillow.** You may solve a problem after a good night's sleep.
3. **Better safe than sorry.** Better to be careful than to take risks.
4. **A bird in the hand is worth two in the bush.** It is better to be satisfied with what you have than to risk losing it by trying to get something better.
5. **Birds of a feather flock together.** People who are alike tend to become friends.
6. **Curiosity killed the cat.** Too much interest in something can put you in danger.
7. **Don't count your chickens before they hatch.** Not to be too sure that something good you hope for will really happen.
8. **Don't cross your bridges before you come to them.** Not to worry about something until it actually happens.
9. **The early bird catches the worm.** To act right now to be successful.
10. **Good things come in small packages.** Size does not always indicate the quality.
11. **The grass is always greener on the other side of the fence.** The things or situations of others look better than your own.

12. **Home is where the heart is.** If you are with the person or at the place you love most, it becomes your true home.
13. **It's no use crying over spilled milk.** Do not worry about something that has already happened.
14. **A kite rises against the wind.** A person grows when he faces opposition and conquers it.
15. **Money does not grow on trees.** It is not easy to earn money.
16. **Necessity is the mother of invention.** If someone has a problem, he will find a way to solve it.
17. **Opposites attract.** People tend to be attracted to those who are not like them.
    Note. "Opposites attract" is the opposite of "Birds of a feather flock together".
18. **An ounce of prevention is worth a pound of care.** Prevent a problem than to deal with it after it has happened.
19. **The pen is mightier than the sword.** Words are more powerful than swords or weapons.
20. **A picture is worth a thousand words.** A picture can give as much information as a written or spoken text.
21. **Procrastination is the thief of time.** Do not delay in doing something that you must do.
22. **Safety lies in the middle course.** Act in a moderate way.
23. **Silence is golden.** Do not say anything if you do not have something constructive to say.
24. **A stitch in time saves nine.** This proverb expresses a similar idea to that of "An ounce of prevention is worth a pound of care".
25. **Too many cooks spoil the broth.** If too many people do the same thing, it will not be done well.
26. **Variety is the spice of life.** Variety makes life interesting.
27. **You can lead a horse to water, but you cannot make it drink.** You can give someone the opportunity to learn, but you cannot force him to learn.
28. **You cannot judge a book by its cover.** Not to judge someone by the appearance.
29. **You can't take it with you when you die.** Do not worry too much about the material things.
30. **You can't get blood out of a stone.** You cannot extract what is not there to begin with.

III. Phrases

1. **A bed of roses.** A pleasant or easy situation.
2. **A cock and bull story.** A fanciful and an unbelievable tale.
3. **A diamond is the rough.** Good at heart but lacks social grace and respect for the law.
4. **A dish fit for gods.** An offering of high quality.

5. **Back to square one.** To start again.
6. **Baker's dozen.** Thirteen.
7. **Call a spade a spade.** To speak plainly, to describe something as it really is.
8. **Cold shouldered.** To treat in an unfriendly way.
9. **Crocodile tears.** Fake tears.
10. **Cut to the chase.** Get to the point.
11. **Day light robbery.** Unfair overcharging.
12. **Excuse my French.** Forgive my swearing.
13. **End of story.** No more to be said.
14. **A face like a bulldog chewing a wasp.** Ugly.
15. **Fall on your sword.** Offer your resignation.
16. **From sea to shining sea.** From one coast to another.
17. **Get off on the wrong foot.** Make a bad start to a project or relationship.
18. **Get your feet wet.** To get your first experience of something.
19. **Have an axe to grind.** Have an ulterior motive.
20. **Hold your horses.** Be patient.
21. **In a nutshell.** Briefly.
22. **In the limelight.** At the centre of attention.
23. **It never rains but it pours.** When troubles come, they come together.
24. **Keep your nose to the grindstone.** Apply yourself conscientiously to your work.
25. **Knee jerk reaction.** An automatic response to something.
26. **Knock off.** To finish work for the day.
27. **Know which way the wind blows.** To understand what is happening in changing circumstances.
28. **Last but not least.** Not necessarily in order of importance.
29. **Laughing stock.** A figure or object of ridicule and laughter.
30. **Learn the ropes.** Learn something new.
31. **Level playing field.** Fair competition.
32. **Lie low.** Keep out of sight.
33. **Let the cat out of the bag.** To reveal a big secret.
34. **Make hay.** To take advantage of a favourable opportunity.
35. **Make a mountain out of a molehill.** To assume something is much worse than it actually is.
36. **Make waves.** To cause a lot of trouble.
37. **Mind one's Ps and Qs.** To behave properly.
38. **Mumbo jumbo.** Nonsense.
39. **Nip in the bud.** Put a stop to something while it is still in its early development.
40. **Not worth the candle.** Worthless.
41. **Off the mark.** Incorrect or inaccurate.

42. **On cloud nine.** To be extremely happy.
43. **On the fiddle.** Engaged in corruption.
44. **Paddle your own canoe.** Act independently.
45. **Pass the buck.** Pass responsibility on to someone else.
46. **Quick buck.** To make easy money.
47. **Rags to riches.** Someone who starts poor and becomes rich.
48. **Red tape.** Bureaucratic Procedure.
49. **Rule of thumb.** Practical rule.
50. **Sacred cow.** Something too highly regarded to be open to criticism.
51. **Scot free.** To avoid payment.
52. **Sleep tight.** Sleep well.
53. **Take a back seat.** Take no active part.
54. **Take with a pinch of salt.** Accept a truth but with reservations.
55. **The full monty.** Complete, the whole thing.
56. **Thorn in the flesh.** A persistent difficulty.
57. **Tie the knot.** Get married.
58. **Top notch.** Excellent.
59. **Turn a blind eye.** To refuse to take notice of a situation.
60. **Up a blind alley.** On the wrong track.
61. **Veg out.** To relax in a mindless manner.
62. **Water under the bridge.** A past event that is no longer worth agonizing over.
63. **Where there's smoke there's fire.** There is always a basis for a rumour.
64. **White elephant.** More trouble that it is worth.
65. **Zero tolerance.** A form of policing that allows no crime to be overlooked.

USE OF WORDS AND SENTENCES IN VERBAL COMMUNICATION

Verbal communication requires the use of words, vocabulary, numbers and is organised in sentences using language. Good linguistic skills help in achieving effective verbal communication.

Everyone's brain is occupied with thoughts which need words to explain them. Words alone will not be sufficient unless they are structured into sentences. Positive well structured spoken or written messages can motivate, inspire and create a lasting impact.

1. Use positive words. A glass can be half full with water or can be half empty. Phrase your words positively. Your words and the emotions which you express through your sentences have the power to create an impact on others. So positive feelings will come out of the positive words creating positive impact on others.

2. Use simple language and simple vocabulary. The purpose of communication is to send a message and not to present yourself a learned man.

3. Use short words and short sentences. Listeners should not have to work hard to understand you.

4. Use of active voice is preferred.

5. Use common words rather than technical jargon otherwise the receiver will be left confused decoding the technical jargon.

6. Ask the right question. By asking questions and wording them specifically, you will invite a positive debate and interaction that will benefit all involved. Unnecessary arguments are reduced when you are able to express yourself with great command of your language skill.

7. Think and plan before you speak. Whether you are speaking in public or talking to your seniors in your office or communicating with your friends or family members, you must think, before you utter those words. Misunderstanding prevails when you express yourself without thinking. Plan words to express your thoughts to give a right message.

8. Avoid long pauses. Do not stop for long during conversation and add 'an', 'um', 'well'. Too many of these create an irritating impact on the listener and present uncertainty on your part. Reduce the unnecessary verbal cues and if you must pause, pause for a short duration and condition yourself to a silent pause.

9. Avoid careless language. Use your words and sentences with care. Give accurate description. Do not expect your listeners to assume or guess.

ENGLISH SPELLING RULES

English spelling often appears to be illogical but some rules can help you to frame the correct spellings. But do not forget that these rules are for general changes. Exceptions are always there.

1. If the word has a consonant before 'y', change 'y' to 'i'.

   Example: Duty = duties

   Mercy + less = merciless

2. If the word has a vowel before 'y', keep the 'y'.

   Example: Toy = Toys

   Employ = employed

3. The final consonant of a word is generally doubled when adding-ed, -ing, or-er.

   Example: Rob = robbing

   Sad = sadden

   Swim = swimming

   Cancel = cancelled

4. Put I before E except before C

   Examples: Achieve, believe, brief, hygiene ceiling but receive, deceive.

5. When adding an ending to a word that ends with a silent *e*, drop the final *e* (if the ending begins with a vowel)

   Example:

   Advancing

Surprising

If the ending begins with a consonant, keep the final '*e*'

Example:

Advancement

Likeness

Drop the '*e*' when the suffix starts with a vowel

Use + able = usable

Judge + ment = judgement

So, if a word ends in a consonant followed by a silent '*e*', drop the '*e*' before endings beginning with a vowel, but keep the '*e*' before endings beginning with a consonant.

Example:

Engage + ing = engaging

Engage + ment = engagement

Care + ing = caring

care + less = careless

6. 'Q' is followed by 'u'

   Example: Queen, Quiet, Queer

7. To spell the sound of '*k*' at the end of a word, we use '*ck*' or '*k*', use '*ck*', after a vowel. After consonants use '*k*'.

   Example: Chalk, clock, talk, bark, stock

8. Words do not end in '*v*' or '*j*' we add silent '*e*' at the end of a word.

   Example: Dove, have, shave, love, daze, summarize

EXERCISE

Answer the following questions:

1. What techniques should you follow to improve your vocabulary?
2. Use the following idioms in sentences of your own.

   (*a*) All the rage
   (*b*) Changed colour
   (*c*) Took to heart
   (*d*) Spread like wild fire
   (*e*) Smell a rat

3. Give examples showing the use and meaning of the following prefixes.

   Auto, Dia, Ex, Hyper, Pro, Super

Chapter 2

ONE WORD SUBSTITUTION

"The fewer words, the better prayer."

—**Martin Luther**

1. **Atheist**—One who does not believe in God.
2. **Theist**—One who believes in God.
3. **Omnipotent**—One who is all powerful.
4. **Omnipresent**—One who is present everywhere.
5. **Omniscient**—One who knows everything.
6. **Convalescent**—One who is recovering from illness.
7. **Gullible**—One who is easily deceived.
8. **Infallible**—One who does not make mistakes.
9. **Mercenary**—One who can do anything for money.
10. **Pauper**—One who has no money.
11. **Turncoat**—One who changes sides.
12. **Volunteer**—One who works on choice.
13. **Bibliophile**—One who loves books.
14. **Bilingual**—One who can speak two languages.
15. **Philanthropist**—One who loves mankind.
16. **Misanthrope**—One who hates mankind.
17. **Optimist**—One who looks at the bright side of things.
18. **Pessimist**—One who looks at the dark side of things.
19. **Egoist**—One who thinks about himself.
20. **Agnostic**—One who doubts the existence of God.
21. **Hypocrite**—One who pretends to be what he is not.
22. **Indefatigable**—One who cannot be defeated.
23. **Samaritan**—One who helps others to do good.
24. **Plagiarist**—One who copies from other writers.

25. **Misogynist**—One who hates women.
26. **Polyglot**—One who knows many language.
27. **Epicure**—One who is fond of sensuous pleasure.
28. **Stoic**—One who is indifferent to pleasure and pain.
29. **Feminist**—One who thinks of the welfare of women.
30. **Effeminate**—One who is quite like a woman.
31. **Eccentric**—One who has strange habits.
32. **Reticent**—One who speaks less.
33. **Fatalist**—One who believes in fate.
34. **Pedestrian**—One who walks on foot.
35. **Valetudinarian**—One who always thinks himself to be ill.
36. **Intestate**—One who dies without a will.
37. **Cynic**—One who questions everything.
38. **Glutton**—One who eats too much.
39. **Immigrant**—One who lives in a foreign country.
40. **Neophyte**—One who is newcomer.
41. **Celibate**—One who is unmarried.
42. **Avaricious**—One who is greedy for money.
43. **Illiterate**—One who does not know how to read and write.
44. **Homicide**—Murder of a human being.
45. **Patricide**—Murder of a father.
46. **Infanticide**—Murder of an infant.
47. **Matricide**—Murder of a mother.
48. **Fratricide**—Murder of a brother.
49. **Foeticide**—Murder of a foetus.
50. **Suicide**—Murder of self.
51. **Anthropology**—A study of man.
52. **Ethnology**—A study of races.
53. **Physiology**—A study of the body.
54. **Zoology**—A study of animals.
55. **Ornithology**—A study of birds.
56. **Archeology**—A study of ancient things.
57. **Astrology**—A study of stars and planets.
58. **Etymology**—A study of the origin of words.
59. **Draw**—A game in which no one wins.
60. **Legal**—That which is lawful.
61. **Illegal**—That which is against law.

62. **Delegate**—To transfer one's authority to another.
63. **Biography**—A life history written by somebody else.
64. **Autobiography**—A life history written by oneself.
65. **Anonymous**—A book written by an unknown author.
66. Posthumous—A book published after the death of its author or award given after death.
67. **Contemporaries**—People living at the same time.
68. **Colleagues**—People who work together.
69. **Insatiable**—That which cannot be satisfied.
70. **Carnivorous**—A flesh eating animal.
71. **Herbivorous**—A grass eating animal.
72. **Monogamy**—Practice of having one wife or husband.
73. **Bigamy**—Practice of having two wives or husbands.
74. **Polygamy**—Practice of having more than two wives or husbands.
75. **Democracy**—Government by the people.
76. **Monarchy**—Government by a King or Queen.
77. **Bureaucracy**—Government by the officials.
78. **Plutocracy**—Government by the rich.
79. **Oligarchy**—Government by few.
80. **Anarchy**—Absence of Government.
81. **Aristocracy**—Government by the nobles.
82. **Autocracy**—Government by one.
83. **Mobocracy**—Rule of the mob.
84. **Opaque**—That through which light cannot pass.
85. **Transparent**—That through which light can pass.
86. **Translucent**—That through which light can partly pass.
87. **Ambiguous**—A sentence whose meaning is not clear.
88. **Indescribable**—That which cannot be described.
89. **Inimitable**—That which cannot be immitated.
90. **Inevitable**—That which cannot be avoided.
91. **Indefensible**—That which cannot be defended.
92. **Orphanage**—A place where orphans live.
93. **Predator**—An animal who preys on other animals.
94. **Sacrilege**—Violating the sanctity of a church.
95. **Idiosyncrasy**—A person with peculiar habits.
96. **Pseudonym**—To write under a different (false) name.
97. **Obsolete**—A thing no longer in use.

98. **Exonerate**—To free somebody from all blames.
99. **Illegible**—A handwriting that cannot be read.
100. **Epitaph**—Words written on the tomb of a person.
101. **Avaricious**—One who is greedy for money.
102. **Chauvinism**—A belief that women are less important than men.
103. **Communism**—A theory where the people or community as a whole are owners of all property.
104. **Dogmatism**—Doctrine of inordinate opinionism.
105. **Eroticism**—Sexual instincts and behaviour.
106. **Fascism**—A system of dictatorship.
107. **Hedonism**—A belief that pleasure is the main aim of life.
108. **Henotheism**—Belief in one God without denying the existence of others.
109. **Materialism**—The doctrine that material is the only reality.
110. **Fatalism**—The doctrine that all events are predetermined.
111. **Nihilism**—Complete denial of social, political and religious authorities.
112. **Pacifism**—A belief that wars and violence are always wrong.
113. **Nepotism**—Favouritism shown to relatives.
114. **Plagiarism**—The act of stealing ideas and writings of others and using as one's own.
115. **Realism**—An inclination towards literal truth.
116. **Secularism**—A belief that religious influence should be restricted.
117. **Sadism**—Deriving pleasure from cruelty.
118. **Spiritualism**—The belief that spirit is the only reality (a belief that spirit exists independent of matter.)

Chapter 3

Homophones or the Words Often Confused

"When all other means of communication fail, try words."

A **homophone** is a word which is pronounced in the same way as another word but differs in meaning, for example—**carat, carrot.** Homophones may be spelled differently, but the term also applies to different words that are spelled identically, such as **rose** (flower) and **rose** (Past Tense of rise). Here are some examples of such words given below:

1. **Accept** (*verb*)—She accepted the salary offer.

   Except (*preposition*)—Everyone has gone home except my boss.

   Expect (*verb*)—They expect to visit Bhopal in summers.

2. **Adopt** (*to take into a family*)—My friend has adopted a child.

   Adapt (*to take up and follow*)—Now we have adapted the changed political situation.

3. **Advise** (*verb*)—He advised his brother to study.

   Advice (*noun*)—Take my advice and work hard.

4. **Affect** (*verb*)—Smoking can affect health.

   Effect (*noun*)—Smoking has a bad effect on health.

5. **All Ready**—The students were all ready for their final examination.

   Already (*adverb*)—He has already written the paper.

6. **Altogether**—His presentation was altogether impressive.

7. **All together**—As soon as the teacher entered into the class, the students alltogether started making a noise.

8. **Allude** (*to refer to*)—She alluded to his height.

   Elude (*to avoid*)—He eluded her criticism by leaving the room.

9. **Allusion** (*reference to*)—Her allusion to his height made him uncomfortable.

   Illusion (*false idea*)—He had no illusion about being very intelligent.

10. **Almost** (*not most*)—Almost all my friends are going in the party.

 Most—Most of my friends are going in the party.

11. **Ambiguous**—(*Ambiguous is used to describe a phrase or act with more than one meaning*). The ending of the movie is ambiguous.

 Ambivalent—(*Ambivalent describes lack of certainity*). The committee is ambivalent about the proposal for starting a new project.

12. **Amount** is used with uncountable expressions—a large amount of money.

 Number is used with countable plural expressions.

13. **Apart** (*adverb*)—The old book fell apart.

 A part (*noun*)—I'd like to be a part of that project.

14. **Bad** (*adjective*)—He has a bad habit of sleeping in the classroom.

 Badly (*adverb*)—He was badly hurt in the car accident.

15. **Because** (*subordinate conjunction*)—He watched T.V. because he could not get sleep.

 Because of (*two word preposition*)—We left early because of the rain.

16. **Belief** (*noun*)—God exists is a common belief.

 Believe (*verb*)—Always believe in what you do.

17. **Beside** (*next to*)—Sit beside me.

 Besides (*in addition to*)—He has no friends besides us.

18. **Cite**—(*to quote*)—Cite an example.

 Site—(*location*)—They visited the site.

 Sight—(*view*)—I saw a beautiful sight on the sea side.

19. **Complement** (*to complete or add to something*)—The wine complemented the meal.

 Compliment (*to make a pleasant comment*)—The guests complimented the hostess for delicious meal.

20. **Compose** (*to make up*)—The conference centre is composed of five rooms.

 Comprise (*to include*)—The conference centre comprises five rooms.

21. **Conscience** (*awareness of right and wrong*)—Her conscience guides her to do right.

 Conscious (*awake or aware*)—The victim was still not conscious.

22. **Continual** (*repetition*)—The continual interruptions made the teacher angry.

 Continuous—The continuous rain filled the pools with water.

23. **Custom** (*tradition*)—It is a custom to enter into a Hindu temple barefoot.

 Customs (*tax on imports*)—The customs department seized heavy smuggled goods.

 Costume (*a style of dress*)—The costumes of the actors have to be designed to suit their roles.

24. **Dairy** (*associated with milk*)—Dairy products are rich in proteins.

 Diary (*daily writing*)—Maintaining diary is a good habit.

25. **Desert** (*verb*)—When did he desert his family?

    Desert (*noun*)—a dry, sandy environment. Camel is called the ship of the desert.

    Dessert (*sweet course at the end of a meal*)—Dessert is usually served at the end of the meal.

26. **Different from**—She looks different from her sister.

    Different than—My performance is different than it was last year.

27. **Discreet** (*tactful*)—Be discreet in your conversation.

    Discrete (*separate*)—John is doing research on five discrete topics.

28. **Each other** (*use with two*)—The twins love each other.

    One another (*with more than one*)—They were dancing with one another when the lights went off.

29. **Elicit** (*to get or draw out*)—The police tried in vain to elicit information from the suspect.

    Illicit (*illegal*)—Their illicit deals landed them in prison.

30. **Eminent** (*well known*)—an eminent doctor

    Imminent (*about to happen*)—an imminent disaster.

31. **Explicit** (*direct*)—She gave explicit instructions.

    Implicit (*implied*)—A tax increase is implicit in the proposal.

32. **Farther**—She lives farther from the college than I live.

    Further—The Principal announced further restrictions.

33. **Fewer** (*with plural countable nouns*)—October usually has fewer working days due to festivals.

    Less (*with uncountable nouns*)—Anil got less marks in the examination.

34. **Flaunt** (*to show off*)—Never flaunt even if you are the best.

    Flout (*to defy*)—Flouting traffic rules can sometimes be suicidal.

35. **Heroin** (*a drug*)—Capital punishments are imposed in the Middle East for smuggling heroin.

    Heroine (*a brave or important woman*)—By being brave, she proved herself a heroine.

36. **Immigrate**—(*To come to another country for the purpose of permanent residence or settling in it.*)

    Emigrate—(*To leave one's own native country to live elsewhere.*) He emigrated from India and immigrated to France.

37. **Imply** (*to suggest in an indirect way*)—You cannot imply different rules to different people.

    Infer (*to draw a conclusion*)—What can you infer from such confusing and contradictory statements?

38. **Incredible** (*difficult to believe*)—The statement of the thief was so incredible that the judge ignored it.

Incredulous (*skeptical, unable to believe*)—The promises made by the politicians are sometimes incredulous.

39. **Kind** (*adjective*)—Always be kind to the old and the aged.

    Sort (*verb*)—I had to sort out my personal file from the big heap.

    Type (*noun*)—So many companies come for the placements that one has to choose a particular type of suiting to one's requirement.

40. **Knew** (*verb*)—I knew I would get placement in Wipro.

    New (*adjective*)—New trains are introduced between Bhopal and Delhi.

41. **Lend** (*verb*)—Kindly lend me your motorbike for a day.

    Loan (*noun*)—Banks provide loans against some securities.

    Lone (*alone*)—India was not lone contender for Security Council.

42. **Lie**—(*to tell lies*) or (*to lie down*) It is better to lie down while recording your blood pressure.

    Lay—Lay them straight.

43. **Loose** (*not tight*)—It is better to wear loose clothes in summers.

    Loss—The death of Kalpana Chawla was a great loss to the nation.

44. **Marital** (*associated with marriage*)—Marital status is usually required on visa forms.

    Martial (*associated with war*)—The warriors of ancient times belonged to the martial race.

45. **Knot**—Tie the knot.

    Not (*negative*)—He is not fool.

46. **Maid** (*female helper*)—Maid did not come for work yesterday.

    Made (*Past of make*)—He made cake from white flour.

47. **Need**—I need your support in my difficult times.

    Knead—Knead the flour to make the chapatis.

48. **Male** (*gender*)—Do not differentiate between male and female child.

    Mail (*associated with post*)—Mail the parcel.

49. **Passed**—He passed his examination.

    Past—She walked past the bakery.

50. **Precede** (*to occur before*)—I preceded back in search of my lost bag.

    Proceed (*to go ahead*)—One has to proceed forward to achieve bigger goals.

51. **Principal** (*main, most important or head*)—The principal hoisted the national flag on Independence Day.

    Principle (*rule*)—He is a man of strong principles.

52. **Quite** (*adverb*)—I am quite well today.

    Quiet (*silent*)—Alok is a quiet boy.

53. **Quote** (*verb*)—Teachers quote great deeds of Mahatma Gandhi even in present era.

 Quotation (*noun*)—Only lowest quotations are accepted in the government departments.

54. **Sale** (*noun*)—The sale is going on in Bhopal.

 Cell (*noun*)—Put the cells in camera.

 Sell (*verb*)—I want to sell my old camera.

55. **Stationary** (*not moving*)—Objects remain in stationary position unless force is applied.

 Stationery (*items used in writing*)—Postal stamps are available in stationery shops these days.

56. **Than** (*used with comparative form*)—It is better to go late than drive rash.

 Then (*time word*)—Britishers have left India but the things have not changed since then.

57. **Their**—Their bags were stolen.

 There—There are many varieties of mangoes available in India.

58. **To/Too/Two**—Divya too gave two gifts to Alok.

59. **Uninterested** (*lacking in interest*)—I am uninterested in watching commercial cinema.

 Disinterested (*impartial*)—The criminal history of the politicians has made me disinterested in politics.

60. **Wear** (*verb*)—The mother asked the child to wear new dress.

 Were (*past tense*)—Many celebrities were not invited on Abhishek's wedding.

 Where–Where do you live ?

61. **Weather** (*noun*)

 Whether (*conjunction*) The weather will determine whether we should go on picnic or not.

62. **Waste**—Do not waste your money.

 Waist—He tied the belt on his waist.

63. **Weak**—He is too weak to walk to his college.

 Week—Our examinations will start next week.

64. **Write**—(*to write*) He writes story books for children.

 Rites—(*the customs*) Rites vary from culture to culture

 Right—(*correct*) Right attitude helps in achieving right targets.

65. **Whole**—(*complete*) The teacher distributed the question papers to the whole class.

 Hole—The holes in the bucket of water are similar to the barriers to communication.

EXERCISE

Use the following homophones in the sentences of your own so that the difference in meaning is made clear:

carat, carrot
told, tolled
see, sea
days, daze
scent, cent
sale, sail
pain, pane
reign, rain
stair, stare
heir, air
dew, due
profit, prophet
piece, peace

prize, price
yolk, yoke
sole, soul
rows, rose
coarse, course
cannon, canon
aloud, allowed
cell, sell
won, one
ring, wring
altar, alter
cot, caught
dissent, decent.

Chapter 4

Prepositional Phrases

"Be careful of your thoughts, they may become words at any moment."

—Ira Gassen

The following are some of the most common prepositional phrases.

At

At first
At least
At most
At times
At any rate
At last
At the latest
At once
At short notice
At an advantage
At a disadvantage
At risk
At a profit
At a loss.

By

By accident
By far
By all means
By heart
By chance
By and by
By the way
By the time
By no means
By name
By sight
By now
By then.

For

For now
For instance
For example
For sale
For a while
For the moment
For ages
For a change
For better
For worse

From

From now on
From then on
From bad to worse
From my point of view
From what I understand
From personal experience.

Under

Underage
Under control

Under the impression
Under guarantee
Under the influence of
Under obligation
Under no obligation
Under suspicion
Under his thumb
Under discussion
Under consideration.

Without

Without fail
Without notice
Without exception
Without someone's consent
Without success
Without warning.

EXERCISE

Choose the correct prepositional phrase to complete the sentences below:

1. The local police is talking to John. I think he is ...... for the crime. (under suspicion/in suspicion)
2. I will make sure your instructions are followed .... (at least, at once)
3. Jack is clearly ...... when it comes to speaking a foreign language. (at a disadvantage, at an advantage)
4. I am sure he did not mean to break the window. It must have happened .... (by accident, by chance)
5. Remember, you are ...... to buy the product. (under obligation, under no obligation)
6. ...... John comes on every function on right time. (without success, without fail)
7. It is ...... an easy task. Make sure to study hard. (by no means, by far)
8. I guess we'll just have to wait for a response .... (at once, for now)
9. ...... he considered looking for a new job, but then he decided to continue in the same company. (at times, at first)
10. We can't do anything about that .... (at the moment, at once)
11. I am afraid you can't enter this bar because you are .... (overage, underage)
12. They learned all their lines .... (by heart, without fail)
13. We are going to have to concentrate on improving customer service .... (from my point of view, at once).
14. Do not worry about the cell phone, it is still ...... we can get it repaired. (at an advantage, under guarantee)
15. ...... I want you to improve your grades in the college. (At short notice, from now on)
16. There are many things you can do ...... you can go to the Engineering College or Medical College. (for instance, by the way)
17. ...... he finishes his lecture, we will have to attend a meeting. (by the time, at time)
18. She was very pleased that she could sell her house .... (at a loss, at a profit)
19. Situation is horrible over here. Things are going .... (from bad to worse, under control)
20. He has been living in Bhopal .... (since ages/for ages)
21. He always comes to my house .... (without warning, without notice)

Chapter 5

PARAGRAPH WRITING

"Broadly speaking, the short words are the best, and the old words best of all."

—Sir W. Churchill

INTRODUCTION

A paragraph is a series of sentences that are organised and related to a single topic or to put it in other words, a paragraph is a collection of related sentences dealing with a single topic. A paragraph may consist of few sentences or many sentences but the sentences should be coherent, united and focused on a single topic. The purpose of a paragraph is to express one point. It must not contain irrelevant facts. Every sentence must contribute to the paragraph by explaining, exemplifying or expanding the main idea *i.e.,* topic sentence. A paragraph may be a part of a long composition or complete in itself. Each paragraph must deal with one idea and the previous paragraph should introduce the new idea if it is being followed in the next paragraph.

PARTS OF A PARAGRAPH

1. Topic Sentence. It comes at the beginning of a paragraph. The topic sentence is the summary of the whole paragraph. It relates to the main idea or central theme the paragraph is going to deal with. The purpose to keep the topic sentence in the beginning of the paragraph is to apprise the readers with the topic to be evaluated in the sentences that follow. This way the readers may understand the details that flow with the explanation of the main point.

The topic sentence should be precise and clear. It should express the central idea and not disclose all the details. The focus should be on the introduction of the main point. Every sentence in the paragraph will support the main idea expressed in the topic sentence. It would be advisable to weigh it properly before putting it down on paper. Do not be confused, always be authentic. Make a bold statement by using strong verbs like 'should', 'must' and not weak verbs like 'I think', 'I suppose', 'It may' etc. Use of weak verbs may make you lose your grip on the reader. Topic sentence is a vital part of a paragraph and it should be presented in a convincing way.

2. Supporting Sentence. They follow the topic sentence. If topic sentence is the beginning of the paragraph, supporting sentences constitute the middle of the paragraph. They form the body of the paragraph. Explain and expand the idea by giving reasons, examples, facts, statistics and quotations. Evidence should be given in support of your explanation. Here, you analyse the topic in detail. Supporting sentences provide support to the topic sentence and help in developing the main idea. Evaluate causes and reasons and use logical reasoning to explain the main idea. Maintain the logical order in writing the body of the paragraph. Do not lose unity.

3. Closing Sentence. The closing sentence sums up the important details mentioned in the paragraph. It should reinforce the point or opinion expressed in the body of the paragraph. It must restate the main idea to make it more convincing. If the paragraph is to be followed by the next paragraph, maintain the unity of idea by the use of appropriate transitional signals. The closing sentence, in that case, must introduce the new idea which is to be discussed in the paragraph following thereafter. You must do this without breaking the unity of the existing element.

FEATURES OF A PARAGRAPH

1. Unity. The paragraph should explain only one main idea which is stated in the topic sentence and develop it further by the proper use of supporting sentences. Unity refers to the proper connection of sentences in explaining the main idea introduced by the topic sentence. Deviating from the main point breaks the unity.

2. Coherence. Sentences should be organised in a logical manner and should follow a definite plan of development. Your paragraph should be easy to understand. The readers should be able to follow your point of view.

3. Development of the Idea. The main point expressed in the paragraph should be adequately explained. Support your point of view through evidence and statistics. Evaluate causes and reasons. Use examples and illustrations. Analyse the topic and then develop it further.

4. Vocabulary Choice. Be very cautious in the use of vocabulary. Wrong use of words may create misunderstanding. Avoid spelling mistakes and carefully use the vocabulary from homophones and the words often confused. Carelessness in the use of confused words may produce a funny, contradictory statement. Words like *expect/accept, bear/beer* etc., need to be carefully selected.

PROCESS OF WRITING A PARAGRAPH

While writing a paragraph, you will have to pass through three stages.

1. Prewriting Stage. Think carefully and organize your ideas before you pen them down on paper. Focus on the facts you are using to support the topic. Evaluate your vocabulary. Collect data, statistics, evidences, facts related to your topic.

Write down the point on a paper. Keep in mind the purpose of writing the paragraph. Find the main idea of your paragraph and concentrate on the main point.

2. Writing Stage. Here, you will have to turn your ideas and the data you have collected into sentences. Write a topic sentence, supporting sentence and a concluding sentence. The expressions should be clear, simple and must not deviate from the main motive. Read and re-read, write and re-write till you feel that you have written what you had in your mind.

3. Editing Stage. Check your language, grammar and structure of sentences. Look for mistakes and correct them. Read the paragraph, evaluate it and find out the vagueness, if there is any. Check the spellings.

TYPES OF PARAGRAPHS

1. Narrative. It is a sequential presentation of the events that add up to a story. It usually contains characters, a setting, a conflict and a resolution. Specific details build up the story.

2. Expository. Exposes things about a subject—an explanatory writing based on facts. It can be an incidental part of a description or narration. It should be clear and credible.

3. Definition. Do not define any thing according to the dictionary. Meaning is found in the world, experience and not in the dictionary.

4. Descriptive. Description requires you to record a series of detailed observations. Success of a descriptive paragraph lies in whether the readers are imagining the same beauty which you saw. Use sensory language.

5. Comparative. Before writing a comparative paragraph, you must have all the elements ready with you which are necessary to write a comparison.

6. Process Analysis. Analyse the process into a series of steps and put the steps into sequence.

7. Persuasion in a Paragraph. Supply the readers with information, which would persuade them to change their mind or take an action. Do not impose your personal opinion on them. Let them make their own judgement and form their own opinion after getting information from your paragraph.

Do's and Don'ts

The following tips would help you avoid problems that may make your paragraph less effective.

Do's

1. Consider and discuss practical application of information you are presenting.
2. Create a strong expression to gain the reader's interest and attention.
3. Limit use of difficult phrases and define where it is needed.
4. Use active voice rather than passive voice.
5. Use good sentence structure and proper grammar.
6. Support your statements with sound evidence.
7. Edit frequently.
8. Consider the value and importance of your explanation and details to the reader.
9. Let the reader know in the topic sentence what the main topic will be.
10. Conclude with strong closing sentences that give a brief sum up of the key points.

Don'ts

1. Do not provide misleading or poorly written introductions.
2. Do not provide weak logical arguments.
3. Do not use too much personal examples.
4. Do not use negative expressions.
5. Do not submit a paragraph which contains poor grammar/syntax.
6. Do not generalise study results.
7. Do not criticise other's ideas or opinions.
8. Do not write in a disorganised fashion, or discuss non-related topics and side issues that do not help in understanding the main topic.
9. Do not introduce acronyms without first defining them.
10. Do not conclude with a weak closing sentence that do not tie back to the topic sentence.

Transitional Signals

Transitional signals are words or phrases that show the reader the relationship between the topic sentence and the supporting sentences. Transitional signals can create relationship of time and space, cause and effect, comparison and contrast. They can show the logical relationship between ideas in one paragraph or in many paragraphs in an essay. The different kinds of transitional signals can be mixed throughout any paragraph or essay.

Transitional signals have been compared to 'Traffic signals'. Like Traffic Signals, transitional signals also tell you to go forward, to turn, to slow down and to stop. They can be classified in the following types.

1. Words that show addition. For example, moreover, first of all, also, another, furthermore, finally.

2. Words that show comparison and constant like. On the other hand, on the contrary, in a same way, equally, although, however, yet, just as, just like etc.

3. Words showing cause and effect. As a result of something, accordingly, therefore, because of etc.

4. Words defining time. Before, after, soon, previously, frequently, immediately.

5. Words that show conclusion. To sum up, in conclusion, all in all, in other words, on the whole, in short etc.

SPECIMEN PARAGRAPHS

Capital Punishment

Capital punishment is the most severe form of justice which means, the death penalty. It is the punishment given to those criminals who commit a serious crime. The capital punishment exists because it is a lesson for the future criminals. It creates a fear in the mind of a would-be criminal. There is a debate going on in the important countries of the world on the issue that the capital punishment should be abolished. People opposing death penalty, believe that capital punishment is not needed in a civilised society. Capital punishment violates the basic human right to live. Capital punishment is the inhumane form of punishment in the world today.

Acid Rain

Acid rain is very harmful to everything. There are many forms of acid rain that we see around us. There is acid rain, acid snow, acid fog, acid gas and acid dust. Acid rain is formed by pollution. The acid rain causes environmental problems. The chemicals in the pollution react with water and other chemicals in the air to form sulphuric acid, nitric acid, and other pollutants. These pollutants travel with the wind for hundreds of miles and eventually return to the earth in the form of acid rain, acid snow or acid fog. Acid rain takes nutrients and important sources from soil and damages the environment.

Success is Different for Everyone

Success means climbing the upward ladder, but success is different for everyone. Success could mean earning money for someone. For others, success could be a happy family. A worker is happy if he succeeds in earning one time meal for his family. A student is successful if he attains satisfactory performance in his institute. The target of success changes at all levels. Success means different to different classes of society. For some success could be a permanent job, for others it could be a big house or still for others, it could be a thatched roof on their heads or inner peace. Success cannot be generalised. Parameters of success are different for everyone. It is in the mind of the achiever and he can define it better. A big achievement for someone can be unimportant for others.

Internet Addiction

Internet addiction is very common these days not only among youngsters but among all ages. The access to Internet has become easier and cheaper. In the modern world, Internet access has become an important part of life. Internet has taken into its grip all age levels. No doubt the Internet is highly informative and entertaining. You can buy tickets, pay bills, do worldwide shopping through Internet. Internet has the multipurpose functions and it has become a necessary skill for those entering the job markets. But excess of everything is bad. We should use Internet for our benefit. One should not become addicted to Internet.

EXERCISE

Answer the following questions:

1. Which points you should keep in mind while writing a paragraph?
2. What do you understand by Transitional Signals ? How can they help you in paragraph writing?
3. What role does unity play in a paragraph?
4. Discuss the different parts of a paragraph.
5. What do you understand by expository type of a paragraph?
6. Write down a descriptive paragraph.
7. Write down a paragraph on:
   (*i*) Science and Religion.
   (*ii*) Beauty and brains go together.
   (*iii*) Hard work and not destiny is important for success.

❑❑❑

Chapter 6
PRECIS WRITING

"Let thy speech be short, comprehending much in a few words."

—Aprocrypha

INTRODUCTION

A precis is the compact summary of a literary text. It is the exact replica in miniature of the original passage. It contains the core essence of the text. Precis is written in your own words in clear and concise manner. It is not an expression of your opinion or ideas or a review of the text but it is a compact version of the original text in your own expressions. A well-written precis is one third of the original passage.

Utility of Precis Writing

Precis writing is one of the most important skills which would increase your concentration and alertness. It teaches you to use the words and expressions economically, to say more in few words. It develops a sense of proportion and emphasis. Precis writing skill would help you both as a student and as a professional.

Qualities of a Good Precis

1. A precis should be limited to one third of the original passage.

2. Use your own expressions and vocabulary. Do not copy the original text.

3. Do not add your own comments or opinions. What you write should be factually correct and exactly from the original passage. Accuracy is a vital part of a precis. Never criticize the author's ideas.

4. Do not use the quotations or phrases cited by the author in your precis.

5. Use short, simple sentences.

6. Try to use one-word substitution.

7. Understand the essence of the text and focus on the central idea of the passage.

8. Write the points in the order in which it appears in the original.

9. Simplify sentences, replace long sentences with compact phrases and phrases with words.

10. Do not repeat because you have to explain a lengthy passage in fewer words. Repitition would be a wastage of words. You have to economise the words and expressions.

11. Come directly to the main point. Avoid examples, illustrations, details, data specifications, evidences, etc.

12. Distinguish between major and minor points and concentrate on the major points.

13. Before writing the final precis, check the draft you have made, review and edit. Make the required changes and write a final version correcting the errors.

Steps to Write a Precis

1. Read the passage, re-read it. Sometime a passage requires several readings before you get an idea about it. So read several times to make sure you have understood it.

2. Concentrate at the most important points contained in the passage. Grasp these points and write on a rough sheet.

3. Pay attention to the author's viewpoint. This will help you in deciding how much detail should be included in the precis you are writing.

4. Each paragraph should have a topic sentence. Underline or highlight the topic sentence or the key points.

5. Note down in the rough draft the key points and the viewpoint of the author.

6. Having understood and written the central idea of the passage, place your ideas in sentences.

7. Arrange your sentences into one unit. Write in your own words keeping the original intact.

8. Review and make corrections. You may have to write and edit several times before the final precis is ready.

Example

If you wish to grow in the spirit of understanding, you must let the other person talk and prove his point to his satisfaction. Do not interrupt him, while he is talking. You know how exasperated you become when someone interrupts you, while you are trying to prove a point. At committee meetings, I have heard those words uttered quite often—"But let me finish". Listen more, talk less. You are made to listen. That is why you are given only one mouth and two ears. If we were meant to talk more and listen less, we would have been given only one ear, right in front and two mouths on the two sides. How funny we would look ! And mind you there is no door with which to close the ears. They are always open. Before a word can be spoken, it has to cross two fences—two rows of teeth and two lips. Therefore, think twice before you talk. Never forget that of the unspoken word you are a master, of the spoken word, you are a slave. Words, once spoken cannot be got back.

(*Words 184*)

—J.P. Vaswani

Title: Try to be a Good Listener

We should listen more and talk less. If we are good listeners, we shall understand others better. We should not interrupt others while they are talking. That is why we are provided with two ears and one mouth. Moreover there are the checkposts of teeth and lips. We cannot take back the words once spoken. So be cautious before taking out the words. (*Words 62*)

EXERCISE

A. Write precis of the following passages:

Passage 1

Gratitude is a beautiful word. Gratitude is a feeling. It improves our personality and builds character. Gratitude develops out of humility. It is a feeling of thankfulness towards others. It is conveyed through our attitude towards others and reflects in our behaviour. Gratitude does not mean reciprocating good deeds. Gratitude is not give and take kindness, understanding and patience cannot be repaid. What does gratitude teach us? It teaches us the art of co-operation and understanding. Gratitude must be sincere. A simple 'thank you' can be gracious. Many times we forget to be thankful to the people closest to us, such as our spouse, our relatives, our friends. Gratitude would rank among the top qualities that form the character and personality of an individual with integrity. Ego stands in the way of showing gratitude. A gracious attitude changes our outlook in life. With gratitude and humility, right actions come naturally. Gratitude ought to be a way of life, something that we cannot give enough of. It can mean a smile, or a thank you, or a gesture of appreciation. Seldom are we grateful for the things we already possess. Think back and recall the people who had a positive influence on your life; your parents, teachers, anyone who spent extra time to help you. They willingly sacrificed their time, effort, money and many other things for you. They did it out of love and not for your thankfulness. At sometimes, the persons realize the efforts that went into help them shape their future. Perhaps it is not too late to thank them.

—*Shiv Khera.*

Passage 2

Until not so long ago, there was always the 'right' age to get married, and a right sequence of priorities, which dictated that a woman's place was with her family. But today, an increasing number of working women are defying this type casting. Meet the eves—the employed, very educated single women. These are professionals who are putting off marriage to pursue career ambitions. Armed with a degree, they are 'work gypsies' by choice and follow promising job opportunities to new cities where they set up home. It is the final step towards real independence—a life where they are their own chief wage earners as well as moral guardians. While the average working women continue to consult parents or husbands for big buys, the eves are the sole decision-makers even for traditionally male-domain purchases like cars and electronics. Most manage their own investments and are fairly savvy about different financial products. This comfort with money is a far cry from the average finance-shy women. Having said this, many eves tend to be living a footloose bachelor existence and spending on themselves comes more easily than saving for later.

—*Ajeeta Bhardwaj*

(from India Today April 16, 2007)

B. Answer the following questions:

1. What do you mean by precis?
2. How can the precis writing skill be useful to you?
3. What are the requirements needed for writing a good precis?

C. Tick the right statement.

1. Precis is one half of the original passage.
2. You can copy the writer's expressions and words while writing a precis.
3. Do not criticise the writers' viewpoint in your precis.
4. One word substitution may help you in economising the words.
5. Your interpretation and judgement of the original passage will make your precis better.

❑❑❑

Unit III
Forms of Technical Communication

Chapter 1
LETTER WRITING

"Keep your words soft and tender because tomorrow you may have to eat them."

INTRODUCTION

Correspondence can broadly be divided into three parts:

1. Personal correspondence, which is between friends and relatives
2. Official correspondence, which is between governments and semi-government offices
3. Business correspondence, when it relates to business companies for trade and industry

We shall deal with business correspondence in this chapter.

The purpose of writing business correspondence is to convey a message by the writer to the receiver without actually contacting him. It is not the exchange of words but the exchange of information.

Importance and Function of Letter

In any business house, correspondence plays an important part. It is true that when there were no letters still the people would conduct business. Nevertheless, with the civilization and coming into force the new laws, business has become easier as well as difficult. Through correspondence, the parties exchange views and come into contact with each other. The parties may be living far away. The correspondence helps to speed up the business and bridge the distance. Of all the forms of written communication, letters are still the most common form.

Several modern means have been invented such as telephone, letter, fax, computer etc. but correspondence through letters is still the most common, cheap and convenient way. Letters are as important as they were centuries ago. Even today, letters are produced in courts as the common evidence to substantiate the claims. The importance has increased with time. Everyday activities in business dealings would not be possible without letters. Letters help in strengthening personal relations in business dealings. They help to improve our knowledge about the organizations.

Essential Features of Letter Writing

Business letters are written to firms when you have not met or you may never meet them. The aim can be to ask for an enquiry, seek information, or give advice or buy a product or sell a product and so on. Business letter must impress the receiver and induce interest in him.

Business letter is different from personal letter or official letter in material and presentations. With time, business community has set some standards and these features are prominent and make these letters different. Such features should be clearly brought out.

1. Direct. The letter should be immediately understood by the reader. The reference should be direct. Vague and ambiguous words should be avoided. The theme should be direct and expressions should be simple. The reader should be able to understand the message in the first reading. Even the ideas should be in sequences and logical so that there is no problem in understanding the letter. Sometimes by the time you read the last paragraph, you forget what was given in the initial paragraphs. The focus should be on the message you are passing on. Details not relevant to the issues can be avoided. You should not forget that people are busy nowadays and companies may be getting several such letters everyday. You may lose message if words with double meaning are used. Meaning should be clear and straightforward.

2. Courtesy. A good business letter should be courteous. Your success may depend upon the dignity you maintain. You cannot find faults in such letters. Be respectful, reasonable and use decent words. Courtesy creates goodwill, helps in making friends, reduces friction and expects to get good response. It always pays to be courteous.

The following are some of the commonly used phrases that may make correspondence courteous.

— Thank you very much for your letter dated 12th March, 2010.

— We are glad to hear that you have started producing yarn.

— We regret to inform you that we did not receive your letter.

— We are sorry to point out that the material has still not arrived.

— You will be glad to know that we have accepted your tender.

— We appreciate the quick response shown by you.

The following phrases may irritate the receiver and should be avoided.

— You are wrong in jumping over the conclusion.

— How can you expect us to agree with you?

— We are shocked to receive your letter dated 12th March, 2010.

— How can you say that we delayed the supply of goods?

— Your claim is beyond our imagination.

The reader may be under no obligation to accept your request and purpose should be to develop long term relations. However, courtesy should be different from humility. Excessive courtesy sometimes lowers your prestige and dignity.

3. Conciseness (brevity). Time is money. Business letters should be brief and suitable to your requirements. The principle should be few words and more meaning. You can achieve this by not repeating the sentences. Avoid unwanted sentences, use appropriate words, and do not deviate from the point. Lengthy letters irritate the receivers. Briefness does not here mean that it should be at the cost of completeness and clarity. Balance should be maintained between these.

4. Completeness. The letter must cover all the materials required in it. Sending incomplete information neither helps the sender nor the receiver. While courtesy and conciseness are important features of letter writing, completeness is the most important out of all these. It is possible that the letter would be direct, clear but lacking the basic purpose of giving the complete information. For example, while placing order for the supply of cement, not only the quantity, quality but the type of bag, (jute or plastic), mode of transportation may be equally important. Insufficient information results in back references and delay.

5. Correctness. Correctness here implies factual truth of the statements being made. There should be no withholding of the information and no misrepresentation of the facts. The figures, rates, sum total, price etc. should be checked twice. It is commonly seen that in business letters, there is usually a mistake in quoting rates in words and figures and working out the amount etc. For example, in supply of materials the following mistake would come to light.

Name of item	Quantity	Rate in figures	Rate in words	Amount worked out
Supply of Taps	5000 Nos.	₹ 25.5 each	₹ Two hundred and fifty five only	₹ 1,27,500

From the above, it is evident that the sender has made a mistake in quoting the rates in words. Instead of mentioning rupees twenty-five and paisa fifty, he mentioned higher rates. However, the amount has been worked out based on the rates quoted in figures. It is better to check the rates in figures and words again before signing the letter. Sometimes dates too can be important. Receiver will not be able to draw any conclusion if you mention 31st June or 31st Nov.

6. Miscellaneous. There are other general issues, which should be kept in mind.

1. Letter should be convincing, impressive and effective.
2. Letter should be neat and clean.
3. Right size of paper should be used.
4. Letter should have correct tone, attitude, and positive thinking.

Form and Structure

By form and structure, we mean parts or elements. Business letters are different from other letters and therefore should contain all elements required for business letters. It is better to divide letter into sections and sub-sections with clear intentions. The usual formats of business letters are shown next page.

Styles

1. Business Letter Styles. The following pictures show what a one-page business letter should look like. There are three accepted styles. The horizontal lines represent lines of type.

Modified Block Style

Full Block Style

2. Semi-Block Style

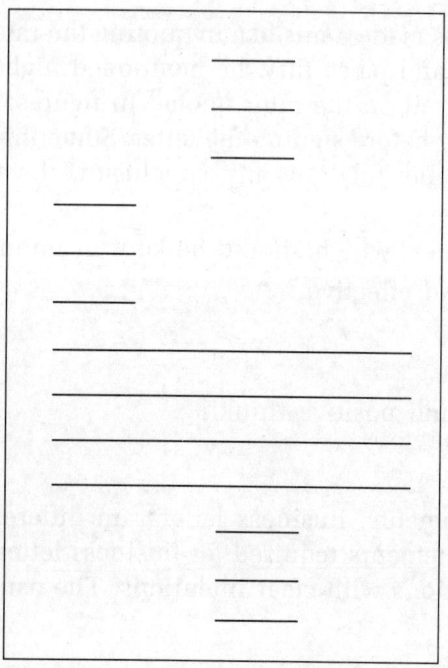

Full-Block Business Letter Format

CORPORATE LETTERHEAD INC
M.G. ROAD, ZONE 11
BHOPAL-2
Tele (0755) 326226 Fax (0755) 326227

corp@rediffmail.com **www.corpo.com.**

(Letter Date)
Receiver's address
(Address line 2)
(Address line 3)
Reference No.:-
Subject: (usually bold, sometimes underlined)
Dear Mr./Mrs./Ms (receiver's last name)
Body of the letter
Sincerely
(Name of the signatory)
(Title of the signatory)
(Reference Initials)
Enclosures (Numbers)
CC:– (Name receiving copy)
(Name receiving copy)

❑❑❑

Chapter 2

BUSINESS LETTERS

A **business letter** is more formal than a personal letter. It should have a margin of at least one inch on all four edges. It is always written on 8½″ × 11″ (or metric equivalent) unlined stationery. There are **eleven** parts to a business letter. The full block style is more commonly used these days.

1. Name, address of the sender. This is the heading and contains the name, address, telephone number, fax number, E-mail address. The receiver on receipt of the letter immediately knows from where the letter has come.

2. Date. All letters have to be sent with dates. Date should contain day, month, and year when the letter is being dispatched. The correct way to write the date is March 14th, 2010 or 14th March, 2010. 14/3.2010 or 14-03-2010 is a wrong way to write the date.

3. Reference Number. This is generally written below date (part 2 above). Please note this is the reference number of the sender and not the receiver. This helps to find out the file number, department, wing etc. From the reference number, we can trace the letter from the dispatch register, hard copies of files or from files in the computer. Only one number is given to one letter. If you are issuing letters away from the office, you can use words such as camp, site etc. For example, HARDA/CPWD/CAMP/2010/1 meaning Harda site, CPWD office, CAMP means you are not in the office, 2010 refers to the year and letter from camp is 1.

4. The Inside Address. The address of the receiver is written inside. It is better to add suitable prefix to the name such as Mr, Mrs, M/s etc. Suitable details of the address may be given in each line such as

Messrs B.S.C.L. Pvt. Ltd.

37, M.G. Road

Bhopal (M.P.)

5. Subject. This is a preamble to the letter. It is a short sentence, which contains the title of the main letter. Sometimes a receiver may receive dozens of letters daily and may pass on the unimportant letters to the subordinates by just reading the subject. For example,

Sub.: Notice of issue under Clause 2 of the agreement—Regarding.

6. Reference. Reference, here, implies the reference of the receiver and not the sender as given above in the third part. If there are more than one references, all or few can be given. This will help the receiver to identify the files and take out the previous letters written by him and understand the subject matter.

7. Salutation. It is a greeting addressed to the receiver. The greeting in a business letter is always formal. It normally begins with the word "Dear" and always includes the person's last name. It normally has a title like Mr. or Mrs. Use a first name only if the title is unclear—for example, you are writing to someone you do not know whether the person is male or female.

8. The Body. This has to be the most important part of the letter. This contains the substance of the message. It is better to sub-divide the body into three parts. The starting part is introductory and contains the main message. The second part is the main part in which all the details are given. It gives the complete detailed message. The substance can be rearranged according to the importance. In the third part, you must mention clearly what action you expect from the receiver. In case the main body is lengthy, different paragraphs can be given different titles. The concluding paragraph should contain the theme of the letter.

9. Complimentary Close. This is a leave taking note. It is either at the left margin or the right margin depending upon the format of the business letter that is being used. Generally it is written two to three spaces below the last line of the main body of the letter. Signatures should be in between the closing and the sender's name. The complimentary close can be Yours sincerely, Yours faithfully, Yours truly.

10. Enclosures. If some documents are to be attached with the letter, the same should be indicated against the enclosures. It is typed two to three spaces below the identification marks. If the documents have been assigned annexure numbers, the same should be put as Annexure 1, Annexure 2, etc. But it is totally optional.

11. Copy to. In case the letter is to be sent to the parties other than the main receiver, the same should be mentioned. If the copies are to be sent to number of persons, it should be serially numbered in each line.

In case you do not want to disclose to the main receiver, the copies being endorsed to others, the words N.I.O. (Not in Original) should be typed in line with 'copy to' so that the receiver of the endorsed letter may not come to know of this.

Chapter **3**

Drafting the Application Letter

"Sweat hard for sweet reward."

There are two ways of writing an Application Letter:

In the first case, your bio-data is given in the letter itself and it forms one composite letter.

In the second case, your personal details such as qualification, experience, your age and other personal details are attached with the forwarding letter and sent as two separate parts. Generally the second part contains.

1. Date of Birth
2. Educational qualifications
3. Experience
4. Seminars/workshops attended
5. Papers/books published
6. Any special achievement
7. Reference of two persons not related to you
8. Salary expected/salary drawn
9. Address
10. Contact number
11. E-mail Id

Sometimes the advertiser may require the applicant to send the application in a particular format. In such a case, it would be advisable to stick to a particular form. The second type of application is more commonly used.

The application letter should be self-speaking, precise but should not leave any important point. It should be polite, dignified and should attract the attention of the reader.

1. Most often application letters are written in response to some advertisement. Application should begin with a reference to that advertisement or the applicant may mention that he has come to know about a vacancy for a particular post in the organization in which he is applying. In either case, the opening paragraph of the application letter should specifically mention that. Some of the common ways of starting an application letter are:

— Please refer to your advertisement in The Hindustan Times dated 14th March, 2010.

— I am applying for the post of Technical Assistant, advertised in The Times of India dated 14th March, 2010.

— I shall be obliged if my application for the post of Computer Assistant is considered.

The opening paragraph should be simple, to the point and should be formal rather than friendly. Avoid using irrelevant phrases and slogans.

2. In the second paragraph, mention briefly your positive qualities *viz-a-viz* the requirements. If you are possessing higher qualification and more experience than advertised, this is the right place to mention it. Since you are attaching your personal bio-data with the letter, mention something which develops interest in the mind of employer to read your full Résume. He should at once get an impression that you are the person he is actually looking for. You may have more years of experience but if it does not suit to the requirements of the employer, there is no point in highlighting the same. Do not forget that specialization is becoming more important these days.

3. You must conclude your application letter with positive tone so that the employer gives you an opportunity to attend the interview or group discussion. Some common expressions to conclude an application letter may be

— I shall be grateful if an opportunity is given to me to be a part of your organization

— I look forward for your favourable consideration

— I hope my application meets the requirements of the advertised job.

Chapter 4

PREPARING THE RÉSUMÉ

"Life is what we make with the possible and how we take the impossible."

By Résumé, we mean the personal bio-data. Your career largely depends on the Résumé you frame. Résumé is more important than your horoscope. Résumé describes your professional details, your personal traits, your special skills and the details mentioned should not be incorrect or misleading. Specific information should be covered under specific head. For example, under 'Educational Qualification', mention only your qualification and not experience. However, additional qualification can be given under this head.

Two examples of Application Letters with Résumé will help you to understand the same. Like in other letters, there is no fixed pattern for writing a Résumé. Résumé is only an analytic record/summary of one's data but impressive writing of a Résumé can attract the attention of the employer. There may be software available in the market, which can be used for writing a Résumé, but again copying these blindly may not be advised since aspirations may differ from one person to another. Further even your own Resume may require modifications since the job requirements may differ from one employer to another.

If you were an employer, you would certainly look at the following qualities in the candidate you would like to select.

1. The Institutes from where the candidate has passed out
2. What course he has attended (Educational/Professional)
3. Your experience
4. Names of the organisations in which he worked
5. Any outstanding achievement
6. Any extra curricular activities
7. Any special skill
8. Age, Marital status, Address for communication, E-mail Id, Contact no. etc.
9. References.

Points to be noted while writing a standard Résumé

1. Educational Qualifications. Start from the highest Educational Degree. Follow the reverse order for example, Post Graduate then Graduate and so on. Name of the Institutes, grades and ranks scored is optional. If it supports your Résumé, go ahead. If these are not in you favour, ignore them.

2. Experience. Use the reverse chronological order, starting from your present employment going backward. In case you are a fresher, and you do not possess any experience, mention the training programmes attended by you. Highlight your achievements. This is the most important part of the résumé. Experience should be related to the job you are applying for and should be drafted accurately and with skill. Be factual, complete and try to give professional look to your Résumé.

3. References. Sometimes the employer, you wish to work with, would want you to give reference of two or three persons. The employer may confidentially try to verify your credentials from them. The referred persons should not be related to you. Give the designation, address, contact no. along with the complete name of the person. You should be careful in giving the names of the references because they should make recommendations in your favour.

Example I

Deepak Gupta
117 B, Tilak Nagar
New Delhi-110058

The Managing Director
DCM Ltd.
Kanchanjunga Building
Barakhamba Road
New Delhi-110001

Sub.: Application for the post of Chemical Engineer

Dear Sir

This is with reference to your advertisement in the 'Indian Express' dated 5th March, 2010 for the post of Chemical Engineer. I shall be obliged if you would kindly consider me for the said post.

I am a Chemical Engineer and I have passed out from a very good Institute. My uncle is already in this field and has a small industry manufacturing vegetable oil. I have developed a lot of interest in this field and have been helping him for the last two years. There has been cumulative increase of 8% during the last two years. Since it is a family business, I am presently not drawing any salary except pocket expenses. My uncle has offered me partnership (small percentage) in his business of vegetable oil unit but I wish to join a bigger organization.

I would appreciate if you give me an opportunity to serve your esteemed organization. I will try to meet your expectations.

Thanking you

Yours faithfully

(DEEPAK GUPTA)

Dated 14th Sept. '11

Encl. Résumé

RÉSUMÉ

1. Personal Details

Father's Name:	Mr. Manoj Gupta
Date of Birth:	10th May, 1985
Age as on 1st Dec. 2006	21 years 7 months
Marital Status	Unmarried
Languages known	English, Hindi
Nationality	Indian
Religion	Hinduism
Category	Open
Address	117 B, Tilak Nagar, N.Delhi-58
Tele No.	(011) 25578034
Cell No.	9425348776
E-mail Id	deep@rediffmail.com

2. Educational Qualifications

Examination passed	Year	Rank/Grade	Institute	Remarks
B.E. (Chemical Engineering)	June 2005	I	BIT, Mesra	II rank in Univ.
12th Std.	May 2001	I	St. Peters Convent Bhopal	I rank in school
10th Std.	May 1999	I	St. Peters Convent Bhopal	secured 97% marks

I am presently learning Computer languages C, C++

3. Experience

From June 2005 till date worked in Haryana Oil Company as Incharge of Extraction Unit. During my two years of supervision, the production went up at the rate of 8% per annum. Even the quality of the oil has improved and has resulted in wider demand in the market. My target is to maintain the growth of 8% on year-to-year basis.

4. Other Activities

(*i*) I have won several prizes in athletics particularly in short races and jumps.

(*ii*) I am a good player of table tennis and chess and have won several prizes in school and college.

(*iii*) I have also participated in inter school and inter college debate competitions.

Example II

Sometimes instead of career perceptions, you may like to send a highly professional Résumé giving more importance to the job you are doing particularly when it is highly technical in nature. In that case the pattern of Résumé may differ and chronological order may start with the Career objectives, Professional Experience, Educational Qualification etc.

Umesh Singh

146, Brindavan Gardens

Bangalore-460072

14th March, 2010

Managing Director

Patni Computers

Pune Hi Tech City

Pune-411007

Sub: Application for the post of Software Engineer

Dear Sir

I have gone through your advertisement in The Times of India dated 2nd April, 2007. I have the required qualification mentioned in your advertisement. I shall feel obliged if my application is considered for the post of Software Engineer in your company.

I am presently working in Wipro, which is a premier Software Company in India. I am working on a project, which is popular worldwide as it deals in printers.

Your company deals in the design of technical software in which I have lot of interest. I am looking for a position in such companies so that I may show my worth.

Details of my experience, educational qualification etc. are attached.

I hope you will give me an opportunity to appear for interview in which I shall be glad to provide you with more information about myself.

Thanking you

Yours truly

(UMESH SINGH)
Email: Umesh@rediffmail.com
Contact +91-9342758901

Encl. Résumé.

RÉSUMÉ

CAREER OBJECTIVES

I would like to forge a relationship with a high growth organization that would provide me an opportunity to leverage my technical know-how and enhance my understanding of business processes. I would like to hold a position that gives me high growth and good learning opportunity. I want to work for the betterment of self and the organization with the qualities like team work, responsibility, reliability and good performance.

PROFESSIONAL EXPERIENCE

1. Got selected in **Wipro Technologies** through campus recruitment and working for the past eighteen months. Currently placed at Bangalore.
2. Undergone training in Wipro Technologies for two months. The following programming languages and software subjects were taught.
   - C
   - C++
   - Win 32
   - VC++
   - Software Engineering Practices
   - Net Framework
3. **Current Work:**
   - I am at present working in Embedded Systems-**MFP** (Multi Functional Peripherals) firmware as a Project Engineer, Responsibilities include feature development and maintenance work. The development is done in **C/C++** on **UNIX** platform. Hewlett Packard (HP) is the client I have been working for.

     I have had the experience of working on different fields of the printers. I joined the team as a developer for the embedded **Analog FAX** portion of the printer. That included the understanding of the complete functionalities of sending and receiving faxes. It has provided sufficient knowledge on how the printer works on fax. Different sub-components under fax were understood and I helped the team in reducing the defects encountered in the product.

     As per the requirements of the project, I started working on the **UI** (User Interface) of the printer. That included a number of defects resolutions and features development. I have worked in a team of three for the development of one of the features. I myself developed three required screens in the feature. I am also a member of the SWAT team which required resolving the number of issues in considerably less amount of time. For the last six months I have been working on the UI and now have good understanding of the user interface working.
   - Have developed good understanding of Clearcase, Debuggers and Emulators.
   - Have exposure to COM fundamentals.

SCHOLASTIC BACKGROUND

B.E. (Electronics and Communication Engineering) from Deemed University **Birla Institute of Technology**, Mesra, Ranchi with an aggregate of 70%. Presently working with **Wipro Technologies** for the last 1 year.

Year	Qualification	University/Board	Institute	Percentage
2005	B.E. (Electronics and Communication Engineering)	Birla Institute of Technology, Mesra, Ranchi Deemed University	Birla Institute of Technology, Mesra, Ranchi	CGPA = 6.4/10 (= 70%)
2001	10 + 2 (Science)	Indian School Certificate [I.S.C]	Hutching's Junior College, Pune	83.3%
1999	10 (Science)	Indian Council of Secondary Education [I.C.S.E]	Boy's High School, Allahabad	86.4%

COMPUTER SKILLS

1. **Operating Systems** : DOS, Unix, Windows 2000, XP and NT
2. **Programming** : C, C++

INDUSTRIAL TRAININGS

1. Underwent industrial training on "**Programmable Logic Controllers**" In Tata Honeywell, Pune.
2. Underwent industrial training for Internet Division in V.S.N.L.(Videsh Sanchar Nigam Limited)

UNDERGRADUATE PROJECT

"**Structural Health Monitoring Using Embedded Fiber Optic Sensors**"

We worked in a group of three, designed and developed a cylindrical model to calculate the strain on an optical fiber (being embedded into the cylinder) after a huge stress provided to the cylinder.

ACHIEVEMENTS

1. Scored the second highest marks in Mathematics [I.S.C.] throughout.
2. Was the winner of the intercollegiate badminton tournament in both doubles and singles.
3. Won the following awards in "BITOTSAV", the all India Cultural Festival of BIT, Mesra
   (*a*) Formal member of the winning team, 2004.
   (*b*) First in the skit presentation and a theme based fashion show.

EXTRACURRICULAR ACTIVITIES

1. General Secretary of the Engineering Society, BIT Mesra. This society was responsible for conducting the various activities like technical workshops and quiz competitions for BE Students.
2. President of the ROTARACT Club. During my tenure various events were organised like Foodotsav, Food Festival and Charity activities for the blind children.

3. Have taken part in the debates during graduation as well as in the present company whenever got an opportunity.

INTERESTS

Playing Badminton, Travelling, Trecking, Driving and Listening to light music.

PERSONAL DETAILS

Date of Birth	:	20th June, 1984
Sex	:	Male
Marital Status	:	Single
Present Address	:	House No. 217, G.F., Brindavan Extension Bangalore 560072

EXERCISE

1. What are the essential features of Letter writing?
2. Discuss the various ways of writing Application Letter.
3. Which points should be kept in mind while writing a Résumé?

❑❑❑

Chapter **5**

PART OF BUSINESS ENQUIRY LETTER

"Strive today and thrive tomorrow."

INTRODUCTION

As the name itself connotes, Enquiry letter is written in business deals seeking certain information or clarification. It consists of written letter requesting for information or clarification. Such Enquiry letters may be addressed to individuals, institutes, companies or departments. Since it is you who are seeking information, such letters should be courteous and ending should be with goodwill expressions. Of course, it should contain the request clearly so that the other person is able to reply to your enquiry. It is the sender who may ultimately suffer if the enquiry is incomplete or incorrect. Why should the receiver bother?

As any other letter, Enquiry letter must contain three vital parts namely.

FORMAT

1. Start. The letter should begin with clear indication as to why this letter is being written. The purpose should be clear in the onset and should be in the opening paragraph. The information or clarifications should be listed in sequences and in specific way.

2. Body. This part is important and should contain the details of the requests. Why such information is being sought? The reasons to seek enquiry should be stated clearly so that the reader may reply in the same way. All the information/clarification should be asked in detail to avoid another reference. Avoid seeking such information which the sender knows that the reader will not be able to disclose. Avoid causing inconvenience to the reader as he may not be liable to respond to your query.

3. Ending. The letter should be closed with thanks and goodwill expressions. Also, specify the exact course which the reader should adopt.

TYPES OF ENQUIRY LETTERS

An Enquiry letter can be classified into two categories:

1. Solicited Enquiry. Sometimes the suppliers directly meet the clients who use their products and directly hand over the price list and catalogues. This has become very common due to competitions and marketing professionals. Salespersons and medical representatives are usually seen with their products. Sometimes the suppliers may send their details by post. In such cases, the suppliers take the initiative. Usually the suppliers are aware of the companies or individuals who may use or buy their products.

The buyers before buying their products may refer to the suppliers enquiring about their prices and discounts available, if any. They may also enquire about the terms and conditions for buying the same product. Such an enquiry letter is called as a Solicited Enquiry Letter.

These days the suppliers are advertising their products on telephones, cell phones, and computers in addition to advertising in the newspapers, roadside signboards, and elsewhere.

2. Unsolicited Enquiry. Unlike the above, the buyer takes the first initiative by contacting the suppliers. For making such an enquiry, the buyer may collect the names of the persons or firms manufacturing the products he needs to buy. This can be done from the various advertisements available with them. Sometimes the buyer may collect the details from the exhibitions or trade fairs. In such places, the buyer gets an opportunity to see the products. He can have on spot discussion with the suppliers to clarify his queries.

Subsequently, when the buyer is actually in need of such products, he may refer to the seller. Such an enquiry is known as Unsolicited Enquiry.

In both the above cases, enquiry is made from a buyer to the supplier, but in the case of Solicited Enquiry, the supplier takes the initiative.

IMPORTANCE OF WRITING ENQUIRY LETTERS

A letter of enquiry is written for enquiry into the terms and conditions and other details of the product proposed to be brought. When bringing vegetables from the market, do we not survey and enquire about the prices and quality before actually buying the same? The purpose here is the same. Through letters, we enquire about the prices, terms and conditions before actually placing the order. Buying without making enquiry can result in procurement of the product not suiting to your requirement. Enquiry letters help in locating the best suppliers in the market. Through enquiry letters you can also negotiate with the seller for correct price and specifications.

Sometimes a particular seller to whom the Enquiry letter has been sent may not be manufacturing products of your choice but can help you to locate another seller manufacturing products of your choice.

This is a world of competition. Both the buyer and seller work for money. Before transaction starts, buyer may have framed his own terms and conditions. Similarly the seller may be having his own terms and conditions. However, through enquiry letters sometimes both may compromise with their terms and conditions and unanimously agree for different terms and conditions somewhere in between. Enquiry letters are, therefore, not only important to the buyers but are equally important to the sellers.

Example 1

Solicited Enquiry Letter

BHARAT STEEL MILLS PVT. LTD.
(Leader in Steel Bars and Billets)
15, M.G. Road
Bhopal-42

15th March, 2011
Ref. No. NEP/234/07
The Steel Authority of India
Bhillai, Durg
Chhattisgarh

Sub.: Regarding Auction of Steel Scrap

Ref.: Your Advertisement in the Hindustan Times Newspaper

Dear Sir

We have read your advertisement in the Hindustan Times Newspaper dated 14th March, 2011.

We are one of the leading retailers of steel bars in M.P. and our annual turnover is about ₹ 150 crores. We supply steel bars, angles, flats, channels to private and government organizations. We are willing to participate in the auction being held on 16th April, 2010. We will be glad to know at what time the auction will be held and the minimum amount of earnest money (bid amount) required to be deposited by the successful bidder.

We shall be grateful if above information is sent to us at an early date.

Thanking you

Yours sincerely

(N.K. PATEL)
for Bharat Steel Mills Pvt. Ltd.

Unsolicited Enquiry Letter

BIJILEE LAMP HOUSE
(Dealer of Electrical Goods)
48, Block 2
Chandni Chowk
Delhi 6
Tele No. (011) 22471368
Fax (011) 22471369

12th March, 2011
Ref. No. BJ/Delhi/04
M/S KK Wires
45, Civil Lines
Allahabad

Sub.: Enquiry regarding prices of various wires etc.

Dear Sir

We wish to purchase electrical wires of the following specifications within one month.

1.	Single wire 0.5 mm..........................	10 rolls (100 m each)
2.	Twin wire 0.5 mm plastic insulation	25 rolls (100 m each)
3.	Twin wire 0.8 mm plastic insulation	35 rolls (-do-)
4.	Cable to carry current of 100-Ampere	17 rolls (15m each)

Please send your price list including the discount you can offer. Please send the terms and conditions and the maximum time you will take to supply the goods.

Thanking you

Yours sincerely

(B.B. RAINA)
General Manager

Bijilee Lamp House

EXERCISE

1. Why are Enquiry letters written?
2. Discuss the various types of Enquiry letters.
3. Write an Enquiry letter to Lotus Computers, Ghaziabad on behalf of Sandeep Software, Bhopal enquiring about HP Printers.

□□□

Chapter 6

QUOTATIONS, ORDERS AND TENDERS

"Good communication is as stimulating as black coffee, and just as hard to sleep after."
—**A.M. Lindberg**

INTRODUCTION

If a company wants to buy any item for their use, they would definitely want that it should be purchased at the cheapest price and its quality is reasonably good. So every company is concerned with the price and quality of the product it purchases. Paying the right price for the right quality is the main aim. By paying the cost price at the lower end, he makes more profit as the selling price is more or less similar to the market price. In order to locate this, the buyer makes correspondence with several producers and also gives the specification and terms and conditions of buying. On receiving the replies from the suppliers, he compares those by preparing a comparative statement of rates, conditions etc. and then selects the best seller *i.e.*, the seller who gives the most competitive rates and whose terms and conditions are most acceptable to the buyer. Next the buyer places an order with the best chosen seller. The seller may totally or partly accept or reject the order. Sometimes due to major market variations, the seller can cancel before or after the acceptance of the order. In case the order of the buyer is accepted by the seller, the seller sends the products in accordance with the terms of the order. When materials are received by the buyer, he makes payments or else lodges complaint in case there are complaints in the delivery. Sometimes advance payments are also made which are adjusted in the amount being paid by the buyer. Sometimes the seller or the buyer defaults and the correspondence has to be exchanged to sort out the issues amicably. In these types of purchase transactions, a few letters are written by buyers and sellers to each other and such letters are called Purchase Transaction Letters.

These letters can be in the shape of:

1. Enquiry letters
2. Quotation letters
3. Order letters
4. Acceptance letters
5. Refusal letters
6. Cancellation letters

7. Complaint letters

8. Clearance of account letters.

Enquiry letter has already been discussed in previous chapter.

I. QUOTATION LETTER

As the final order is placed on the basis of the quotation received, it is necessary that all the vital parts concerning the deal are mentioned in the quotation. There should be no misunderstanding or ambiguity, otherwise, it may result in disputes which may prolong for years.

1. Inviting Quotations. Letters are written by the firms/companies for obtaining rates, conditions of payment etc. It is necessary that not only adequate care should be taken to draft such letters but at the same time, it should be exhaustive and no room should be left with the sellers to manipulate afterwards.

The Inviting Quotation letters should include the following points:

(*a*) **Specify the item and its specification clearly.** For instance, if you want to buy invertors, give the exact numbers, watt-hours, size, guarantee period, shape, make and quality.

(*b*) **Request the seller to quote price.** Based on the specifications, the sellers may be asked to quote the rates. Conditional rates should be neglected and discouraged. For example, in case of Invertors and Air-Conditioners, rates fall during winters as demand is low but rates rise during summers. The rate should be delivery rate and not ex factory rate.

(*c*) **Mention the time period.** Your enquiry should invariably contain the period in which you wish to get the supply. Sometimes, the supplier may not be in a position to supply bulk quantity in short period and such prospective suppliers can judge their capacity and may not offer. Time period is an important parameter and time should always be the essence of the contract. Sometimes compensations are levied for not supplying the goods in time. If that is so, it should be clearly indicated in the Inviting letter.

(*d*) **Ask for Installation charges.** Sometimes goods such as Air-conditioners, Invertors, Refrigerators, Computers are required to be installed by expert technical persons. In such cases, ask the supplier as to how much he will charge for the same and whether or not there will be repair charges.

(*e*) **Independently ask for the tax components.** In addition to the basic price of the good, there shall be few taxes such as Sales Tax, Central Sales Tax, VAT etc. which may be paid by the buyers. Normally such tax component is included in the price because the delivery is at your notified place but certain relaxation is given to government departments and charitable institutions. Hence, asking for separate tax component would be advisable.

(*f*) **Ask for the validity of the quotation.** The supplier may not keep his rates open for infinite period. Normally the rates are valid for thirty or sixty days. In such cases the buyer should place his order within the period for which the rates remain valid. He should, therefore, ask the seller to mention the period for which his quotations are likely to remain valid. In few cases the validity can be extended with the consent of the buyer and seller.

(*g*) **Sample of material.** Sometimes the buyer may already be possessing the sample and in the Inviting Quotations, he can specify that the sample can be seen from his office before quoting rates. In case, he does not have the sample, he can ask for a sample, if required. Use of sample helps in case of beds, sofa-sets, cupboards, carpets for which the item cannot be completely reproduced in words.

2. Sending Quotations. The supplier sends his offer after he receives the Inviting Quotation Letter and this is called as Sending Quotation.

Quotation. The letter should be properly drafted because any mistake in rates or conditions can put the supplier to disadvantage. This is nothing short of sales letter. Please indicate.

(*a*) The rates preferably in words and figures. If possible work out the total.

(*b*) The time required for supplying the goods.

(*c*) The place where goods are to be delivered.

(*d*) Work out the charges of taxes, freight, octroi etc.

(*e*) Work out loading, carriage and unloading charges.

(*f*) Insurance charges, if not added, then work out the risk elements particularly for brittle and precious items being destroyed in transit.

Following examples shall make it easy to understand.

Look at the following examples:

Note: The examples below may not contain the eleven parts of a business letter, but these must be incorporated while drafting such types of letters.

Examples of Inviting Quotation

Example I

S.V.N. College
T.T. Nagar
Bhopal-4
Tele No. 2771833
www.sun.com

Dear Sirs

We intend to buy the following items for our new college building located in T-T. Nagar, Bhopal. The quantity and description of the items are given below. The quantity can deviate by 5% to 10%. Please quote your lowest rates giving full technical details. The rates shall remain valid for a period of two months from the date of receipt.
The items should be supplied within a maximum period of twenty-five days from the placement of the order.

Description of the item	**Quantity**
Arm chairs for students	500 Nos.
Desks with shelves for students	500 Nos.
Tables for teachers	15 Nos.

Easy chairs for staff	45 Nos.
Central tables	15 Nos.
Sofa-sets	5 Nos.
Blackboard to be fixed 6′ × 3′	10 Nos
Call-Bells (electronic)	3 Nos.
Water Coolers (200 lts.)	3 Nos.
Asian Carpet 25 mm thick	50 sq. meter
Electric fans (Usha Make 48")	2 Nos.
A.C. (1.5 ton) voltas	2 Nos.
Wooden Benches (3 seaters)	5 Nos.

Conditions:

(1) Only 75% of the payment shall be made on receipt and remaining 25% after a maintenance period of three months.

(2) Buyer reserves the right to accept or reject any item in full or part.

(3) Please indicate the tax component separately.

(4) Samples of some of the items can be seen from the office of the Principal.

We look forward to a reply from you.

Thanking you

Yours truly

S.N. SHARMA

(Principal, SVN College)

Example II

Punjab Engineering College

(Maintenance Deptt.)

Chandigarh.

Sub.: Providing and fixing of

(*a*) 10 Nos. 1.5 ton Window Air-Conditioner

(*b*) 5 Nos. 3 ton Split-Air-Conditioner.

Dear Sirs,

We are immediately in need of the above items to be fixed at various locations within our Engineering campus. We shall be grateful if you will please send us your lowest quotations together with the details, date of delivery and the brand name of the Air-Conditioners within ten days of the receipt of this letter.

Window A.Cs are to be fixed in the windows after removing the shutters and grills. Wooden ply all around the A.C. shall be required to make it airtight.

As regards the Split A.Cs, mechanical part is to be fixed at the terrace of the double storey building to be connected to the A.C. by insulator.

Nothing extra shall be paid for installation, fixing and accessories.

Thanking you

Yours truly

(B.N. DAS)

Head Maintenance Dept. P.E.C. Chandigarh.

Examples of Sending Quotation

Example I

Dear Sir

Thank you for your letter no. 243/10/06 dated 12/02/10. Please find below the following quotations submitted for your kind consideration.

Description of Item	**Rate of site**
Bricks 10″ × 5″ (50 strength)	₹ 2000 per 1000 bricks
Grey Cement (Birla make) 50 kg	₹ 235 per bag.
White Cement (Birla white) 50 kg	₹ 450 per bag.
Steel	₹ 20 per kg.
Coarse Sand	₹ 450 per cu.m.
Stone Aggregate (40 mm)	₹ 675 per cu.m.
Binding Wire (GI)	₹ 35 per kg.

Conditions

1. The above rates are inclusive of all taxes, carriage etc.
2. 90% payment should be made within five days of the receipt of the material and remaining 10% within twenty days of the receipt of material.
3. The above prices shall remain valid for two months.
4. Any government increase shall be paid extra.
5. The unloading of the material shall be done at site by your staff.
6. Material shall be supplied from 8 a.m. to 12 noon only, due to traffic restrictions in the area.
7. All disputes shall be settled through arbitration.

We look forward to receiving order from you.

Thanking you

Yours faithfully

(N.K. SHUKLA)
Sales Manager

Example II

To
M/s Deepak Consultants
49, Defence Colony.
New Delhi

Sub.: Regarding Quotations for Various items.

Ref.: Your No. DP/1002/FC/01 dated 15/01/10.

Dear Sir

With reference to your letter cited above, please find below the quotations for the various items. We hope that you will find these rates reasonable and place order with us.

Item detail	Rate Exsite
Screw drivers 10″	₹ 250 per Dozens
Nails 2″ (length)	₹ 500 per 100 Nos.
Plier 8″ length	₹ 420 per Dozen
Electrical Tester (5 Ampere)	₹ 84 per Dozen
Pipe Wrench 24″	₹ 360 Each
Jack (5t Capacity)	₹ 780 Each
Electrical Insulator Tape	₹ 150 per Dozen

Conditions

1. Packing charges are included in the above rates.
2. The rates are inclusive of all Taxes, Carriage etc.
3. Payment in full to be released within twenty days of the receipt of the material.

In case of any further information, please do not hesitate to write to us.

Thanking you

Yours faithfully

(B.B. DHAR)
Sales Manager

II. LETTER OF ORDERS

1. Placing Orders. On receipt of the Quotations, next step is to place an order. This is done after all the Quotations have been received. The lowest rates are worked out and the decision is taken to place an order. For doing so, the following points should be kept in mind.

(*a*) The order should be firm and clear.

(*b*) Mention the quantity and rates. Check the units whether they are in numbers, sq. meter or otherwise.

(*c*) Mention the quality, specifications, make, sample and other details accurately. These parameters should tally with the quotations already invited.

(*d*) Mention the period of executing the order, mode of payment.

(*e*) Give the full address of the place where goods are to be received. The seller may be genuine but due to wrong address or change in address, goods may be stolen.

(*f*) In case you want the goods in phases, spell that out in the orders you place. It is always better to do so. This will help in making payments in parts.

(*g*) Goods may sometimes get destroyed during transportation. Hence proper packing and safe transportation should be made the responsibility of the seller. Mention that in the order. If desired, get them insured against fire, theft and damage.

(*h*) If required introduce compensation clause. In case the supply is not received on time, suitable compensation shall be levied.

Examples of Placing Orders

Example I

Dear Sir

This is with reference to your quotations bearing no. BD/1041/Arc dated 15/01/10. We are pleased to place an order for the following items on the terms and conditions already specified in the quotations. Please ensure that the goods are received by us within one month of the receipt of this letter.

Name of item	Quantity	Rate
Godrej Soap 75 gm	1000 Nos.	₹ 8.50 Each
Godrej Soap 100 gm	1000 Nos.	₹ 11.20 Each
Toothpaste 150 gm (colgate)	500 Nos.	₹ 37 Each
Toothpaste 150 gm (close up)	500 Nos.	₹ 43 Each
Palmolive Powder 100 gm	500 Nos.	₹ 55 Each
Vim Bar 200 gm	1000 Nos.	₹ 25 Each
Tooth Brush (Raja Make)	2000 Nos.	₹ 23 Each

Sales Tax @ 4% shall be paid extra over and above the rates mentioned. Entire payment shall be released through ICICI Bank within ten days of the receipt of the goods.

Thanking you

Yours truly

(VAISH P)
General Manager

---

2. Acceptance of Order. Sometimes after the issue of place order, the buyer waits for confirmation from the supplier. If the supplier rejects the order then all the exercise done earlier by the parties shall be futile and end without the transaction coming through. However, sometimes the supplier does not confirm the order and still supplies the material and transaction takes place.

So acceptance of order needs to be studied and understood in following aspects:

(*i*) **Importance of Acceptance.** This provides legal status to the order. In other words, the acceptance of the order by the supplier makes the order a contract. It is the act of acceptance that makes the purchase order a legal contract. Therefore, acceptance is necessary without which an order cannot become a contract.

(*ii*) **Results of Acceptance.** In case of contract, both the parties are legally tied up to honour his or her commitments and violation of anyone of the terms shall amount to violation of the provisions of the contract and would invite legal action. The choice to accept the order lies with the supplier who can refuse also. Therefore the supplier shall accept the order only and only if it is beneficial to him. In case the order is not profitable or in case material differences have taken place between the submissions of the quotation and receipt of order, the supplier can reject the order. The consequences of acceptance of order are fully known to the supplier.

(*iii*) **Method of Acceptance.** This can be done firstly by sending the original copy of the order alongwith one more copy to the supplier by putting across the stamp of acceptance duly signed with date or the supplier can write a letter to the buyer indicating his acceptance. Whatever may be the mode of acceptance, an order shall become a contract after it is accepted and further action to purchase goods can be done.

(*iv*) **Is it Compulsory to Accept?** Some suppliers may not send acceptance letter and remain quiet even though they have agreed to accept the order. Nevertheless, written acceptance is necessary so that both the parties have in their hand copy of the agreement enforceable by law. By this, both the supplier and buyer will be free from worry in case the acceptance was conveyed. Buyer will not be able to issue orders again to other suppliers once the agreement is drawn. Similarly, the supplier will be assured of the assignment and can make arrangements accordingly.

Examples of Acceptance Orders

Example I

Deepak Chemicals Pvt. Ltd.
15 A, Janakpuri
New Delhi

The J & K Paper Mills
Civil Lines
Kanpur

Sub.: Regarding Acceptance of Order

Ref.: Your order no. JKP/125/CD/125 dtd 25/12/09

Dear Sir

We are in possession of your order indicated above. We thank you for the same. We are pleased to accept the order and have started manufacturing the goods. We promise to deliver the goods within the period stipulated in the order.

We assure you that we shall carry out the orders to your entire satisfaction.

Yours truly

(ALOK BANSAL)
Manager
Deepak Chemicals Pvt. Ltd.
Enclosures—Copy of the Order duly stamped and signed

Example II

Vaishali Trading Co.
15 Jor Bagh
New Delhi

M/S V.S. and Co.
5 Park Street
Kolkata

Sub.: Order regarding purchase of woolens.

Ref.: Your letter no. TC/Purchase/287.dtd. 28/12/09.

Dear Sir

We are pleased to accept your quotation cited above and place the following order.

1. Pattern no. 463 Dhariwal Suiting @ ₹ 290 per m. (5 rolls)
2. Pattern no. 687 Raymond Suiting @ ₹ 197 per m. (15 rolls)
3. Pattern no. 467 DCM Suiting @ ₹ 283 per m. (7 rolls)
4. Pattern no. 063 JK synthetic @ 700 per m. (2 rolls)
5. Pattern no. 101 Oswal Suiting @ ₹ 200 per m. (6 rolls)
6. Pattern no. 303 Mayur Suiting @ ₹ 590 per m. (7 rolls)

Conditions

1. Discount @ 15% is allowed for making payment within 15 days of the receipt of the material.
2. Sale Tax of 4% shall be paid extra after deducting discount.
3. Date of delivery.
4. Measurement shall be taken jointly with our representatives.

Please acknowledge the receipt of this letter.

Thanking you

Yours truly

(ASHOK SINGH)
Manager

III. INVITING TENDERS

Quotations are generally invited for supply of the goods etc. The tenders are invited for undertaking specific type of jobs. This can be, for example, construction of quarters or bridges. This does not mean that tenders cannot be called for supply of goods. However, generally tenders are invited for jobs which are of slightly longer durations. Notice regarding tenders is given in the newspapers and through websites. Most departments have, with the passage of time, framed their own standard form for inviting tenders.

Examples of these forms used by various departments are given below. These forms are sometimes in abbreviated form and most of these do not contain the conditions and default clauses. The advertisement has to be precise because these have to be published in the newspapers. Sometimes they mention that for detailed conditions, the contractors can refer to the detailed conditions and terms available with the department.

Example I

Notice Inviting Quotation

The ______________________ invites on behalf of the President of India item rate quotations in sealed cover upto 3.00 pm. on ________ and will be opened at 3.30 pm. on the same day from the approved and eligible agency.

Name of Work: ______________________

AS PER SCHEDULE ATTACHED

Conditions

1. The work shall be completed within 01 month.
2. The work shall be executed as per the direction of Engineer-in-Charge.
3. TDS will be deducted as per rule.

Government of India
Executive Engineer
Bhopal Central Division-II, CPWD,
201, Nirman Sadan, Arera Hills, Bhopal

No. 63(2)/EE/BCD-II/2010/ Dt:

Executive Engineer
BCD-II, CPWD, Bhopal

COPY TO

1. Notice Board.
2. The Assistant Engineer, BCSD-I, CPWD, Bhopal.

Executive Engineer

Example II

NOTICE INVITING TENDER

____________________ invites, on behalf of the President of India, sealed item rate tenders from approved and eligible contractors of CPWD and those borne on the appropriate category of Department of Telecommunications, MES, Railways and M.P. State PWD upto 3.00 pm. on, for the following works.

Name of Work/ NIT No.	Estimated Cost	Earnest Money	Time Allowed	Last date of receipt of Application	Last date of issue of tender Documents	Last date of receipt of Tenders	Time & date of opening of Tenders
N.I.T. No.:	₹	₹	_____ Months	_____ upto 16.00 Hrs.	_____ upto 16.00 Hrs.	_____ upto 15.00 Hrs.	_____ at 15.30 Hrs.

Tender document shall be issued from the office of The ________________, during the hours (11.00 am. to 04.00 pm.) everyday except on Sundays and Public Holidays, on payment of the following:

(*i*) ₹__________/- in cash as cost of tender and

(*ii*) Earnest Money of ₹ __________/- in the form of Receipt Treasury Challan/Deposit at Call receipt of a scheduled bank/fixed deposit receipt of a scheduled bank/ demand draft of a scheduled bank issued in favour of ______________ .

Tender forms shall be issued to the Class-I CPWD Contractor. Class-II Contractors of CPWD & Non CPWD contractors shall also be eligible to tender provided they have satisfactorily completed three similar works each of ₹ __________ lakh or one similar works of ₹ ___________ lakh in the period of last seven years ending _________ (**'Similar work'** means **Building Works** with or without Electrical works). The enlistment of the contractors should be valid on the last date of the sale of tender. In case only the last date of sale of tender is extended, the enlistment of contractors should be valid on the original date of sale of tenders. In case both the last date of receipt of application and sale of tenders are extended, the enlistment of contractor should be valid on either of the two dates *i.e.*, original date of sale of tender or the extended date of sale of tenders.
This Notice may also be seen on websites at www. tenderhome. com & www.cpwdwr.nic. in

Inviting tenders is one of the most important constituent of business correspondence followed by submission of tender document and placing of order and issue of award letters.

The sole purpose of inviting tenders is to get competitive rates from the eligible agencies. Therefore, while inviting tenders, care should be taken to specify the name of work, its location, approximate cost put to tender, period of execution, depositing of earnest money, eligibility criteria and so on and so forth. Since the notice for call of tender is to be sent to the public at large; it should be published in leading newspapers of that locality as well as big cities. Advertisement should also be given in magazines and websites. The notice should be put on the notice board of the office calling tenders. In short, wide publicity should be given and adequate time period should be available between the date of advertisement and purchase of tender. Similarly, time should be given between the last date of sale of tenders and receipt of the tenders so that contractors are able to fill up the tenders.

GOVERNMENT OF MADHYA PRADESH
PUBLIC WORKS DEPARTMENT DIVISION RAISEN

Tender Notice No. 692 (2009-10) Dated 29.01.10

Sealed tenders on "A"-Form are invited on behalf of Governor of M.P. for the following works in three cover system on Road and Bridge SOR. Issued by Engineer-in-Chief M.P. P.W.D. Bhopal w.e.f. 01-04-08 with all amendments issued upto the date of issue of this NIT from the Registered Contractors with the Govt. of M.P. P.W.D. in appropriate class. The tenders will be received through Registered A.D. Post or Speed Post service only in the office mentioned. The department will be responsible for any postal delay.

S. No.	Name of work	Cost of Tender Form (₹)	1. Probable amount of contract 2. Earnest Money (₹)	Last Date & time of issue of blank Tender Form	1. Date & time of receipt of Tender 2. Office	(1) Date & time of opening of Tender 2. Office	1. Period of completion of work 2. Class of Contractor 3. Call No.
1	2	3	4	5	6	7	8
1.	Construction of Junia to Bamhori via. Choka Khamria Singhpur Hameerpur Road including Bridge and culverts Length 23.00 K.M. Under Naward	5000	1. 551.85 Lakhs 2. 551850	12.3.10 upto 5.00 pm.	1. 21.3.10 upto 5.00 pm. 2. C.E. PWD. (C.Z.) Bhopal	1. 22.3.10 11.30 am. 2. C.E. PWD. (C.Z.) Bhopal	1. 10 Month including rainy season 2. A 5 3. First

Notes: (1) Blank tender form can be obtained on payment of non-refundable cost shown above from, E.E. P.W.D. Dn. Raisen during office hour (2) Validity of tender will be 120 days from the date of opening of tender. (3) In case of holidays the tender shall be received/opened on the next working day. (4) Application for purchase of blank tender form shall accompany with following documents. If the contractors fails to submit these required documents tender form will not be issued to the applicant. (*i*) Copy of the valid Registration Certificate as a contractor with Govt. of M.P. Registered in appropriate class. In case of firm of partnership submit copy of DEED & Power of Attorney. (*ii*) Current Income Tax clearance certificate. Registration and clearance certificate as per clause 36 of M.P. , Vanijyak Kar Adhiniyam. (*iii*) Valid Revenue Solvency (No older than 6 Months), Blank Solvency of any Schedule Bank for **₹ 25.00 Lakh** which is not older than 12 months. (*iv*) No relationship certificate. (*v*) Documentary proof of owning plant & machinery like Hot Plant, Vibratory Rollers, Mechanical Paver Finisher, Bitumen/Emulsion Mechanic Sprayer as per MOSRT & H Specifications required for the work. (Affidavit shall not be treated as proof of possession).

Note. This notice can also be viewed on government Website: http:/www.mp.nic.in/pwdmp.

G-25147/07 विज्ञापन को www.mpinfo.org पर देखा जा सकता है। "दहेज लेना एवं दहेज देना दण्डनीय अपराध है"

EXECUTIVE ENGINEER PWD. DIVISION, RAISEN

By now we have discussed about inviting quotations, sending quotations and placing orders. But it is important to understand few more things.

Comparative Statement

This term has already been used. It is a statement in which the rates of all the sellers are copied along with the terms and conditions. First of all the conditions are evaluated and then added to the amount. For example, two suppliers may have charged Sales Tax extra while the third did not and their rates were included in the offer. Some suppliers may not have quoted rates for one or more items. Therefore, it becomes necessary to compare the rates of all the suppliers after bringing them to a level field or after evaluating their conditional offers in terms of the amount. The supplier, who offers the best price and the terms, can be selected. The comparative statement helps to do so.

Sometimes the quotations are sent by suppliers in different forms, in their own handwriting. It becomes difficult for the buyer to compare the terms directly from the quotations and hence comparative statement is prepared in which the rates and terms and conditions are copied. In short, the purpose of preparing comparative statement is to make the job of the buyer easier by drawing comparisons. The statement can be prepared product-wise or order-wise.

EXERCISE

1. Mention the points to be kept in mind while sending Quotations.
2. Give three differences between Quotation Letter and Notice Inviting Tenders.
3. Draft a letter inviting quotations for supply of goods.
4. What should a good placing order include?
5. Prepare a tender for the construction of 30 feet bituminous road from 0 km. to 120 km. for sending it to the Executive Engineer, CPWD, Pune. Assume that you are a Manager in Bharat Construction Company, Pune.

❑❑❑

Chapter **7**

COMPLAINT LETTERS

"We can do more good by being good, than in any other way."

INTRODUCTION

Normally a buyer after the receipt of the material should make payment to the supplier as per the conditions already agreed upon. Sometimes the buyer may get the damaged goods or the quantity may be less. The buyer finds this on inspection. Before making payment, the buyer inspects the quantity and quality and tallies with the Invoice. The Inspecting officer of the stores who certifies that the goods received are to their satisfaction does inspection on behalf of the buyer. During inspection, he will be able to find out the mistakes and the shortcomings and record those on papers. Sometimes there can be mistakes in totalling or in discounts offered. Inspection has to be with respect to the order placed with the seller as well as with the Invoice received from him. The damage or bad condition is common in case of materials prone to damage by wind, fire, water etc. Cement bags are damaged by rainwater. Glass breaks by mishandling. Paint, petrol, diesel easily catch fire.

Hence, it becomes the duty of the buyer to immediately check the products and shortcomings should be intimated to the seller without loss of time through letter. Law fixes responsibility on the buyers for buying carefully the goods through caveat emptor clause. Any letter written for the above purpose is called a complaint letter.

Complaint letters are written for pointing out the defects or the shortcomings or for getting the errors rectified. It is not meant to find undue faults or quarrels with the supplier. Complaint is warranted only when it is essential and causes pecuniary loss or causes inconvenience. While writing complaint letter, the nature of defect should be specifically highlighted. Complaint should not be based upon presumptions and assumptions. Any unwise complaint cannot only spoil relations but affect the reputation of the parties. Complaint should appeal to the supplier's sense of honesty and integrity. Any prudent person not connected with the case should appreciate the complaint if it is realistic.

When complaint is made, it should be supported with revised invoice calculations or defective materials should be asked to be withdrawn. Complaint should be correctly worded and reference to the original item be given with units of measurements.

IMPORTANT FACTORS

Complaint letter is expression of dissatisfaction. Complaint letters are to be written with an expression of goodwill and not provoke anger.

The following factors should be kept in mind while writing complaint letters:

1. Give the purpose of making the complaint.
2. Explain the real solid complaint. Give full information. Do not presume or guess anything.
3. The words and expression used should be convincing, tactful, polite, and non-provocative. Avoid the word 'complaint'.
4. Send the statements of damages or loss suffered because of the mistake/defect.
5. Make an appeal for rectification of the situation or for adjustment of the dues. It should be fair and just.
6. Complaint letter should not spoil the future relationship.
7. Mention the less quantity received. Give details of defective material.
8. Explain the nature of defect—whether it is a manufacturing defect, or defective packing, wrong mode of transportation etc. If it is due to late delivery, mention that.
9. Errors in calculations/overpricing should be clearly stated.
10. Violation of any other term and condition of the order should also be mentioned.

Complaint is always due to non-fulfillment of the terms and conditions of the contract. The violation can be of one clause or more than one clause. Therefore, the complaint letter should briefly discuss the terms and conditions and support the complaint with sufficient data to make the complaint clear. For prompt and satisfactory reply, address the complaint to the head of the unit who may be responsible for the mistake.

DRAFTING THE COMPLAINT LETTER

A letter of complaint may be broadly divided into three parts:

1. Start. Start the letter with a direct statement bringing home to the reader the exact nature of complaint.

2. Main part. Discusses the terms and conditions of the agreement. Mention exact paragraphs, clauses, numbers. Explain the factual position with documents and establish that the complaint is genuine. Language should be polite but straight.

3. End. Request the reader for rectification of the mistake or provide alternatives and solutions. Work out the financial aspects. Close the letter with an expression of goodwill.

In addition to the above parts, a letter has to be drafted without explosive words or expressing anger or accusations. Such letters do not help. We all are liable to make mistakes. The purpose of making a complaint is to solve the problem and to secure the service you need. So be straight, precise, true to yourself, and courteous in your approach. If letter has been written in anger, hold it and give a second thought. This will not only yield better results but increase your credibility in the organisation you work.

Example I

Letter of Complaint on the quality of goods

Gupta Construction Corporation Ltd.

Ref.: GCC/2009/AB/2010
15th March, 2011
M/S Associated Cement Corporation
75 M.G. Road
Pune

Subject: Regarding defective delivery of grey cement

Ref.: Your consignee no. 72 of Feb. 2010

Dear Sir

We are in receipt of 1000 MT of grey cement (20,000 bags) and thank you for the same. While unloading the cement in our godowns, we found some set bags of cement and noted on the invoice the same day.

As per the agreement, 20,000 bags of grey cement were to be received by us from you in good condition. Each bag should have weighed 50 kg. Considering your good reputation, order was placed with you by us. Our past experience has been good. However, unfortunately the experience this time has not been that good. Out of the total of 20,000 bags, 79 bags were found to contain set cement which cannot be used for any purpose in our constructional activities. The defective set bags were counted at the time of unloading of the cement bags and was intimated to your representative and recorded on the invoice returned to you.

We, therefore, request you to either take back these bags and substitute with good quality or else modify the bill excluding 79 bags, so that full and final payment can be released to you.

An immediate action is solicited.

Thanking you.

Yours faithfully

(N.K. SINHA)

General Manager
for Gupta Construction Corporation Ltd.

Example II

Letter of Complaint of late delivery

Deepak Trading Company

(Dealers in all Kinds of Woollen Goods)

Ref. No.: DTT/Camp/I
14th March, 2011
M/S Radha Kiran & Co.
5, Park Street
Kolkata

Subject: Regarding late receipt of goods

Ref.: Your compliance letter no. RKC/sd/304/06

Dear Sir

We are in receipt of the goods sent by you and thank you for the same.

However, we are not happy, as there has been inordinate delay in receiving goods. As per the terms and conditions, we should have received the goods in the month of August. Manufacturing normally starts by us in August so that woollens are dispatched by early October to reach the users before the onset of winters. Manufacturing takes one and half month. We are sure that you will be able to understand our difficulty in receiving the consignment so late.

We, sincerely, hope that you will not disappoint us in future due to late delivery.

Thanking you

Yours faithfully

(R.DUTTA)
Manager
Deepak Trading Company

On the above lines complaint letter can be written for supplying the materials not ordered by you.

EXERCISE

1. What is a complaint letter?
2. Which points should be taken into consideration while writing a complaint letter?
3. Draft a complaint letter complaining about the quality of the products received by you.

Chapter **8**

ADJUSTMENT LETTERS

"Communication is not only the essence of being human but also a vital property of life."

—**John A. Piece**

INTRODUCTION

Adjustment letter is a letter expressing clear understanding of the issues conveyed by the buyer and providing reasonable solutions to it. In other words, it deals with the claims for adjustment.

When a buyer has made a complaint, the supplier is left with few options. The supplier must know that the fault lies with him for violating the provisions of the agreement. Therefore, the seller should treat the complaint letter in a positive manner and draw a balanced conclusion. It will emerge from the complaint letter that

1. Mistake has been committed.
2. Whether such a mistake was due to the negligence on the part of a buyer, seller, or third party such as transporter. It can also be due to natural calamity.
3. How to solve such a complaint.

If the fault lies with the supplier, the best way is to accept the mistake in a polite manner. In such a case, settle the claim as quickly as possible. He should also apologise for the inconvenience caused to the buyer. The claim as well as adjustment should be fair and not the policy of caveat emptor. The supplier, even otherwise is legally duty bound to do so as he is on the receiving end since the buyer will not pay for the defective goods. Sometimes, it is uneconomical to receive back the defective goods.

Therefore, apart from the above, the supplier, on receipt of the complaint, should

1. Hold an enquiry to locate the mistake and inform the buyer. At the same time should apologise for the mistake.
2. Take the complaint in good spirits. Buyers can spread words about the supplier's mistakes and spoil his reputation.
3. Try to settle the complaint even if it has to be at the higher costs.
4. At the end of the day, the buyer should feel satisfied that the supplier has handled the complaint to his satisfaction.

Sometimes the complaint letters are welcomed as they provide the supplier with an opportunity to monitor their work more seriously. They may carry out necessary changes, if required. In this era, complaints remaining unattended or unanswered are brought before the media and other forums. The result of a good adjustment letter would bring back the buyer to the same supplier to buy the goods. Therefore, great care is needed in drafting the adjustment letter.

Important Factors

1. Immediately reply to the complaint and thank him in pointing out the defect/ mistake.
2. Offer reasonable adjustment gracefully. Offer further cooperation and assistance. If complaint is unreasonable, give reasons and refuse adjustment.
3. State measures adopted by you to improve your product and assure that no such inconvenience shall be caused in future.

Example I

Municipal Corporation of Delhi
(East Delhi Zone)

16th July, 2011
Mr. V.K. Banerjee
14, GF, Aditi Apartments
New Delhi-92

Dear Sir

Thank you for your letter dated 21st June, 2011 wherein you have pointed out error in our bill of May.

We are sorry for the inconvenience caused to you. The problem was discussed with the junior accounts officer of the department who intimated that due to non availability of the previous records available with the other wing such mistake took place. There had been redistribution of the works among various wings of the corporation in April, 2011.

The error has been rectified and the modified bill is enclosed herewith. In the meanwhile, no additional interest for late payment is to be paid by you until September 2011.

Thanking you for your cooperation.

Yours Sincerely

(N.M. SINGH)
Joint Assessor and Collector
East Delhi Zone
MCD
New Delhi-92

EXERCISE

1. What is an adjustment letter?
2. What constitutes a good adjustment letter?
3. As a supplier, you have received a complaint from the Principal of a college about the supply of wrong and defective books. Draft an adjustment letter.

❑❑❑

Chapter 9

Settlement of Account Letters or Remittance Letters

"Of all the words of tongue or pen, the saddest are those... it might have been."

—J.G. Whittier

INTRODUCTION

It is obligatory on the part of the buyer to make payments for the products received by him after the complaint has been settled. Such letters giving the details of payment for example, cheque or draft, amount, name, full or part payment are called Remittance letters.

FEATURES

Such letters must contain

1. Details of payments whether by cash/cheque/draft.
2. Give details of cheque/draft etc. such as number, date
3. The amount of payment
4. Name of the person in whose favour cheque/draft has been issued
5. Whether full and final payment or part payment
6. Reasons for part payment and likely date of payment of balance amount.

Example

Punjab Shoe Company

45, Upper Hills

Indira Chowk

Shimla-3

23rd Jan., 2011

Ref.: Your bill no. 47 dated 14th December, 2010

M/S Leather House
Neelkamal Market
21/3 Sadar Bajar
Kanpur

Sub.: Settlement of Accounts

Sir

Please find enclosed herewith a crossed cheque bearing number 217584 drawn on State Bank of India payable at Kanpur in favour of your company.

The amount of the cheque is ₹ 2.5 lacs (Two and half lacs only). This is in full and final settlement of our dues. Kindly acknowledge the receipt of the cheque.

Yours truly

(M.K. SHARMA)
Manager
For Punjab Shoes Company
Enclosures: Cheques as above

EXERCISE

1. What is Remittance Letter?
2. Draft a remittance letter for making full payment.

❑❑❑

Chapter 10

DEMI-OFFICIAL LETTERS

DEMI-OFFICIAL LETTERS (D.O.LETTERS)

- Such letters are written to attract the personal attention of the addressee. Use active voice for example "I feel pain to write this ....". Similarly, write I notice rather-than it is noticed. The wordings should be direct, more friendly and should give personal touch. Such letters should preferably be one or one and half page, brief, to the point. Therefore, it is a must that the point should be brought home straight way. Lengthy letters should be squeezed/condensed. Incase elaborate datas are to be sent, the same should be attached with the D.O. letter as exhibits. It is necessary to avoid detailed arguments.
- Usually black or blue ink is used in such letters. Leave adequate margins one to one and half inches on all sides. Should start with the salutation. My dear ...... and terminating with yours sincerely etc., should be personally signed and not innitiated. Letters are to be written in first person and tone should be friendly. In case it is to be drafted, it should be drafted by Branch Officers and above. Since note has to be friendly, it should be addressed by an officer of equal designation in the Ministry/Department or else not more than one level below to whom such a letter is being written to. As far as possible use one and half or double spacing.
- As the name itself indicates, these letters are totally informal and devoid of formal laid down procedures. Mostly used between government officers for communications. But communication to non-government officials can also form D.O. letter. These are not normal or routine types of letters but are written when it is to be brought to the personal notice of an officer a case in which appropriate action has been delayed and even various reminders have not produced results or where suitable report or compliance or reply is required without any further delay. These can also be written in case of extreme secrecy.
- We must bear in mind that like any other correspondence D.O. letter is an official letter and as files, notings, documents, agreements etc. are not exempted in courts/ commissions, even D.O. letters are not exempted. But if disclosure of the stipulated information in such letters impedes any ongoing investigation, the same can be

denied. Demi-official letters are to be supplemented by official letters. As per the government orders, D.O. letters are not to be quoted in newspapers or official communications without seeking permission from the authorities.

– Given below is an example of D.O. letter.

Govt. of India
Central Public Works Department

Er. R.S. Gupta
Chief Engineer

My Dear Shri Ranglal Ji,

I am writing this D.O. letter in connection with the reimbursement of expenditure incurred for the various institutes at Lucknow, Meerut and Balrampur.

As per the Memorandum of Understanding between your department and the C.P.W.D., liability in excess of the funds received is not to be incurred by us, but in the aforesaid schools/institutions we have spent more than the funds which were allotted to us. May it be informed that all these works are in full swing and barring unforeseen circumstances, we are planning to complete all works by December, 2010.

Incase adequate funds are not allotted, the progress is likely to suffer and we shall not be responsible for the same. For completing these works, our minimum requirement is about 400 lacs.

It is therefore requested that suitable funds may please be arranged without further delay.

With Regards,

Yours

(R.S. Gupta)
Chief Engineer
Lucknow

Shri Ranglal ji,
Asstt. Commissioner
Kendriya Vidyalay Sangathan
Aliganj, Lucknow.

LETTERS TO AUTHORITIES

Letters written by individuals, firms, companies, N.G.O.s etc., to the persons holding position in government or authorities is called letters to Authorities. The authorities can be government departments, politicians and the like. Letters can be about events of public interest, corruption, complaints etc. But any such letter to very senior authority such as the Prime Minister, Chief Minister is normally sent below to the concerned department for reports and comments. The letter finally reaches the lowest level and he is asked to draft the reply and passes upward hierarchy (modified at various stages). It sometimes becomes impossible for any Minister to read enormous letter received by him not to talk about sending replies to all those letters. Hence the reply of your letter is finally the produce of a public servant. Is it then not advisable to meet the Minister personally and followed by a letter which is bound to have more impact? The system is same virtually everywhere. The problem is how to meet these politicians.

With the coming into force of Right to Information Act, at least obtaining documents or information has become easier because information has to be supplied within a reasonable period. This however does not solve your complaints because for that you will be required to send complaint letter. Most of the letters written to the authorities pertain to the complaints, seeking fund grant and inaction of the departments.

Example of Letter to Authorities

December 15, 2011
Shri Vinod Vats
Municipal Counsellor
First Floor, Municipal Corporation of Delhi
Town Hall,
Delhi–110006

Subject: Regarding non-covering of manholes in Ashok Nagar Pocket–B.

Dear Sh. Vats,

We the residents of Pocket-B of Ashok Nagar, Delhi are facing extreme hardship due to open manholes of sewer lines in our area. These manhole covers are either missing or are broken. These results in foul smell and are hazard to the residents. Even though no casuality has taken place uptill now but the possibility is not ruled out.

We request you to kindly direct your good officers to immediately attend to our problem. Sketch plan giving the exact location is attached herewith.

Yours sincerely

(Residents of Pocket-B Society)

Enclosure– As above

Copy for Information and Action to

(1) Superintending Engineer, West Zone, Town Hall, MCD, Delhi.
(2) Executive Engineer, Maintenance Division II, MCD, Ashok Vihar, Delhi.

(Residents of Pocket B Society)

From the above example, you should first identify your problem, find the source who can attend to your problem, though not desired you can give your suggestions and or send photographs explaining the seriousness of the problem. Do not forget letter etiquettes, howsoever serious the problem may be. Send cc (carbon copy) to juniors who may be connected with the problem.

LETTER TO A GOVERNMENT OFFICIAL

Writing a letter to a government official is the most common method of allowing your voice to be heard and is most sensible and active participation. Personal contacts again have to be followed with written letters. Letters were substituted with telegrams and telex but with internal facilities, letters through mails are becoming more frequent. Each topic has to be addressed through separate letter. Respect, hatred, disrespect, anguish all can be depicted in letters. You can win the confidence of a person and doubtful gaps can be eliminated through letters.

IDEAL INSTRUCTIONS

(1) Preliminaries

- Write the date at the top.
- Write address below the date leaving slight gap.
- Write the subject and if required the subhead. Subject should be of one or two lines only like title.

(2) Main Body

- Before proceeding with the main part, you should draw an outline and ideas on what you wish to write.
- Each idea or point has to be in different para.
- Begin the letter with salutation as such "Dear ...."
- Write main part based or the ideas created. Start with background, reasons for writing, detail letter, your request/demand.
- End with "Sincerely".
- Write your name and put signature.
- Endorse copy to concerned persons.

(3) Tips

- Avoid lengthy letters.
- Leave adequate space between body and signature.
- Be to the point. Most of the officials may not have enough time to read entire letter. Each para should have one point. Stick to this principle.
- Use computer for spellings, meanings.
- Use address book and telephone.
- Write your telephone number at the end for response.
- Good etiquettes matter.
- Use letterhead if required.
- Expect favourable response and mend your language.

- Do not use threatening or abusive language.
- Try sending through registered cover.
- Avoid hand-written letters.
- Language should match with your purpose.
- Note that these are no readymade rules. You can tailer the format as per your preference.
- Write to the person who is closely related to the issues.

Example of Official Letter

Government of India
Sports Authority of India

No. 18/6/2011–Wi/Dir/69 Date: 16 Jan., 09

To

1. Chief Engineer NZ I CPWD, Sector 9A, Chandigarh.
2. Chief Engineer WZI CPWD, Old CGO Blding, Mumbai.

Subject: Works related to Commonwealth Games 2010.

Reference: This office earlier letter no. 18/6/2011–Wi/Dir/1154, dated 15th Nov, 2011.

Sir,

Please refer to the above mentioned letter wherein request for current status of the projects within your zone indicating construction/preconstruction was called.

It is seen that the status report has still not been sent. These are time-bound projects and are monitored by the senior officers.

You are therefore again requested to send the report immediately and such report may be sent every fortnightly.

(Sh N.S. Reddy)
Director, Infrastructure

Copy to:

1. P.P.S to I.G (W) for information of DG (W) CPWD.
2. Director (Works) CPWD, Nirman Bhawan, New Delhi.

Director, Infrastructure

❑❑❑

Chapter 11

TECHNICAL REPORTS

"It is the framework which changes with each new technology and not just the picture within the frame."
—**Marshall McLuhan**

INTRODUCTION

In this unit we will discuss the reports written by engineers, doctors, scientists, executives etc. These reports may contain the details of their own work or they may discuss the functions/activities of their organisations. These reports are, therefore, different from the general reports and lot of technical effort is required in writing such types of reports. These reports are the backbones of an organisation and many vital decisions are taken based on them. The future planning depends upon the quality of such reports. The importance of such reports increases when the managers are far away from the sites where activities take place.

Reports have to be written or studied at one time or the other by the technical officers no matter what their profession is. Statistics show that on an average, officers spend half the time in writing or studying the technical reports. In this competitive world, you may require the data or reports of other organisations for comparisons.

Reports not only reveal data but also fill in the gaps and correlate activities. For example, the percentage progress needs to commensurate with the percentage expenditure. With the advancement in technology, preparation of reports has become easier and evaluation has become complex due to variety of pictorial analysis of reports.

TYPES OF TECHNICAL REPORTS

Based on the simple classifications, Reports can be **written** or **oral.** Written reports can be further divided into different types as shown below:

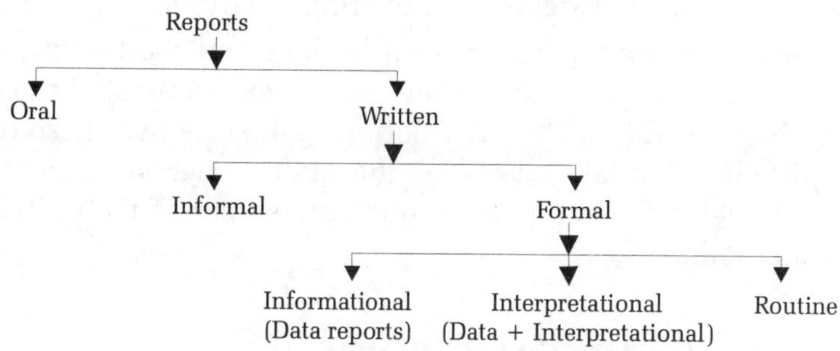

1. *Oral Reports*

In oral reports, facts are stated verbally and communication is not through written means. Unless it is visually recorded, it is as ephemeral as any oral communication. The receiver has to carefully listen to each and every word and hence is more time-consuming. Since it is only verbal, there may be chances of failure to corelate the activities. It is useful for the reporter as his time is being saved.

2. *Written Reports*

Written report is relatively permanent. The reader may read only the relevant abstract and may skim through the irrelevant material. It is more formal and can be gone through again and again. There are certain written reports which are informal in nature such as report of vacancies in a department or comments on the items published in the newspaper etc. Such informal written reports can be in the form of letters.

(*a*) Informal Reports

Such reports are sent by one person to another communicating certain data or information. These reports are usually in the form of letters. The format may vary according to the objects, contents etc.

(*b*) Formal Reports

A formal report is present in a definite format. Its preparation is based on the established procedure. Such formal reports can be statutory ; which are prepared as per the procedure established by the law. For example, reports submitted to the shareholders, director's report given at the time of the annual general meeting, auditor's report etc. Formal but non-statutory reports may not be prepared in accordance with an established procedure of law.

(*i*) Informational, Interpretational Reports. An informational, as the name indicates, is a report in which only the data or information is sent. This is done after the investigation, survey, research and it pertains to the facts observed or recorded. It does not contain inferences, conclusions or recommendations. Rather, it represents a situation as it is. Examples of such types of report may include data pertaining to the expenditure incurred on a work, the amount of deposits or advances received during a year.

(*ii*) Interpretational or **Interpretative Reports** are those reports which not only contain facts or data but also evaluation or the interpretation of the data. If the Interpretative report contains only recommendations, it is called Recommendatory Report. Such reports are a result of survey, investigation, reasoning, analysis.

(*iii*) Routine Reports. Some reports are sent in the usual routine manner to conduct business. These are written in prescribed or standards forms. In most of the cases, reporter has to only put a tick mark or fill up the information against items. These reports are sent regularly, for example confidential reports of the staff, progress reports of the work, inventory reports etc. Usually, these reports contain statement of facts, and are devoid of recommendation or opinion.

CHARACTERISTICS OF TECHNICAL REPORTS

1. Accuracy. Based on the data contained in the report, many vital decisions are taken. If the report is inaccurate, the entire effort is wasted. A good report should contain accurate data leading to correct decisions. The information should be accurately worded.

2. Brevity. Due to lack of time, brief reports are preferred compared to the lengthy ones. Brief does not mean incomplete. Brevity is a comparative word. It must contain all the information desired by the reader but should be precise and clear.

3. Simple. Complex reports are offensive. Simpler the report, better it is. Language should be comprehensive. One reading should give a clear understanding of the report.

4. Complete. Incomplete report is of no use. This point is generally forgotten by the sender. Good report must be complete from all angles, must contain the desired information, facts, conclusions and recommendations.

5. Co-Relation. By co-relation, we mean mentioning various points and drawing relationships between each other. For example, if column number seven (7) of a report is the total work done in lacs and column number 8 is the value of work done last year, then column number nine (9) should be mentioned as column seven minus eight (col. 7 – col. 8) and is the value of work done in the current year.

6. Clarity. The report should not lack clarity. It should be clear in data, conclusions and recommendations. If required, title should be given to each heading or sub-heading. For quick understanding, facts may be arranged in sequence and divided into paragraphs.

7. Attractive. A good attractive report immediately catches the attention of the reader. Give subject, name, serial number, column number, designation and put signatures. Report can be made multi-coloured or multi-dimensional. In short, it should appeal to the reader.

8. Recommendations. Recommendation should be consistent and should match with the data inbuilt in the report. It should be impartial, workable, feasible and logically derived. Try to analyze the data and arrive at a conclusion. Avoid guess work.

MEANING OF REPORT

There can be endless ways of defining a report but in very broad terminology, *"A report is an account of events or collection of data, presented in desired form followed by analysis, conclusions and recommendations, if required."* This definition is best suited for Technical Reports.

NATURE OF REPORT

The main features of a report are:

1. It is a formal statement of information, facts, data, account of events, activities of the departments etc.

2. Report is prepared for a specific audience depending upon the requirement. It can be a one page report to a voluminous report consisting of three hundred pages or more.

3. Report is prepared for a specific purpose. Specific purpose implies specific need. Hence there has to be a technical approach, prescribed style, effective communication, photographs and diagrams if required. Reports should fulfill the required purpose.

4. It should be unbiased and present true picture. The process of decision making starts from the report, therefore, it must depict true events whatever the consequences may be.

5. Reports contain analysis and conclusions. From data, you cannot jump to the conclusion. The data has to be analyzed. Analysis may contain detailed calculations, charts, graphs etc. If the data is technically analysed, you will reach conclusions scientifically.

6. Report is submitted by a junior officer to senior officer. It moves upwards.

7. Report often includes recommendation. Conclusions are different from recommendations. Construction of a dam at a place may be technically suitable from civil engineering aspect but recommendations involve finances, policies and actual requirements. But a report should usually include recommendation as this motivates and persuades the reader. It should give effective solutions. There can be more than one recommendation depending upon the circumstances.

PRINCIPLES OF DRAFTING

1. Preliminary Work. By preliminary work we mean planning. Effective technical report can only be prepared by detailed preparation. This should constitute more than half your efforts. The various steps can be:

- Lay down the requirements
- Determine the audience
- Obtain/collect the data
- Draw broad outline.

— Unless you know the requirements, you cannot find the scope of the report or its purpose. Sometimes from the reference made, the exact scope can be known but if the instructions are not clear, clarifications may have to be obtained. If you are in marketing you may be required to submit a report on the fall or rise of the demand of the product and may have to state reasons for the same. The goal in such reports is defined. Standard proformas may be available for routine types of reports.

— Determining the audience means the audience to whom the report is required to be sent. He can be the head of the department, your immediate boss, the colleagues in other wings of your own organisation, shareholders, members of the public etc. Having done this, you need to know what they know and what they do not know of the contents which you are ready to present in the report. You may have to amend your report according to the audience.

— Data collection or gathering information may not be as simple as it appears. The exact source has to be searched. Even the means of obtaining datas can be explored. The source should be reliable. The most common ways of collecting data/information can be through Internet, library, telephones, manually, prior records etc.

Next step is to determine the data as to whether it is correct or incorrect. Evaluate with respect to the reputation of the sender. Basis are the same as required by you. Is the data co-supported with the facts? Does data contain lots of variations etc.

— Before finally drafting the report, note down the important points. Arrange them in some order and number. This outline will give you the vital parameters of the report which can be further expanded. Do not get lost in data only and ideas may not come to you in series. Therefore the only method is to prepare the outline of a report before you actually start writing. Outline will act as a framework within which you have to work. The outlines will give you the starting and ending parts. This way you can reject the material which is infructuous and not required. Like compilation of data, the outline is one of the important parts of drafting a report. This should not be taken as rigid base but if some new point comes to your mind, the same can be included. The outline is very useful in oral reports/presentations and provides safety in not forgetting the ideas.

The above parts if properly considered can lead to effective report writing.

2. Report Writing. The next step is to write a report. It is always better to prepare a rough report first and then make necessary corrections. There may be no hard or fast rules for writing a report but few points should be kept in mind such as:

— From the drawn outline proceed with various topics, headings and sub titles etc. Discuss and complete one topic before passing on to the other. Follow same sequence and path.

— Read and re-read the report as you go forward. Follow suitable style, clear language which is readable, precise and scientific oriented; choice of words, grammar, phrases, paragraphing is important.

— Most of the technical reports require the use of tabulation (arrangement in columns and rows). Such tables explain better than paragraphs. If required, present your data in graphical form, charts, maps, drawings or even photographs.

— The subject matter should not be lost sight of. Concentrate on it as you proceed. Analyse the data, use technical words while describing events. Support you analysis with calculations. Draw conclusions and sketch recommendations.

— Prepare a rough draft. Visualize the report in entirety. See that all your thoughts and ideas have been incorporated. The ideas should be correlated, coherent. Follow certain order.

— Before writing final draft, give a pause between the rough draft and final as checking will be more effective. In case you have missed out something, the same can be added. Compare the final draft with the already available check list.

TYPES OF REPORT

(*i*) Laboratory Report

By laboratory report we mean the reports of the tests or experiments conducted by the scientist. There can be no uniform pattern of such reports.

Specimen of a Laboratory Report

Concrete is one such material which is used in every building and to ensure good quality of concrete certain standards have been fixed and the proforma below gives the work test of concrete both for 7 days' and 28 days' strength.

Register of Work Test of Concrete

	Concrete mix (By volume)	Compressive strength in kg/cm² on 7 days
(*a*) Name of work		
(*b*) Name of contractor	1:1:2	210
(*c*) Agreement No.		
(*d*) Sample No.	1:1 1/2:3	175
(*e*) Identification mark		
(*f*) Portion of work and quantity represented by sample	1:2:4	140
(*g*) Date and time of casting cube		
(*h*) Proportion of mix		

7 Days' Test (C1.5.4.10.3)

1. Due date of test — Cube No.
2. Actual date of test
3. (*a*) Minimum Strength
   (*b*) Maximum Strength
   (*c*) Average strength of three cubes
   (*d*) Difference between 3*a* and 3*b*
   (*e*) Difference in % age in terms of average strength

   $$i.e., \quad \frac{3b - 3a}{3c} \times 100 =$$

4. Specified compressive strength of concrete mix used
5. (*a*) If 3 (*e*) is more than 30% — Sample is not acceptable, then 28 days' strength test shall be carried out.
   (*b*) If 3 (*e*) is equal to or less than 30% than proceede as below:
   (*i*) Difference between column 4 *i.e.,* specified comp, strength and column 3(*c*) *i.e.,* actual average is higher, it will be denoted (+) and (–) if it is less.
   (*ii*) Difference in column 5(*b*) (*i*) in terms of % age of specified strength — $\frac{3(c) - (4)}{4} \times 100\%$
   (*iii*) If the difference in col. 5 (*b*) (*i*) is +ve and the same in terms of % age of specified strength (4) *i.e.,* value of col. 5 (*b*) (*ii*) is with in (+ 15% range) — Acceptable and Strength is considered in order

JE AE/AEE EE

Register of Work Test of Concrete

	Concrete Mix (by volume)	Compressive strength in kg/cm on 28 days
(*a*) Name of work		
(*b*) Name of contractor	1:1:2	315
(*c*) Agreement No		
(*d*) Sample No.	1:11/2:3	265
(*e*) Identification mark		
(*f*) Portion of work and quantity represented by sample	1:2:4	210
(*g*) Date and time of casting cube		
(*h*) Proportion of mix		

28 Days' Test (Cl. 5.4.10.4)

1.	Due date of test	Cube No.
2.	Actual date of test	
3.	Actual comp. strength of cubes (Min No. of cubes to be tested-three)	
	(*a*) Minimum Strength	
	(*b*) Maximum Strength	
	(*c*) Average Strength of three cubes	
	(*d*) Specified compressive strength of concrete mix used	
	(*e*) 70% of specified strength	*i.e.*, 70% of 3(*d*)
	(*f*) 130% of specified strength	*i.e.*, 130% of 3(*d*)
4.	If 3(*b*) = 3(*f*) and 3(*a*) ≥ 3(*e*)	Value of 3(*c*) shall be compressive strength of sample.
5.	If 3(*c*) is more than 3(*f*)	EE may order further investigation
6.	If any test value exceeds 3(*f*)	It should be restricted to 3(*f*) for computation of strength.
7.	If 3(*c*) ≥ 3(*d*) but < 3(*f*)	Strength is in order and concrete accepted at full rates.
8.	If 3(*c*) < 3(*d*) and > 3(*e*)	Concrete may be accepted at reduced rates in accordance with para 5.4.13.2
9.	If 3(*c*) < 3(*e*)	Work represented by this sample shall be rejected and action taken as prescribed in clause 5.4.10.4

2. Observation Report

Observation report is a report of collecting data by human, mechanical or electronic means. There can be different ways of collecting data. Data can pertain to people or events or occurrences. The actual recording is the most useful method and is advantageous too. With advancement in technology, cameras and microphones, it has become possible to gather significant information to take a decision.

Newton began his study of falling bodies not by making statements but by observations and by performing experiments.

Observation Techniques

- The simplest method is to ask people questions.
- The other method is to just observe which can be formal or a informal.
- Sampling with formal observation.
- Automatic observation: using paper, mechanical counters, calculators etc.
- Mechanical observation: with counters, presses button each time activity takes place.
- Audio tape: Small recorder with microphone.
- Videotape: Cameras at safe place and record for fixed time.
- Still cameras: snapshot method.
- Self observation: Getting respondents to observe themselves.
- Domestic observer: Observe people at home.
- Combining observation: Response: combining two or more methods.

3. Inventory Report

By Inventory report we mean the report of the list of goods and materials which are available in stock by a business. Inventory is prepared to manage the goods and to ease the effect of imperfections in supplying the goods.

The contents may include

1. The reasons for keeping stock
2. Special items of the stock
   (*a*) Manufacturing
   (*b*) Supplying
3. Financial aspects

In the reasons for keeping the stock, mention can be made for buffer stock, safety stock, overproduction, demand fluctuation, change over. Manufacturing units divide their goods into Raw material, Work in progress, Finished goods. So far as financial accounting is concerned, it counts as an asset on the balance sheet.

Many companies follow standard form to track inventory and accept or reject goods. Some of the forms are as follows.

Inventory control is a term commonly used in such reports and is connected with minimizing the total cost of inventory. Some call it stock control and to weigh this we need to find the cost of holding, cost of placing an order and cost of shortage.

INVENTORY REPORT

Date							
Item							
Depth/Location							
Received				Shipped			
Date In	P.O.#	Amount	Received By	Date Out	Invoice	Amount	Stock

Out-of-Stock Notice

Order #		Date	
Customer		Phone	
Address			
City		State	ZIP
Qty.	Item/Description	Estimated Shipping Date	

We cannot fill your order at this time. The items listed above are temporarily out of stock. We apologize for the inconvenience.

PHYSICAL INVENTORY COUNT SHEET

Sheet # ____________________

Location ____

Item Number	Description	Quantity	L

Counted by ______________________________ Date __________

LIST OF INVENTORY

Name of work

S. No.	**Name of articles**	**Quantity handed over**	**Remarks**
1	Aluminium handles		
2	Aluminium sliding door bolts		
3	Aluminium Pull bolts		
4	Aluminium Tower bolts		
5	Aluminium hanging floor door stoper		
6	PVC door with frame and shutter		
7	M.S. Oxidised casement fastner (for window and ventilator shutter)		
8	M.S. Oxidised pege stay (for window and ventilator shutter)		
9	Steel cupboard shutter with double leaf and three way bolting device six lever lock and key		
10	Flush door shutter with aluminium beading		
11	Wire gauge shutter bija wood		
12	Orissa pattern W.C. pan with low level tank		
13	Wash basin with C.P. brass piller tap C.P. brass waste		
14	Beveled edge mirror		
15	Towel rail		
16	Stainless steel kitchen sink		
17	Ball valve (in polyethylene water tank)		
18	PVC connection 15 mm N.B.		
19	C.P. brass shower		
20	Polyethylene water tank-500 ltr.		
21	Brass bib cock		
22	Brass stop cock		
23	PVC waste pipe-32 mm		
24	Stainless steel jali-100 mm		
25	Manhole cover		
26	Gully trap cover		
27	M.S. pipe curtain rod-20 mm		
28	Curtain-vista levelor		

Handed Over — Taken Over

Assistant Engineer (Civil) — Client

4. Project Report

Each project report may require a different format but every format shall contain

1. Cover page and Title page
2. Bona fide certificate
3. Abstract
4. Table of contents
5. List of Tables
6. List of Drawing/figures/sketches
7. Chapters
8. List of Abbreviations
9. Appendices
10. References

Well planned project report is important for the success of the project. The size of the report depends upon the targets and points to be considered. Managerial skill is required to prepare the report. Many project report software are available in the market.

The most common project report is a report of the project yet to be commenced or when it is in planning stage.

The project report given below is for the Construction of Administrative Block for Sport Authority of India at Bhopal (M.P.).

B & R

Estimate No: 45/BPL/2009-2010

Work: C/o Administrative Block for Sports Authority of India, Udhav Das Mehta (Bhaiji) Central Regional Centre at Bhopal (MP).

Expenditure to be charged to

4055—R.B. (Non-Plan)

Estimate is framed by Er. Sharma, Executive Engineer, Bhopal for the probable cost of ₹ 2,08,52,500/- including contingencies.

Report

History: This preliminary estimate amounting to ₹ 2,08,52,500/- including contingencies has been framed to meet the probable cost of the above mentioned work and for obtaining administrative Approval and Expenditure Sanction of the competent authority.

Work has been requisitioned by the SE(Infra), SAI, New Delhi vide letter No. Infra/SAI/2005/542 dated 27.09.2009.

Design and **Scope:** This preliminary estimate for Construction of Administrative Block for SAI is based on following architectural drawings:

(*i*) Ground Floor Plan No. /403/80

(*ii*) First Floor Plan No. /403/81

(*iii*) Front elevation and sections on A-A No. /403/82

The proposed Administrative block shall be two storeyed RCC framed structure with total plinth of 1414 sqm. It has entrance lobby, conference hall, library, director's room, seminar hall, physiology hall, X-ray store, Wax and ward room at ground floor and staff cabins, officers' cabin, store along with attached toilets at first floor.

In view of poor quality of bricks available in Bhopal, RCC framed structure building is proposed.

The site of construction is having black cotton soil, it is considered necessary to moorum under the plinth and provide RCC plinth protection with RCC curtain wall and drain all around the building. Provision has also been made in the estimate for protection against black cotton. Provision for internal electrical installation, necessary development work and bulk services has also been made as detailed under sub head II and III of abstract of cost respectively.

The brief specifications to be adopted in this work are appended as Annexure 'A'.

The cost of project is liable to revision due to probable escalation in cost of construction other reasons such as changes in scope, area, design and specification etc. if so desired by the client at a later date.

SPECIFICATION	: Work shall be carried out as per CPWD specification 1996 Vol. I to V and revised specifications 2002 for cement mortar, cement concrete and RCC works with upto date corrections slips.
RATE	: Based on DPAR 1.1.92 plus duly enhanced for Cost Index for Bhopal @ 230.00 as on 01.06.09 and DSR 2002 duly enhanced for Cost Index @ 38.55%.
COST	: ₹ 2,08,52,500/-including 3% contingencies.
METHOD	: By Contract after call of tender.
W.C. Staff	: Shall be met out of contingent provisions.
T AND P	: No special T and P required.
LAND	: Available with the client deptt.
TIME	: 4(Four) Months for planning 14(Twenty) Months for execution Total **18(Eighteen) Months**

ANNEXURE – 'A'

BRIEF SPECIFICATIONS (OFFICE BUILDING)

Name of Work: C/o Administrative Block for Sports Authority of India, Udhav Das Mehta (Bhaiji) Central Regional Centre at Bhopal (MP).

Sl. No.	Items	Specifications
1.	Structure	Two storeyed RCC framed structure having brick masonry filler walls.
2.	Foundation	Isolated footings at 2.00 metre depth.
3.	Plinth and Floor height	Plinth height of 0.60 m and Floor height 3.30 mt.
4.	Flooring	Kota stone and Marble pattern flooring in passage and staircase. Granite flooring in main entrance hall. Terrazoo tile flooring for all office rooms except Seminar Hall, Library, Director's room, Conference Hall and PA's room.

		Vitrified tile flooring for Seminar Hall, Library, Director's room, Conference Hall and PA's room.
		Cement Concrete Paver Blocks in open courtyard.
		Toilets shall have white marble flooring.
5.	Structural glazing and Aluminium cladding	Front face of the building shall have aluminium Structural glazing and aluminium composite panel cladding.
6.	Door	Door and window frames shall be of powder coated aluminium box section. Main entrance door of aluminium and other doors of 25 thick prelaminated particle board factory made shutter with aluminium 'U' beading.
7.	Windows	All windows shall be of aluminium with glazing.
8.	False Ceiling	Conference Hall, Seminar Hall and Director's Room— Gypsum Board False Ceiling.
9.	Wall Panelling and partitions	Wall paneling in Conference Hall, Seminar Hall and Director's Room with Pre-laminated particle board on hard wood backing. Aluminium frame and pre-laminated particle-board partitions for officers at first floor.
10.	Dome	Multi-walled Poly carbonate sheet dome.
11.	Internal Finish	Acrylic washable distemper and synthetic enamel paint on steel work. White washing on ceiling.
12.	External Finish	Textured Acrylic exterior paint.
13.	Roofing	Integral water proofing treatment on RCC slab.
14.	Sanitary fitting	Vitreous China wash basin, mirror and WC pan with low level PVC flushing cistern with sensor.
15.	Water Supply	Through water storage tank at terrace.

GENERAL ABSTRACT OF COST

Name of Work: C/o Administrative Block for Sports Authority of India, Udhav Das Mehta (Bhaiji) Central Regional Centre at Bhopal (M.P.)

Details of Subhead	Civil	Electrical	Total
I: Main Building	16019100.00	2560200.00	18579300.00
II: Development of Site	953500.00	185500.00	1139000.00
III: Bulk Services	100000.00		100000.00
Total	**17072600.00**	**2745700.00**	**19818300.00**
Add 2.5% of project cost (Civil Portion) for Horticulture operations on ₹ 17072600/.			426815.0
	20245115.0		
Add 3% Contingencies			607353.4
			20852468.4
		Say	**20852500.00**

5. Progress Report

Progress report is prepared either for the work which is in progress or for pre construction stage. Mostly these reports are prepared every month for slightly bigger projects. The progress report gives an idea whether or not the work is progressing on schedule. In case of delay, the reasons are also given and sometimes remedial measures are also proposed. These reports can be prepared for research works also. Such reports must be inspiring and not irritate or serve as impediment. Normally a progress report should contain:

(*i*) Name of the work
(*ii*) Heading and subheading
(*iii*) Date of start and stipulated data of completion
(*iv*) Percentage of progress
(*v*) Value of the work
(*vi*) Likely date of completion
(*vii*) Reasons for delay
(*viii*) Remarks

There can be no fixed pattern of the progress report, the person who wants the report has to state what information he wishes to seek. Two examples of progress reports on pre-construction and construction stage for CPWD works are given below which are exhaustive.

6. Survey Report

A survey may focus on facts or opinions depending upon its purpose. Most of the surveys involve questions to individuals. Statistical surveys are used to collect quantitative information about items in a population.

Uses of Survey

- It is the most efficient way of collecting information from people. Very large samples are possible.
- Wide range of information can be collected. They can be used to study values, beliefs, attitudes and behaviours.
- Errors are eleminated because questions are standardized.
- There is an economy in data collection due to standard questions.

Disadvantages

- Totally depends upon honesty, motivation, memory of the respondents.
- The validity period is less.
- Could lead to vague data set.

Surveys can be

- **Structure and Standardization.** Questions and orders are standard and does not influence the respondent.
- **Serial Survey.** In which same questions are repeated producing time series data.

Methods

There can be several ways

- On telephone
- On time surveys
- Mail
- Personal

A report on subsidy drawn units in Jammu and Kashmir

Over 16,000 industrial units in Jammu and Kashmir that have drawn subsidy, being offered by the Centre and the state government for promotion of industries in the state, exist only on papers. The States Directorate of Economics and Statistics, in its latest economic survey report for 2006–2007, has pointed out–that "of the total 36,520 units surveyed, 16219 were untraceable." Most of these untraceable units are those that are registered to take advantage of incentives given to small scale industries in the state, adds the report. Though the exact amount of subsidy drawn by those non existent industrial units is still not known, official sources said details are being looked into. The state Government has also asked the Industries Department to look into the matter. Minister of State for Industries said. "An inquiry is being conducted into the matter and once it is completed action shall be taken."

And the report runs in few pages.

7. Report of Trouble

Trouble report is a report sent regarding some failure or mistake. Generally these reports are in the form of letters or memorandums.

Specimen of the Trouble Report shall make the matter clear.

PROGRESS REPORT OF NON-CPO WORKS COSTING MORE THAN RS. ONE CRORE (CONSTRUCTION STAGE)

Month : APRIL 07

(A) WORKS UNDER CONSTRUCTION (ALL AMT. IN LACS OF RUPEES)

Sl. No.	Name of Work (I/s Sub Heads)	Location	Client	Zone	A/A & E/S Amount	A/A & E/S Date	Date of Start (as per agmt.)	Stipulated date of completion (as per agreement)	Head of A/c.	Budget allotment	Expdr. upto last year = x	Expdr. upto reporting month in current year = y	Expdr. upto date total expdr. = x + y	Upto date Physical Progress (%)	Target date of physical	Remarks (Present stage of work i/c reason of delay, if any & action proposed)
1	2	3	4	5	6	7	8	9	10	11	12	13	14	15	16	17
1	C/o. J.N.V. at Dharmagaon Dindori (MP) (Phase-A)	Dindori	JNV	CZ	550.99	July-05	Aug-05	Nov-07	Deposit		128.78	0.15	128.93	30%	April 08	Work in progress
2	**Civil Work**															
	(a) Boundary wall				15.00		Dec-05	Jun-06						100%	Completed Jul 06	Work in progress
	(b) 4Nos. Type-I, 4Nos. Type-II, 8Nos. Type-III & Principal Residence.				67.43		Apr-06	Apr-07						40%	Sep-07	Work in progress
	(c) Kitchen & Dining hall				51.10		Apr-06	Feb-07						44%	Aug-07	Work in progress
	(d) Dormitory				179.00		Oct-06	Dec-07						10%	Mar 08	Work in progress
	(e) School Building				124.89		Nov-06	Nov-07						8%	Mar 08	Work in progress
	(f) Development & Play fields				58.00											To be taken up in Jun 07
	(g) OHT & UG sump.															Tender received and under scrutiny
3	**Electrical Work**															
	(i) Internal El & Fans				43.60										Dec 07	Tenders Under security
	(ii) Service connection & development				22.00										Dec 07	Demand Note from MPSEB shall be obtained in Mar. 07

PROGRESS REPORT OF WORKS COSTING MORE THAN ONE CRORE (PRE CONSTRUCTION STAGE)

Month : APRIL 07

(C) (WORKS FOR WHICH P.E. SENT BUT NOT SANCTIONED)

(AMT. IN LACS OF RUPEES)

Sl. No.	Name of Work	Location	Client	Zone	Date of Requisition	P. E. Amount	Date of submission of P.E.	Detailed Remark on the present Status of
1	2	3	4	5	6	7	8	9
1	C/o Record Room for Income-tax	Bhopal	IT	CZ		381.58	Dec. 02	A/A & E/S awaited
2	C/o Office Complex for the office of the RLC (C) Jabalpur & CGIT cum Labour Court	Jabalpur	Labour	CZ		133.42	Mar. 03	A/A & E/S awaited
3	C/o Office Building For Vocational Regional Centre for Handicapped (VRCH)	Jabalpur	Labour	CZ		1003.46	May 03	A/A & E/S awaited
4	C/o Office Building for Central Excise Bhopal	Bhopal	CE	CZ		560.68	Jul. 06	A/A & E/S awaited
5	C/o Office & Resdl. Complex for SIB	Ambikapur	SIB	CZ	Aug. 05	107.58	Oct. 06	A/A & E/S awaited
6	C/o Office & Resdl. Complex for CBI	Jabalpur	CIB	CZ	May. 06	472.61	Jul. 06	Reply on observation furnished
7	C/o Office Bldg C.C.I.T at Raipur.	...	...	...	...	...	...	PE being prepared

Specimen of a Trouble Report

To
The Engineer in Chief
Public Health Engineering Deptt.
State of Tamil Nadu
Chennai

Subject: Investigation in the cause of failure of shaft type overhead tanks.

Sir

The failure of the various shaft type overhead tanks in the state has been carefully investigated. In all, about 62 tanks, small and big, have collapsed during the last 3 years in the state. The datails are

Year of collapse	No. of Tanks collapsed	Capacity	Year of construction
2004	25	2 lac to 5 lacs	1986 Annual
2003	18	1 lac to 4 lacs	1980 Annual
2006	19	1 lac to 5 lacs	1990 Annual
	Total 62 Nos.		

We have the photographs of such fallen tanks and detail reports from the concerned executive engineers.

Causes. The main reason appears to be settlement of the soil, poor quality of material, poor workmanship and carroding of the steel bars. Thickness of the shaft is also a cause. Two tanks collapsed during construction stage itself.

There were hardly any casualities indicating that before collapse, there were signs of failure.

Suggestions

1. It is suggested that instead of shaft type overhead tanks, we should construct overhead tanks with columns and beam arrangement.
2. The material required for construction should be issued departmentally, particularly cement and steel.
3. Stronger design is proposed and soil strata should be carefully analysed before giving the design.
4. The superintending engineers must record structural certificates before handing over the tanks.

(Signature)
Chief Engineer
P.H.E. Deptt.
Chairman

EXERCISE

1. Prepare a project report of Assembling of Computer units. Assume necessary data.
2. Give benefits of Observation Report.
3. Discuss the advantages and disadvantages of Progress Report.
4. Choose a problem of your interest and write a report.

Chapter 12

TECHNICAL PROPOSAL

TECHNICAL PROPOSAL

Broadly speaking a proposal needs to have two parts namely Technical Proposal and Financial Bid. Technical proposal implies Technical bid. Suppose you want to construct 2000 quarters for the Tsunami affected people in Andaman Island. For doing this, you will have to decide.

(*a*) The area of each quarter,

(*b*) Specifications of quarters such as flooring details, brick or stone walls, number of floors, external and internal finishing details, the types of doors and fittings, kitchen details and finishing, toilet types etc.

(*c*) The layout or Master plan of the plot where construction is to be started. This will include parks, boundary wall, road details, water supply and sewerage details, storm water details, street lights, transformers and so on and so forth.

(*d*) Source of water supply, electricity and disposal of sewerage etc., and any other detail which may be required depending upon the site conditions. If it is a hilly terrain, then levelling etc. has to be done and quarters shall be constructed at different levels.

For finalising all the above details, you need the help of Engineers and Architects. The documents prepared by them would be called "Technical proposal." Once the Technical Proposal is through, the contractors or the departments can be asked to send their cost or price bid or financial bid/offer.

DEFINITION

A Technical Proposal is a document which is used in two step bidding process through which only technical information is solicited. A Technical Proposal is necessarily a document that explains the technical requirements of the project and fully explains the approach and the plans which have been formulated to address the issues. Generally it is the buyer or investigator who prepares the Technical Proposal but depending upon the requirements,

Technical Proposal can be invited from the vendors also. In such cases, you, as a prospective buyer, are required to give the final minimum requirement. In mega projects such as construction of dams or railway lines below the oceans, the vendors are called upon to send their technical proposals because they may have more expertise when compared with you. On receiving various technical proposals, the best one or the combination of the various technical proposals will give you the final Technical Proposal. The technical proposals do not only indicate that you have understood the project but may invite innovative ideas. Such proposals importantly improve the quality of the project.

SIGNIFICANCE OF A TECHNICAL PROPOSAL

1. **Offer to undertake project.** Technical Proposal may contain several elements which are totally technical in nature. It could be a result to extensive survey, data collection, information about its feasibility, meticulous estimation, study of alternatives etc. etc. Through technical proposal, you may fetch a contract or it may slip from your hands. The document has to be impressive and technically sound.
2. **Vital for Organizational Success.** Technical proposals are important for the success of the organization as these documents are vital tools to assess your capabilities. Some firms even hire people for their special skills in writing these proposals. In short it fetches you business.
3. **Helps in future projects.** Sometimes, particularly in government contracts, the technical proposals are extended upto three to five years because inviting technical proposal again every year may not be possible as it requires lot of homework and time and money for advertising. Hence the duration of survival increases.
4. **Valuable tool for studying alternatives.** Unlike ordinary proposals such as marriage proposal, a technical proposal invites suggestions from the audience to approve or modify the technical proposal drafted by the buyer. In this bargain you get to know several alternatives and can choose the best one. Gathered solution capabilities are put into decision-making.
5. **Helps to cell financial bids.** Without clear and detailed technical proposal, you cannot invite financial bids. Therefore, this is a prerequisite for inviting price or financial bid. It technically grants permission to undertake the project.

WRITING OF TECHNICAL PROPOSALS

This is the most important part. It is an art different from research work. It is a bridge between the buyers requirements and solutions proposed.

1. Identify Basic Ingredients

(*a*) **Why:** You as a buyer must mention as to **why** you require technical proposal. Why could this not be done in house by you?

(*b*) **Who:** Who are you? Give brief description about your firm or organisation and how long you are in this profession. Some may not like to submit their proposals in case your description does not suit their requirements.

(*c*) **When:** This gives the time indication. When to submit the technical proposals and when to buy the documents. How much time you will take to decide about shortlisting the firms. How much time do you require to prepare the technical proposal and whether the same can be extended and if yes by when.

(*d*) **What:** What is the nature of your proposal, your needs and desired results. What is the scope of the work and what are the alternatives?

(*e*) **How:** Having received several technical proposals, how you are going to evaluate those, the award process? Broad terms of the contract are known, payment schedule, incentive, compensation etc.

2. Use Standard Forms

Avoid handwritten material and as far as possible use standard forms as templates. Most of the technical proposals contain printed schedules and annexures and these are only required to be filled in. Wherever expressed opinions and technical details are required, the same should be given under the selective headings.

3. Parts which are Common

(*a*) **Objective of the Technical Proposal.** This has to be unambiguous and clear. Any contradictions incase can render the objective futile. Describe the extent of the problem or the services you are looking for.

(*b*) **Scope of work.** Narrate the specific duties you are looking for and expected outcome. List the responsibilities and incase you are employing subcontracts, their responsibilities should also be included. Can the scope of work be enlarged? Provide alternatives to the originals.

(*c*) **Background Information.** You may wish to engage and receive proposals, from the selective class of people. Hence you need to fix same minimum criteria and essential and desirable conditions. Obtain overview of your organization and expect the same also. Mention your strength and inform what you do not want. In order that no back references are made for reconfirmations, ask for certified copies of the documents.

(*d*) **Outcome Standards.** The quantity and quality targets should be fixed. Specify the outcome targets. Some minimum benchmark can be fixed.

4. Ask these Questions and Answer Them

- Have you given some suitable title?
- What was the problem and have you assessed that?
- The result of the project given or not?
- Have you given the concept, goal and approach?

– What risks are attached with the problems and have you discussed?
– Have you given the time schedule and your own expenses to be incurred?

5. Some Fundamentals

– Good Technical Proposal has to be concise and coherent.
– Be specific and reasonable.
– Methods used to achieve the goals should be clearly stated.
– Technical Proposal must give convincing need for the proposal.
– Technical Proposal should be such that it is easy to evaluate.
– Say forcefully, particularly the opening paragraphs.
– Do not leave the buyer with something more to ask.
– Aim clarity and establish goal.
– Try new approach/methods.
– Give concluding note and capture others' attention.
– Put yourself in recipient seat and think which information would need to feel safe hiring you to undertake the project.

INVITATION FOR BID

1. The Executive Engineer, Allahabad Division, Allahabad, on behalf of the President of India invites the bids from firms/contractors of repute in two envelope system for the following work:

Sl. No.	Name of work	Estimated Cost		Period of completion
1.	C/o Floating Jetty on the river Ganga at Allahabad.	Civil	₹ 2,005.50 lacs	17 Months
		Elect.	₹ Nil ..lacs	
		Total	₹ 2,005.50. lacs	

2. Contractors who fulfil the following requirements shall be eligible to apply. Joint ventures are not accepted.

   (*a*) Should have satisfactorily completed three similar works each costing not less than ₹ 803 lacs or completed two similar works each costing not less than ₹ 1,204 lacs or completed one similar work costing not less than ₹ 1,605 lacs of the following nature during the last seven years ending last day of the month Sept. 2008.

   (Similar work means Jetty or bridge work with pile/well foundation.)

   (*b*) Should have had average annual financial turnover of ₹ 1,003 lacs on construction works during the last three years ending 31st March 2008.

   (*c*) Should not have incurred any loss in more than two years during the last five years ending 31st March, 2008.

   (*d*) Should have a solvency of ₹ 803 lacs.

3. Bid documents consisting of plans, specifications, the schedule of quantities of the various classes of work to be done and the set of terms and conditions of contract to be complied with by the contractor whose bid may be accepted and other necessary documents can be seen in the office of the Executive Engineer, Allahabad Division, Allahabad between hours of 11.00 AM and 4.00 PM from ....*........... to ....*.......... everyday except on Sundays and Public Holidays. Bid documents, excluding standard form will be issued from his office, during the hours specified above, on payment of the following :

   (a) ₹ 1,500/- (non refundable) in cash as cost of bid and

   (b) Earnest money of ₹ 30.06 lacs, in cash (up to ₹ 10,000/-)/Receipt Treasury Challan/Deposit at call receipt of a scheduled bank/fixed deposit receipt of a scheduled bank/demand draft of a scheduled bank issued in favour of Executive Engineer, Allahabad Division, Allahabad. A part of earnest money is acceptable in the form of Bank Guarantee also. In such case, 50% of earnest money or ₹ 20 lacs, whichever is less will have to be deposited in shape prescribed above and balance in shape of Bank Guarantee.

4. Application supported by prescribed annexure and the financial bid shall be placed in separate sealed envelopes each marked "Technical Bid" and "Financial Bid" respectively. Both the envelopes shall be submitted together in another sealed envelope. The bids will be received upto 3.00 PM on ....*........ The envelope marked "Technical Bid" shall be opened by the Executive Engineer or his authorized representative in his office on the same day at 3.30 PM. The time and date of opening of financial bid shall be communicated at a later date.

   (a) Pre Bid Conference shall be held in the chamber of The Chief Engineer Lucknow at ..... * .... on ...*...... to clear the doubt of intending tenderers, if any.

   (b) The department reserves the right to reject any prospective application without assigning any reason and to restrict the list of qualified contractors to any number deemed suitable by it, if too many bids are received satisfying the laid down criterion.

5. If any information furnished by the applicant is found incorrect at a later stage, he shall be liable to be debarred from tendering/taking up of works in PWD. The department reserves the right to verify the particulars furnished by the applicant independently.

6. This notice can be seen at **www.tenderhome.com** too.

After finalising the technical proposal, the next step is to scrutinise financial bids or price bids. Because for awarding the work, you need to compare the quotations of the firms and select the lowest.

TYPES OF PROPOSALS

(A) Internal or External

When the technical proposal is within your organization (government, business, agency etc.) it is called Internal Proposal. In such cases you need not ask for the personal details or other exhibits which are already available with you.

In case the proposal is made by one organization to other or individual e.g., a consultant proposing to take a project for another firm or individual. Such proposals are External Proposals. Exhibits requiring details may be received from the firm.

(B) Solicited or Unsolicited

In case of Solicited Proposals, the recipient of the proposal in one way or the other, is requested for such a proposal through mail, newspapers or publication etc.

In case of Unsolicited Proposals, the recipient does not request for proposals. The sender has to explain that problem exists before he starts with the main part of the proposal.

(C) Depending upon Specific Purpose

- Auction proposals
- Proposals seeking funding
- Engineering proposals
- Business proposals
- Formal and non-formal

FORMAT FOR PROPOSAL

Format will be different for different proposals. But each proposal should have at least

- Title page
- Main body
- Budget details
- Number of Proposals or alternatives
- Time frame
- Miscellaneous information
- Conclusion.

But other materials may be added such as

- Research methodology
- System of evaluation
- Activity or Bar charts
- Technical assessment

- Bibliography
- Future prospects

EXERCISE

1. What do you mean by Technical Proposal and what does technical signify in this?
2. What points should be kept in mind while writing Technical Proposal?
3. Give three significances of Technical Proposal.

❑❑❑

Unit IV
Presentation Strategies

Chapter 1

ORAL PRESENTATION

"A spoonful of humour makes the message go down easier." **—Frank Leehy**

INTRODUCTION

An oral presentation is a formal way of conveying your message to your audience. Oral Presentation is different to communication. While oral communication is an interactive process of sharing information, oral presentation is formal, structured, systematic and intended to raise a particular issue for discussion.

It is important to be able to present your thoughts and ideas effectively. You will need to develop and use this skill when you attend job interviews and especially when you start working. You may start with short presentation in your college and gradually build up. Each presentation gives you an opportunity to enhance your technique and confidence.

Importance of Oral Presentation

Oral Presentation can inform, motivate and convince more effectively than any other single form of communication. Employers place great value on presentation skills. Your ability in this area can make or break your career. You may be very efficient in your specific field. You may be hard working too, but if you lack in the skill of presentation, you may not grow in your career. As an employee in an organisation, you will be expected to attend seminars, workshops, symposiums, conferences, general meetings. You will have to organise departmental presentations, team presentations, product launches. If you have acquired the skill of oral presentation, you can use each presentation as an opportunity for your professional growth.

Although there are certain people who have a natural potential for communication, but the techniques involved would benefit them to brush up their skill. The others may benefit from hard work and practice. Oral Presentation is an acquired skill which can be enhanced with practice. Oral Presentation is becoming an essential part of working life.

The organisations rank oral presentation as the most important skill responsible for their growth. Oral Presentation may help you in your meetings with your juniors in which you can collect ideas. Ideas are discussed, evaluated and then selected. Effective Oral Presentation would make you popular among your juniors.

This may help you to get the desired task done in the fixed time. Effective Presentation would present your best before your seniors. Oral Presentation is beneficial for the growth of the organisation in which you work.

If you are important for the growth of your organisation, you will get the due acknowledgement.

Factors Important for Effective Oral Presentation

1. **Purpose.** Clarify your purpose, prepare accordingly. Whether your presentation is intended to motivate, inform, persuade, teach or just to convey a message.
2. **People.** Know your audience, their mental level, their expectations from you. Use the language appropriate to the audience. Keep your audience's interest intact. Provide variety and relief if possible. If you are presenting before an enlightened audience, your research should go into more details. You must know beforehand the age level, the educational level, the special interest, the cultural background of your audience. Tailor your presentation accordingly.
3. **Planning.** Outline your topic, gather information, do sufficient research. Plan to add stories, anecdotes, demonstrations, testimonials. Plan effective introduction and ways to encourage audience's participation.
4. **Preparation.** Planning the presentation would help you in the preparation. You can start the preparation by using the gathered material, the researched material. Make note-cards to avoid last minute humiliation. Do not go too much into the details of the topic that it may become vague. Prepare for the unexpected queries. What if the audience is more prepared than you expected? What if there is an unexpected question—prepare accordingly.
5. **Practice.** Always practice before the final day. Review your notes beforehand to avoid last minute changes. You may be brilliant in your presentation but practice would boost your confidence.
6. **Be Positive.** Treat the topic of your presentation with positivity. Do not take the negative questions as personal offence.
7. **Personal appearance.** Your audience would know about your ability only after you start delivering your presentation. Before that they will look at you; pay attention to your personal grooming. Always wear a formal dress but never overdo your grooming.
8. **Preach not.** Convey controlled enthusiasm for your subject. Have confidence, be assertive but do not preach. Be concrete, specific, relevant and practical but do not preach. Audience like to be treated on equal level.
9. **Place.** The use of audio-visual aids must correspond with the venue of the presentation. How can you use your audio-visual aids in that particular place? How can you plan and adapt to the logistics of that place?
10. **Punctuality.** Be in time for your presentation. Don't go over the time allotted. If you have been allotted two hours for your presentation, keep the last half an hour for feed-back. There should be no shortfall or time overrun. Division of allotted time would make you more confident.

11. **Posture.** Maintain a balanced posture. Don't lean. Try to position yourself that you can see the audience properly and you are also viewed by them. Maintain eye contact. But don't stare too much. Use gestures naturally. Do not block the visual aids.
12. **Pretend not.** Be honest. If you do not know an answer, say so.
13. **Physical mannerism.** Be your natural self. Don't over-act. The focus should not be on you but the subject.
14. **Panic not.** Maintain the confidence. Being nervous is natural. Everybody gets panicked, but proper preparation, planning, practice should boost your confidence.
15. **Proper Feedback.** Question answer session is an important part of any presentation. Plan the last part of your allotted time for feedback. Anticipate questions and prepare answers. Be firm and assertive without being aggressive and defensive. Do not let interruptions disturb you. Avoid circumstances that require an apology. Answers to the questions asked by the audience should be thought-provoking and not a show off of your knowledge. If you have to ask the questions, ask friendly questions, don't question to embarrass. Conclusion should include the summary of your presentation.
16. **Language.** Use only professional language in professional presentations otherwise use language appropriate to the audience and the topic. Make sure that correct grammar and word choices are used throughout the presentation. Avoid the use of colloquialism or the slangs.

Do's for Oral Presentation

1. Be positive, firm and relaxed.
2. Take a deep breath before you start.
3. Anticipate questions, plan answers.
4. Practice.
5. Use note-cards.
6. Speak clearly.
7. Maintain eye contact.
8. Structure your presentation.
9. Do research on the topic.
10. Speak clearly and correctly.

Don'ts for Oral Presentation

1. Do not rely on one source of data.
2. Do not panic.
3. Do not be boring.
4. Avoid using technical terms not familiar to your audience.
5. Do not read from a script.
6. Do not speak too fast or too slow.
7. Do not go over the allotted time.

8. Do not forget your audience.
9. Do not forget to have a bit of fun.

EXERCISE

A. Answer the following questions:

1. How is oral presentation different from oral communication?
2. Discuss the features important to make an oral presentation effective.
3. Can effective oral presentation help you in the growth of your career? How?
4. What role does Feedback play in a presentation? How can Feedback help you to achieve the desired goal.
5. Prepare a presentation on the disadvantages of the excessive use of cell phones.

B. Assignments:

1. Which points will you keep in mind during the preparation of your presentation?
2. How can you maintain a balance between talking and listening during presentation?

C. Which of the following statements would help you in your presentation:

1. Never say no to any question, even if you do not know the answer.
2. Always dress up formally for your presenation.
3. Use difficult vocabulary and go into the deep details of the topic.
4. Humour blocks the flow of presentation.
5. Too much visual aids may deviate you from the actual purpose of presentation.

❑❑❑

Chapter 2 COMMUNICATION

"Communication leads to community, that is to understanding, intimacy and mutual valuing."

—Rallo May

"I just wish my mouth had a backspace key."

"Communication is the real work of leadership."

"Communication works for those who work at it."

"Self expression must pass into communication for its fulfilment."

—Pearl S. Buck

INTRODUCTION

Communication is the process of exchanging information and ideas. The information is transmitted through a common system of symbols, signs, behaviour, speech, writing, or signals. Human communication refers to the social interaction of sharing information for the purpose of understanding and social connection. Communication happens at many levels, in many different ways and for all beings. The word communication is derived from Latin "Communicare" which means "to impart, share".

IMPORTANCE OF COMMUNICATION IN AN ORGANISATION

1. To impart Information. The basic function of the communication is to impart information to the receiver. The information is required both ways–from sender to the receiver and *vice versa*. In an organisation if the manager does not impart information to his juniors about the work to be done, he will not achieve results. Similarly he is required to inform his seniors about his performance. When the employers are well informed about the various aspects of the work, they perform well. To get good appraisal, the employees in turn should apprise their seniors about the work they have done, otherwise they will not get the due benefits.

The information may be collected from outside as well as inside the organisation. Internal information may include the qualification and skill of the employees, production of Sales data, Absentee statement, Performance data, Budget statement, Accounts etc. The external information includes knowledge about the market, sources from outside, policies of the government survey of the public, future prospects of the company etc. Information, of whatever kind, must be concise, accurate, up-to-date and reliable to avoid misunderstanding of any kind.

2. To Impart Education and Training. Communication plays a vital role in imparting education—both formal and informal. Information for the purpose of education can be given through lectures, class notes, seminars, study-tours, T.V., newspapers, press, journals, Internet, Websites, E-mails etc.

Take the example of modernisation of agriculture or family planning or personal hygiene or eradication of epidemics like polio, bird-flu etc. The public in rural areas is educated through television, radio, advertisement, personal interaction. Mass media helps in providing education for family-planning, hygiene, road-safety, child abuse, child-labour, foeticide, different addictions, pollution control etc. Inside an organisation the employees are informed about the rules and procedures of the company. They are given formal training in which communication plays its role.

3. To Issue Orders and Instructions. Orders and Instructions may be sent orally or in written way. They may be in the form of notices, circulars, oral, e-mail, telephone, manuals, hand-books. Annual reports can also be prepared to issue instructions, rules and procedures. Orders and Instructions are authority based and the employees cannot ignore them.

4. Counselling. Majority of the problems in an organisation can be resolved through psychological counselling. Effective communication can help in this direction. Employees can be counselled to perform better. The team leader can be counselled with effective counselling, not to be dominating. Counselling may produce cordial relationship among the different levels of employees in an organisation. Counselling also increases the creativity, bring out the hidden potentials and brings the positive change in the behaviour of the employees.

5. Persuasion. Persuasion is the art of influencing the attitudes, opinions and actions of the people. Politicians persuade people to vote. A salesman persuades the customers to buy the product. The companies persuade the public to take their product through advertisements. Companies spend millions of rupees on advertisements to persuade the public. Persuasion is very important when the company decides to bring some changes in the administration or in its rules and procedures. Persuasion should be convincing and cordial.

6. To Provide Advice. An employee may be very good in his work but if he is not friendly with his colleagues, juniors or seniors, the advice may help him to develop friendly attitude. The advice must be friendly and not dictatorial. It should be for the betterment and not to show superiority.

7. To Receive Suggestions. An employee should be receptive. Suggestions may come from any quarter, from juniors or seniors. Useful suggestions should be implemented and the sender should be rewarded. The betterment of the organisation is always above your personal ego. Suggestion boxes should be installed at the workplace to encourage the employees to suggest openly. The management must welcome the suggestions and act against the complaints.

8. Motivation. The employees may be motivated to perform better by getting the due recognition for their work. Timely due appraisal from the management motivates others to perform better. Organisation is like a family. If the manager gives his hundred percent for its growth and the management treats its employees like family members, the motivation to do better, increases.

Due rewards for work, cordial relationship between management and the employee, sympathetic ear towards the problems of the workers, timely and deserved appraisal, motivate the employees to do better for the organisation in which they work.

9. Improve Discipline. Discipline is an integral part of the growth of any organisation. Discipline may be taught by issuing warning and notices.

CYCLE OF COMMUNICATION

Human life is interactive and communication spins the web of interaction. In order to make interaction effective and reduce the chances of misunderstanding, we need to analyse the cycle of communication. If we understand the importance of the cycle of communication and filter our communication to make it healthy, we can transform ourselves and our environment by changing the way we communicate with others and ourselves.

The communication cycle starts with a knowledge carrier—Verbal or Non-Verbal. The communication cycle is a basic process for interacting. It applies to almost every environment and circumstance where communication is required, from the basic two person verbal exchange to the network of communication involving thousands or millions of people. The communication cycle helps in identifying and defining the information needs and desires of the individuals or groups who will be participating in the communication.

We interact with so many people daily, formally or informally, and sometimes we fail to understand what went wrong in the conversation. This happens because very few of us recognize and understand the cycle of communication. We may share the same language but the communication pattern may be different. To avoid the psychological, emotional or even physical stress arising out of the misunderstanding, we should be sensitive towards the cycle of communication.

The cycle of communication involves the message, → sender → medium of communication → receiver → message → medium of communication → sender. So, this is a cycle of give and take. The message is passed from one person to another and unless the sender gets the feedback from the receiver, the cycle is left incomplete. If you fail to complete the cycle as a sender, you will need to brush up your communication cycle. In this cycle of communication, one is active, and the other is receptive.

Active Listening is very important to achieve the target conceived in the communication cycle. The sender transmits the message with an intention of being understood by the receiver. If the receiver does not pay attention or he is lost in his own thoughts, there will not be any communication. Communication cycle must involve the participation of two parties—if one is active, the other should be receptive. The message sent should never be ignored by the receiver. The cycle of being ignored results in **Anger, Rejection**

and **Hurt** feelings—the damage caused may not be repaired. A good way to avoid ignoring others would be to directly focus on the person speaking.

The most difficult aspect of human life is to sustain relationships at work, at home and with friends. People experience serious difficulties because of the poor communication, which may temper sometimes one's growth in career too. Ability to communicate well is a skill which can be achieved if an understanding of the communication cycle is developed.

The cycle of communication defines the goal of transmission of message which is to exchange ideas, and not to win an argument. Since feedback is a part of the cycle of communication, the receiver's feelings are equally important in this process. If both the sender and the receiver are sensitive about the personality traits of each other, if they understand the complexity of transmission of message, the cycle of communication may bear the desired results.

The channel of transmission should be appropriate to the situation. The congenial environment brings the desired results. Offering some level of humility will create an arena fit for communication.

Process of Communication

The communication process is that process by which a message, encoded by a sender is transmitted through a medium to a receiver, who decodes the message and provides feedback. So, communication process may be understood as a description or explanation of the chain of events involved in communicating information from one party to another. The communication process has been analysed from time to time. In 1940s and 1950s, researchers like **Claude Shannon, Warren Weaver, Wilbur Schramm** offered models describing the process of communication.

Communication can best be summarized as the transmission of a message from a **SENDER** to a **RECEIVER** in an understandable manner. It is through the communication process that the sharing of a common meaning between the sender and the receiver takes place. Those who follow the communication process are more productive in every aspect of their professional communication. Effective communication leads to understanding. Knowledge about the communication process helps the communicator to choose a proper medium and guard against the errors so that the right message is received and proper feedback is sent back.

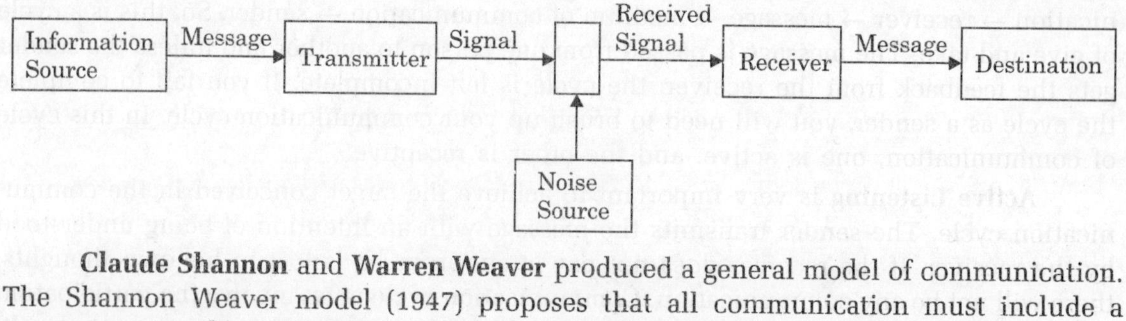

Claude Shannon and **Warren Weaver** produced a general model of communication. The Shannon Weaver model (1947) proposes that all communication must include a source, an encoder, a message, a channel, a decoder and a receiver.

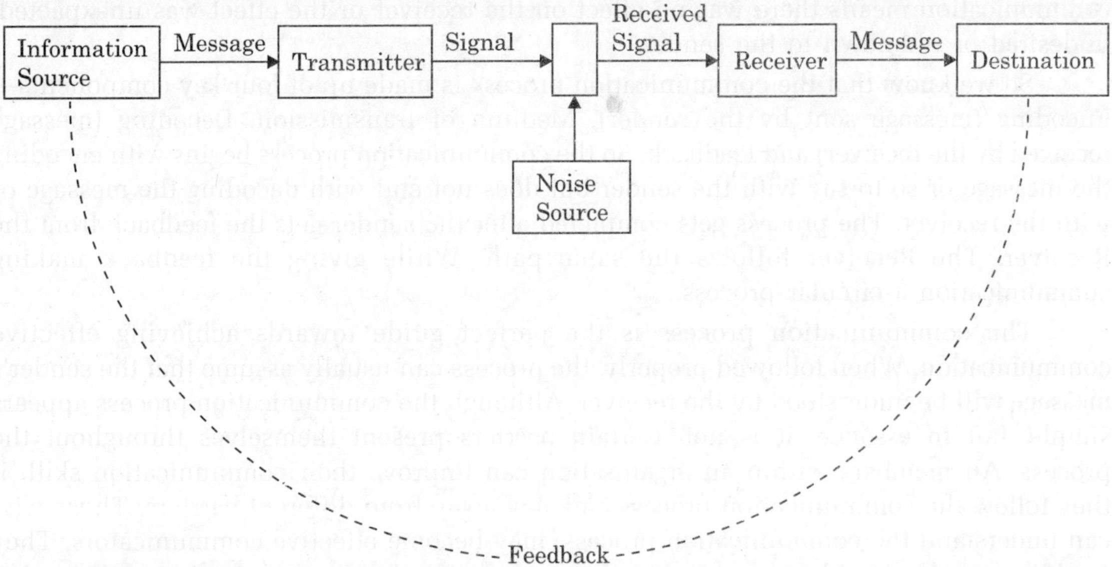

Feedback is included in the modern process of communication. The **Shannon Weaver** model is often referred to as an 'Information mode' of communication. It looks at communication as a one-way process. This is remedied by the feedback as an integral part of communication which makes communication a two way process (Look at the 2nd model).

Shannon's model of the communication process was, in important ways, the beginning of the modern concept of the communication process. It provided, for the first time, a general model of the communication process that could be treated as a common ground for such diverse disciplines as journalism, rhetoric, linguistics and speech and learning sciences.

The process starts with a SENDER who has a MESSAGE for a RECEIVER. Two or more people are involved in this process. The sender has the responsibility for the message. His message travels to the receiver through one or more channels chosen by the sender. The channels may be verbal or non-verbal. They may involve only one of the sense for example hearing or they may involve all the five senses for example, hearing, seeing, touch, smell and taste. Non-verbal communication, primarily, relies on seeing rather than hearing. After sending the message, the Sender becomes a Receiver and the Receiver becomes a Sender through the process of feedback. Feedback is the receiver's response to the attempt of the sender to send a message. Feedback is the key to determination by the sender whether or not the message has been received in the intended form. Feedback involves choice of channels to be opted by the receiver of the original message. The channels for feedback may be quite different from the channels adopted by the sender of the message. A puzzled look may be the feedback to what the sender considered a perfectly clear oral presentation or instruction. Effect on the receiver completes the communication process.

Effective communication brings the desired effect on the receiver. Communication, at its best, minimizes misunderstanding between the sender and the receiver. Ineffective communication means there was no effect on the receiver or the effect was unexpected, undesired or unknown to the sender.

So we know that the communication process is made up of four key components—Encoding (message sent by the sender), Medium of transmission, Decoding (message received by the receiver) and feedback. So the communication process begins with encoding the message or so to say with the sender but does not end with decoding the message or with the receiver. The process gets completed after the sender gets the feedback from the Receiver. The Receiver follows the same path. While giving the feedback making communication a circular process.

The communication process is the perfect guide towards achieving effective communication. When followed properly, the process can usually assume that the sender's message will be understood by the receiver. Although the communication process appears simple, but in essence, it is not. Certain barriers present themselves throughout the process. All members within an organisation can improve their communication skill, if they follow the communication process and stay away from different barriers. Those who can understand the communication process, may become effective communicators. They can diagnose the problems coming in the way of effective communication and develop plans for improvement.

HOW TO MAKE THE COMMUNICATION EFFECTIVE

When we learn to communicate effectively, our confidence about our prospective success in interactions increases. Lack of communication skills often result in depression, shyness, stress, negativity, loneliness etc. On the other hand the ability to communicate well not only sustains relationships but also promotes effectiveness on the job. The organisations look for those employees who can communicate effectively and assertively.

The following points may help you to make your communication effective:

1. Self Awareness. Understanding your personal style of communication will help you to create desired effect on others. If you are aware of the fact how others perceive you, you may adapt readily to their styles of communicating. This way you can create a comfortable, congenial environment.

The right message may be transmitted. Select and emphasize the behaviour that fit within your personality and that corresponds with the receiver of the message too.

2. Express Yourself Clearly. Sometimes the way you say something may not mean what you intend to say. Organise thoughts in your mind. This will give proper shape to your expressions and your listener would understand you better.

3. Active Listener. Active listening means that you are paying attention to what others say—you are listening with a purpose. Active listening helps you to gain information, obtain directions, understand others, look at the things from sender's point of view. Active listening is not so easy as it sounds. It is very difficult to concentrate on what someone is saying since only a part of our mind pays attention. Our mind is constantly thinking about other things while listening to someone. To control the mind from drifting, try to repeat the words of the sender in your mind. This helps in concentration. Human mind cannot hold two thoughts at one time. So if you are listening, do not indulge yourself in other activities.

4. Be Positive. Positive communication is always encouraging. It can be hard to see the positive in everything, but if you try to find positivity, you will definitely find it out. If you go into a conversation with a negative or a defensive tone, your message may not get desired result. Positive attitude must be applied to the listening as well. Do not take positive things for granted nor negative as personal offence.

5. Be Honest. If you do not know something, never hesitate to say '**NO**'. People can identify with a communicator who can admit he is wrong. It will give you credibility in future communication.

6. Be Humble. People may be better at doing something—should always be kept in mind. Offering some level of humility will make the environment congenial, encouraging the flow of communication. Treat others as you would yourself.

7. Use Non-Verbal Communication Effectively. Great deal of Communication is non-verbal like facial expressions, tone of voice motions, gestures, smiles, posture, eye-contact etc. It may also include the way we wear our clothes. Be sensitive to non-verbal messages. Co-operation in an organisation improves if we recognize and respond appropriately to non-verbal cues.

8. Speak Directly and Assertively. Speak for a purpose and the body language should correspond with your words. Too much communication can be counter-productive. Communicate in the clearest possible way.

9. Avoid Pre-determined Notions. Being receptive always makes communication easier and effective. Be open to every suggestion and every criticism. Never frame in your mind the pre-determined idea about the people you are communicating with. This may make you prejudiced and the flow of communication may get disturbed.

10. Feedback. Effective feedback is always specific and not general. "Your project is well-written, understandable and contains the important points"—is specific. Do not say "your project is good". Feedback should not contain advice. Constructive feedback is not criticism. Feedback should always be directed to the action and not person.

Recognition for effective performance is a powerful motivation. Most people want to obtain more recognition. So recognition encourages more of the appreciated actions.

BARRIERS TO COMMUNICATION

Proper communication is an art which is natural as well as acquired. There are some barriers which block the flow of communication. The barriers may be external as well as internal. They may relate to the sender, the receiver or the circumstances. Understanding the communication process and then working at improvement provides a recipe for becoming more effective communicators. Knowing the common barriers to communication is the first step to minimize their impact.

There may be the following barriers to organisational communication.

1. Muddled Messages. Muddled messages are a barrier to communication because the receiver does not get the intended message from the sender. Contrast these two messages, "You are invited to attend the seminar at about 2.00 in the afternoon" or "You are invited to attend the seminar at 2.00 in the afternoon". The one word difference makes the first sentence muddled and the second clear. Muddled messages may take place because of many reasons. The sender may be confused in his thoughts. He may be at loss of appropriate words or he carelessly uses the language without knowing that one word here or there may change the meaning of the message.

2. Weak Delivery. It does not matter how important or impressive the subject of your communication is, if you deliver it without any 'push', you will not get the desired result. It is important not to get confused between delivery and presentation. Good presentation may lack a suitable structure, still it can be impressive. I know of a friend who is not a powerful orator but due to her strong delivery of message, she creates a strong impact on the audience.

3. Improper Channel. Varieties of Channels help the receiver understand the nature and importance of a message. A teacher may write "Good morning" on the blackboard as she enters into the classroom. Writing "Good morning" on the blackboard is not as effective as a warm oral greeting. In choice of a medium, the sender must consider the knowledge, skill and ability of the receiver. Writing "Good morning" for a deaf and dumb class is a better medium than oral greetings.

4. Language Problems. Language is the most important medium of communication. Language is an arbitrary code that depends on shared definitions, but there is a limit to how completely any of us share the same meaning for a given word. To overcome language barriers, use the most specific and accurate words possible. Always try to use the vocabulary and expressions your audience will understand.

5. Listening vs Hearing. Audience may not pay attention to what you deliver—then you lose the objective of your communication. People are likely to drift off when they are forced to listen to information that is monotonus, or difficult to understand, or too technical, or too philosophical. To make your audience listen carefully, you must view the situation through the eyes of the receiver. Add lightness to your communication, clarify meaning by asking non-threatening questions. Humour appeals to everybody. Plan comic element in your communication.

6. Incorrect Filtering. Filtering is screening out before a message is passed on to someone else. There are many filters between the sender and the receiver in an organisational communication—Secretaries, Assistants, Receptionists, Answering machines etc. Try to establish more than one channel. If possible, try to have direct approach by eliminating the role of intermediaries.

7. Varied Attitudes and Perceptions. You see a situation according to your own way of thinking. Your attitude and thoughts are unique and they may not match with other people. Why force your opinion on others?

Others may have different perceptions. As senders we choose the details important to us. As receivers, we try to fit new details into our existing pattern. If a detail does not fit into our pre-determined notion, the message may take a distorted shape.

8. Lack of Feedback. Communication is a two way process but without feedback, it remains one way. Both sender and receiver can play an active role in using feedback to make communication two way. Feedback should be helpful rather than hurtful. Immediate feedback is more useful than waiting for the 'right' moment.

9. Varied Backgrounds. Age, education, gender, social status, economic position, cultural background, temperament, health, popularity, religion, personal beliefs, beauty, even the mood-swings—all separate one human being from another and make understanding difficult. Imposing one's personal background, beliefs or culture onto others is a great barrier to communication.

10. Distracting Environment. Physical disturbance like too many people talking in the room, police and ambulance sirens creating noise, mobile phones keep ringing, will not make communication audible. Slow Internet connections, if you are using the one, unfavourable climatic conditions in the room, etc. may hamper the flow of communication.

11. Varied Emotional Behaviour. Every message has a content meaning and a relationship meaning. The relationship meaning suggests the nature of interaction between the sender and the receiver. You may have to deal with the people when they are upset. Be sensitive towards the feelings that may arise in yourself and others as you communicate. Negative emotional outcomes during the process of communication may distort the message.

OVERCOMING THE BARRIERS TO COMMUNICATION

1. Positive Attitude. Defensive and negative attitude interferes with communication. Always look at the positive aspect of the things unless the limits are crossed.

2. Improve Communication Skills. It requires knowledge and practice. The awareness towards the importance of achieving communication skill is the first step to better communication. Read books meant for this purpose or don't hesitate to go for professional training.

3. Consider Communication Skills as a Professional Skill. Include Communication as a skill to be evaluated along with all the other skills in each person's job description. Help other people improve their communication skill by helping them understand their communication problems.

4. Use of Vocabulary. Use the most specific and accurate words possible. Always use those words and expressions which your audience will understand.

5. Feedback. Feedback from the receiver is the best way for a sender to be sure that the message is clear.

6. Communication to be Goal-Oriented. Make communication goal-oriented. Relational goals come first and pave the way for other goals. When the sender and the receiver have a good relationship, they will accomplish their communication goal.

7. Active Listening. Concentrate on the speaker's words and restate them to be sure that you heard them correctly.

8. Say No to (improper) Wrong Behaviour. Recognize the kind of behaviour that makes you defensive. When someone displays that behaviour, tell openly that you are uncomfortable.

9. Communication—a Creative Process. Experiment with communication alternatives. Communication is a creative process rather than simply a part of the chore of working with people. Creativity in communication helps in dealing differently with different people.

10. Varied Channels. Use varied mediums according to the situation. Varied listening techniques, varied feedback techniques will take away the boredom.

11. Proper Encoding. Use the language familiar to the audience. Proper encoding process facilitates the flow of communication.

12. Be Semantic. Be clear, simple and brief to send the message as is meant. Do not use the words which have two meanings.

13. Maintain Goodwill. Do not act on predetermined notion, assumptions or impulses. Have an open outlook. Do not restrict yourself to your own beliefs.

14. Be Cautious. Take care of the feelings that arise in yourself and others as you communicate and try to control the unwanted feelings in you and unhealthy responses from the receiver.

15. Avoid Misunderstanding. Be concise, clear and accurate so that the right message is sent.

16. Positive Environment. Create healthy and positive environment by encouraging open communication and interaction.

17. Do Spiritual Exercises. To maintain the concentration and to overcome the emotional and psychological barriers do spiritual exercises like meditations. This actually helps to maintain calmness and balanced temperament.

EXERCISE 1

A. Answer the following questions:

1. What do you understand by communication?
2. How can communication skill help in the growth of an organisation?
3. Discuss the different barriers to communication.
4. What can management of an organisation do to improve the efficiency of its employees?
5. How can you overcome the barriers to communication?

B. Assignment:

1. As a manager of an organisation, what role can you play for its growth?

C. Say True or False:

1. The employees of an organisation should be dominated at work.
2. Listening is an important aspect of any communication.
3. The performance of an employee depends on his efficiency of work and not his relationships with his juniors.
4. It is always better to maintain a distance between seniors and juniors.
5. Communication is a creative process.

EXERCISE 2

A. Answer the following questions:

1. What do you understand by the process of communication?

2. Define cycle of communication. Discuss the role of feedback in the cycle of communication.
3. Discuss the role of a sender in the process of communication. What can a sender do to send the right messages?
4. How can you minimise the communication gap between the sender and the receiver?

B. Fill in the appropriate word:

1. Shannon's model of communication did not include ....
2. Communication cycle is a ....
3. The message travels to the sender through the ...... chosen by the ....
4. Effective communication brings the ...... results.
5. Certain .... come in the way of effective communication, hindering its process.

C. Assignment:

1. Draw and explain the process of communication.

❑❑❑

Chapter 3

VERBAL AND NON-VERBAL COMMUNICATION

"You can communicate without motivating, but it is impossible to motivate without communicating."
—John Thompson

"Use Non-Verbal Communication to SOFTEN the hardline position of others: S—Smile, O—Open posture, F—Forward lean, T—Touch, E—Eye contact, N—Nod."

Communication can be divided into two classes:

I. Verbal Communication

II. Non-verbal Communication.

I. VERBAL COMMUNICATION

Verbal communication is the most popular means of carrying information from one person to another. Verbal communication is when we communicate our message verbally. It requires the use of words, vocabulary and the symbols. Since language is the necessary instrument of verbal communication, mastering linguistic skill is important to improve interaction.

The principal function of verbal communication is to transfer information, which may be factual or specific. It may also convey emotions, attitudes, beliefs, hopes desires etc.

Categories of Verbal Communication

1. Discussion. The motive of discussion is to discuss actions, suggest ideas and come to decisions. Let others speak too. Listen to others with openness and always be ready to accept their viewpoint.

Exchange facts and opinion. The purpose is not to win an argument but to come to constructive conclusion. Discussion must lead towards one 'right' answer. Discussion is individual opinion, individual knowledge. Always respect and value others' opinion with open attitude

2. Debate. Constructive communication is productive dialogue and skillful discussions where new insights can emerge through healthy give and take. In debates you are visualising both pros and cons, negative and positive of a situation. Do not try to knock each other out. Your opponent may be right in his perspective. Your ego will not hurt if you say, "You are wrong". Debates should not create a close-minded attitude, a determination to be right. Do not listen to find flaws and counter arguments. As compared to discussion, debate tends to be competitive. Always use the competitive nature of debate to your advantage.

3. Dialogue. Dialogue is designed to promote a free flowing interchange of ideas and create an open-equal and collaborative conventional climate. The purpose is to share perspectives and understanding. We talk with others to develop new ideas and concepts. You can explore issues creatively if you give an ear to other's points of view. Dialogue creates an open-minded attitude, an openness to being wrong and an openness to change. Dialogues respect all other participants and never seek to offend. Dialogue is mutual enquiry and collective knowledge.

Importance of Verbal Communication

Verbal Communication includes the following components (1) Information or message (2) Communication means (3) Communication network and (4) Communication activity.

Message is converted into a language by a sender and transferred as a text via a particular channel to a receiver. Message may be sent through different modes. Message with high information density like research articles are printed out and stored in libraries for future reference. In contrast, message with low information density like casual conversation is used in spoken verbal words along with non-verbal gestures. Besides language, verbal communication utilizes gestures such as using fingers when counting or pointing with fingers at something, or eyegaze, head nod, leaning forward etc. The gestures and word combined together strengthen the intended meaning. Feedback is a response that a sender obtains from a receiver. It provides information about success or failure of communication and accordingly enables a sender to monitor or change his message. So verbal communication is a circular and continuous process.

To make communication effective statistics show that words play only 7% role, Tone of voice 38% and Non-verbal cues play a role of remaining 55%. So how you deliver your material is more important than what you have to say.

II. NON-VERBAL COMMUNICATION

When Demosthenes was asked what was the first part of oratory he answered "actions" ; which was the second and which was the third, his answer remained same "action". Does that mean "Actions speak louder than words"? We have read in the earlier chapters that communication is the transfer of information from one person to another. Unconsciously we are transmitting our thoughts, ideas, expressions, to others through non-verbal means of communication. Non-verbal communication includes facial expression, gestures, tone, body-movement, eye-contact, mannerism, paralinguistics, humour, language of touch etc.

So, in Non-verbal communication, we do not use words but convey our message through other means. The most important thing in a communication is to understand what is not being said. We can express our emotions, feeling, attitudes, opinions views through non-verbal communication in a better way because words can be framed. The body and its movements substitute words. Our body movements can converse better than words with the advantage that this dialect does not need dictionary but is understood the world over.

Categories of Non-verbal Communication

As per a famous linguist **G.W. Porter** there are four categories of Non-verbal Communication:

1. Physical—It includes our body-movements, facial expression, tone of voice, eye movement, the way we touch, we smell etc.

2. Aesthetic—We can convey our message through creative art like painting, music, dance movements, dramatics, sculpture.

3. Signs—A mechanical type of non-verbal communication which may help the disabled to use sign-language to communicate. It may also include the other signs like road signs, signs of red cross, arrow for direction, different signs denoting different places like church has a different sign than temple.

4. Symbolic—This type of non-verbal communication is implied in religious, spiritual cultural symbols—the way we pray, the way we show respect, we celebrate our events, saying goodbye, greeting people, etc.

Factors Important for Non-verbal Communication

1. Kinesics. The different ways in which people move their bodies like postures, gestures, head nods, leg movements are called kinesics. The best way to assess the personality and behaviour of a person is not to listen to what he says but to observe what he does. Gestures are of three types.

(*i*) **Emblem**—Direct verbal translation like yes, no, hellow, bye used in place of words.

(*ii*) **Illustrations**—They accompany us during our speech for the purpose of emphasizing our point like close our palm in fist or bang the table or use the rod for threatening.

(*iii*) **Adaptors**—Unconscious movements of body that originate from the nervous state of our mind like shaking legs, crack fingers, tap foot shows our lack of confidence.

Using Kinesics positively, you can enhance the quality of your personality. For example with practice you can get rid of the unconscious movements of your body which shows lack of confidence on your part.

2. Occulesics. This is the science of movement of our eyes and of facial expressions. Facial expressions usually convey emotions. The expressions tell the attitude of the communicator. Facial expressions are a better indicator of the meaning behind the message than his words. Eye contact is a direct and powerful form of non-verbal communication.

The direct stare conveys openness.

Eyes rolled upward are associated with fatigue.

Long stare shows lack of respect for others or superiority.

Downward glances are associated either with modesty or shyness.

Withdrawl of eye-contact is a sign of submission.

Frequently looking at people from a distance—Sign of extrovert behaviour.

Scarcely looking at people—Introvert behaviour.

Too little eye contact shows shyness, insincerity, dishonesty. Research shows left lookers are more emotional, subjective while right lookers are influenced by logic.

3. Paralinguistics. Refer to the pitch, tone, intonation, modulation, rate of speech etc. The emotion conveyed through paralinguistics can be accurately judged regardless of the content of the message. The voice is important because it complements the message we intend to convey. The tone, pitch and quality of your voice has a great influence on the interpretation of your message.

4. Personal space (proximity). Cultural norms dictate a comfortable distance for interaction. Proximity is the space you place between yourself and others. The impact of use of space on the communication process is related directly to the environment in which the space is maintained. You can divide the space zones into intimate, personal, social and public according to the situation. Your personal space and environment would facilitate the communication process.

5. Artifactics. Personal appearance, the style of dress up, personal hygiene say a lot about you. Once your personality attracts the people, you start scoring immediately. Your appearance, clothing, style, the perfume you use, the cell-phone you are carrying, your pen, your briefcase—your shoes, polished or unpolished—all transmit a message. Even small details about your outward appearance carries a message.

6. Silence. Silence can be a positive or negative influence in the communication process. Sometimes it creates peace, at other times it may send a cold response resulting in tension.

7. Time. How much do you value your time? Do you maintain a schedule? Always take an appointment if you want to meet somebody. If you are conducting meetings, inform about the duration of meeting. Do not divert from the main point while conducting meeting. That will be a wastage of time. Making people wait for you may not raise your status. Be punctual.

8. Tactilics—Communication through touch is obviously non-verbal. Use this science of touch properly. If it is used improperly, it can ruin the relationship. Touch therapy can heal the emotional wounds too. For example, a pat on the shoulders sends a message of encouragement, holding hands shows goodwill, stepping on someone's feet is an example of carelessness. So be careful in your Tactile communication and send the positive waves.

Non-verbal communication is a reflection of your inner-self. Verbal communication may be fabricated, you can hide your feelings, your attitude by selecting the words of your choice but unconsciously you present a true picture of yourself through non-verbal means of communication. Brush up your non-verbal communication so that a positive personality is reflected.

EXERCISE

A. Answer the following questions:

1. What do you understand by verbal communication?
2. How can you improve verbal communication?
3. Discuss the different types of verbal communication.
4. What is the difference between discussion and debates?
5. What will you do to avoid sending the wrong message?

B. Answer the following questions:

1. What do you understand by non-verbal communication?
2. How can you improve the non-verbal communication?
3. What do you understand by Tactile Communication?
4. How can kinesics help you win confidence?

C. Say true or false:

1. Long stare sends a message of intimacy.
2. Your personal appearance does not play any role in non-verbal communication.
3. Proxemics is a study of distance.
4. If you touch somebody with affection, you will annoy him.
5. Always make your subordinates wait for you.

Chapter 4
PRESENTATION

"Think like a wise man but communicate in the language of the people."

—W.B. Yeats

INTRODUCTION

Presentation is the process of presenting information to an audience, possibly enhanced with visual or audio material. As students, it is very important to present your thoughts and ideas effectively, using a variety of tools and mediums. You need this skill in your academic career, when you attend job interviews and especially when you start working. Presentation is the first managerial skill which a working executive must acquire.

Management is the art of getting things done. A presentation is a quick and productive method of getting things done. Presentation is used as a formal method for bringing people together to plan, monitor and review the work progress. Any successful presentation needs impressive material and attractive process. While hard work and good ideas are essential for your success, your ability to express those ideas effectively is equally important.

In today's competitive and rapidly changing world, the organization looks for the employees who can think creatively and act ethically and responsibly. Presentation skill has become a way to develop competence to communicate ideas with diversity and to create impact. To keep your audience with you. You will have to plan a strategy for your presentation. You will have to develop verbal as well as non-verbal skills to make your presentation effective.

PLANNING AND PREPARING A PRESENTATION

Presentation is a skill which is developed through experience and training. But we cannot take this skill of presentation for granted because like all other skills the presentation skill can be improved and adapted according to the context within which it is used. A presentation in your organisation may require a different approach than one you had at college level. The following points would help you to plan your presentation effectively. Keep these points in mind while preparing your presentation to get the desired results.

1. Determine the Main Purpose. Identity the purpose of your presentation and state it in a single sentence. When you know the objective of the presentation, all your efforts, the materials which you use, illustrations, aids will be focused on the desired result.

2. Assess your Audience. "Success depends on your ability to reach to your audience" Assess the knowledge level of the audience. How large is the audience? Know about their educational background, their age group, their interests and their expectations. This will help you to motivate them. The more you know about your audience, the better you will be able to plan your presentation.

3. Evaluate the Environment/Space. Familiaze yourself with the presentation environment before you start preparing your presentation. Keep in mind the seating capacity of the room, seating arrangement, distracters. How is the room organised? Have you checked the Audio/Visual equipment? Will you be able to operate them confidently? Prior planning will let you know of the shortcomings which can be rectified in time. Besides boosting your level of confidence, this saves you from the last minute embarrassment.

4. Preparing Visual Aids. The Visual Aids act as a trigger for the speaker and keep the presentation focused. They make presentation interesting and provide an additional way of receiving the message.

5. Planning the Content. Determine main points. Do not gather too many points which will create confusion. Find supporting evidence to prove your points. Examples create interest, you can use quotations, interesting facts, relevant statistics, bold statements, current events, stories and anecdotes to make your presentation interesting. Always draft a rough outline. Start by identifying your most important argument which supports the goal of your presentation.

6. Research the Information. Use key words from the topic. Begin your research with the prescribed texts. Scan recommended material, conduct a library search, consult journals, articles, newspaper; do net surfing. As you research, take notes, add reviews, make a rough draft.

7. Structuring the Content. Presentations are structured with Introduction, Body and Conclusion. First introduce yourself to build rapport with the audience. Then introduce the topic. Define any ambiguous terms. Outline the scope of the presentation. Give a plan of the main points to be addressed. Expand main points in a logical sequence. Provide supporting evidence from your research with references. Use humour, examples, statistic to get the response of the audience. Invite participation through questioning or short activities. Inform audience that you are about to conclude. Summarize main points. Evaluate the importance of the information before concluding the presentation.

8. Final Preparation. Practise in front of a friend or mirror. Record your voice. Ask for a feedback. Review and make corrections. Keep in mind the time element. Ensure that the presentation is within the time allowed. Organize your notes, slides, transparencies in the order the information will be presented. Number the pages. Have confidence and positive attitude. Think of the positive response you will get from the audience.

If you are well prepared and know your topic, confidence will came automatically. Present the right information in the right format in the right amount of time. Prior planning and preparation will give you success.

ORGANIZING YOUR PRESENTATION

1. Introduce the topic in clear words. Use your introduction to motivate the audience besides presenting the problem. Be strategic. Avoid technical details.

2. Do not give too much information. Give only important points. Too much details would create confusion and they would not be remembered.

3. If you are using slides, use only one idea per slide.

4. Visualize your key points. Once you are clear about your key points, the presentation will develop easily. Write your summary slide of the key points.

5. Be authentic and add authority to your tone. Let your audience know that you know your topic well.

6. Be selective in the use of aids. Use minimum slides for maximum impact.

7. Be sure to label and number each overhead transparency, chart, or flip charts used. Make them large enough so that you can read them clearly even in imperfect light conditions.

8. Preview the main supporting points so that your presentation will be easy to understand.

9. Emphasize the main point by using different tones or pitches of your voice. Change the rate of your speech. Listing and numbering points would help.

10. Use descriptive language to support your points with examples. This builds interest and makes the presentation more interesting for you and the audience.

11. Make smooth transition to next section. Let everyone know you are about to go to a new topic. This makes your audience mentally prepared to understand the new idea you are going to explain.

12. Summarize the main points while concluding your presentation. Wrap up by restating the whole idea, emphasizing the main points. Conclude with a positive note and an open, platform for the feedback session.

IMPORTANCE OF GESTURES, POSTURES, BODY MOVEMENTS, EYE-CONTACT

Communicating with other people would become a much easier task, if we understand the importance of gestures, posture and body movement. If we apply body language techniques to convey our intentions, it will lead to a successful career and fruitful relationships. People tend to understand and remember messages better if they are accompanied by the body language.

Importance of Gestures

"The key to effectively using gestures is to know your material so well, to be so well prepared, that your gestures will flow naturally." If we use our gestures rightly, we will create an enhanced impact. Use of gestures give more clarity to your words, produce dramatic effect and stimulates the participation of the audience. Keep in mind the following points while combining gestures with your speech.

1. Be natural. Don't invent artificial gestures. Be real, genuine. Let the gestures come out of you spontaneously.

2. Your gestures should suit to what you say. You might make a fool of yourself if your gestures do not suit to the occasion and to your words.

3. To make your gestures appear convincing, involve yourself completely with your message. Let your gestures arise from your thoughts, feelings, emotions and not from your efforts.

4. Do not impose gestures on yourself. Use your gestures only when you are comfortable with their use.

5. Make your gestures well timed. They must come at the exact time, otherwise you may send a wrong message or create a negative impact.

Types of Gestures

1. Descriptive Gestures. Descriptive gestures clarify and enhance your verbal message.

2. Emphatic Gestures. They help you in putting force in your words for example, you can pound the podium or bang the table to emphasize your message.

3. Suggestive Gesturers. These gestures are the symbols of ideas and emotions. They create a mood or express a thought for example, you nod your head to show approval or shrug your shoulders to indicate confusion.

4. Prompting Gesturers. Prompting gestures evoke a desired response for example, you raise your finger to point at something. To appreciate you may clap or raise your hand if you want your audience to follow you.

Gestures are a personal trait. What works positively for one, may not do the same for you. So avoid imitating gestures. Be natural, spontaneous, genuine and not artificial.

Some gestures create negative impact. Avoid following gestures:

1. Do not cross your hands behind your back. This position of standing at ease would not correspond with the presentation as presentation is a formal activity.

2. Do not cross your arms over your chest.

3. Fist raising can be interpreted as hostile or threatening.

4. Do not put your hands in your pockets.

Your gestures should be varied. Don't use the same motions over and over again. If you use your gestures effectively, you will project confidence and efficiency and in return will get a positive response from your audience.

POSTURES

Your posture and the way you present yourself on the platform is as important as your gestures. To have a right posture, keep in mind the following points.

1. Stand up straight and face the audience head on. Keep your posture open with arms relaxed and hands hanging down at your sides.

2. Spread your feet six to seven inches apart. They should be parallel to each other and your toes should be pointed straight ahead. This way you will have a comfortable speaking position.

3. Stand erect but not stiff. Standing erect will stop any swaying motion. Put your weight on the soles of your feet. An erect posture shows high spirit and confidence.

4. Hold your head with your chin up. Raised chin shows confidence.

5. While communicating, lean forward. It implies that you are open and interested.

6. Do not speak with your back turned or looking at the floor or at the ceiling.

7. If your hands are clasped firmly in front of you, your feet are crossed and your body is tight, you present a picture of the one who lacks confidence.

8. Your hands on hips present a picture of dominating character, crossed arms will not invite others to talk. Your hands crossed in front of you would make you look timid and weak.

9. Do not fold your arms while speaking. Folded arms show that you are bored, tired or not interested in your presentation.

10. Maintaining a rigid posture implies that you are defensive while a relaxed posture presents openness.

11. Crossed arms and legs indicate a defensive position, while uncrossed arms and legs present your willingness to listen.

Posture has been considered as an expressive medium for presentation. Your posture reflects your self-confidence and your enthusiasm for the subject you are dealing with. Postures can convey your feelings and emotion, your interest in the subject. Postures can even be used to establish the relationship with your audience.

Look at yourself in the mirror and see how it feels to stand with the varied postures. You may feel awkward looking at yourself in the mirror but it helps. Look at the various postures that look appropriate and natural. Make appropriate postures a part of your personality.

BODY MOVEMENTS

Body movement is an essential part of a presentation. Proper body movements can enhance the quality of a presentation. They can help you explain the words you use to create pictures in the minds of your audience.

1. Do not repeat the same movements. Practice a variety of movements.

2. Practice a speech by clasping your hands behind your back. This way you can control meaningless repititive hand and arm movements.

3. Make your body movements relevant to the words. Movement rehearsal would help you use the right movements at the right time.

4. Avoid too much movement during your presentation. Excessive body movement is as undesirable as no movement at all. Continuous pacing back and forth or sideways may distract your audience.

5. Adjust your movement to the size of the audience and the nature of your topic. Some subjects call for considerable action while some topics expect calm consideration.

6. Never move without a reason. Do not sway, rock or shake your leg. The purposeless movements indicate nervousness.

7. Step forward to signal that you are arriving at an important point. Step back to conclude a point. Step sideways to indicate a change from one idea to another.

8. Your movements should be natural, informal, spontaneous and smooth.

9. Body movements carry true messages about feelings because emotions cannot be masked.

10. The message sent by body movements travels faster than spoken words. Wrong body movements may carry wrong messages which cannot be rectified.

11. Few movements of the hands, fingers and arms are directly related to what is going on in the mind. Hanging hands signify restlessness or tiredness. Hands which move little show confidence and calmness.

Facial Expression

Facial expression is the chief component of your presentation. Your facial expressions add meaning to your words, express your attitude, feelings, emotions, your likes and dislikes. Your facial expressions may present you as a confident speaker or a nervous speaker before your audience.

1. Keep your facial expressions relaxed and flexible.

2. Do not lick, bite or click the lips or tighten the jaws. Do not frown. These expressions indicate nervousness and lack of confidence.

3. Your face will reflect good thoughts and emotions if you are confident about the subject you are dealing with. Believe your message and practice thoroughly. This will relax your facial expressions.

4. Keep a smile on your face. Smile will bring warmth but it should be appropriate and according to the situation.

5. Change your facial expressions according to the message. Flat expressions distract the audience and create monotonous atmosphere.

Eye Contact

Proper eye contact maintains the flow of communication. It creates interest in others and increases the speaker's credibility. Strong, direct eye focus is one of the most important elements in building a relationship with your audience. Proper eye focus will help you achieve effective communication. Right eye contact with your audience will help you in the following ways.

1. It encourages communication. If you look at someone, you establish a connection. This connection breaks the ice and initiates communication.

2. Strong eye focus engages your audience and helps you to stay in control. This reduces the distraction of your audience and makes them attentive towards your message.

3. Eye contact with your audience brings confidence in you. You can control your stage fright also.

4. People on the receiving end of good eye focus feel comfortable with you. They will develop a sense of intimacy with you.

5. Your strong eye focus at the right time creates a feeling of trust among your audience. They believe you, they agree with you, they receive the positive waves.

Keep in mind the following points to maintain the right eye contact with your audience.

1. Do not stare but give a comfortable, natural, spontaneous look to your audience. Your audience deserve your attention. By looking at them, you make them feel that they are important for you.

2. Do not limit your focus to just few people or just one person. Change your focus from one direction to another. Focusing on some people repeatedly may create negative impact.

3. Focus on one person at one time when you are speaking to small groups. Finish a point and then change your focus to someone else.

4. If you are talking to a large audience, start your eye focus with one person at the back of the room. This would lead you to reach out to the entire audience.

5. Use the three second method. Look straight into the eyes of a person in the audience for three to four seconds at a time. Adopt this method and maintain eye contact with a number of audience. Glance at the whole audience every now and then. Your audience will feel involved.

6. During presentations, split the room into three parts. Move your eye contact from one part to another. The people around that part would feel that you are speaking directly to them.

Maintaining eye contact throughout your presentation requires preparation. You will be required to remember some part of your material otherwise you will be left reading the material instead of connecting.

VOICE MODULATION

Your vocal quality is a key element in presenting your message. Speak naturally as if you are conversing with your audience. Do not try to make your voice artificial. Speak from the diaphragm and not from the throat. If you are communicating with a large number of audience, you will have to increase the volume of your speech. Put vocal variety and emphasis in your speech. Avoid speaking in a monotonous, flat tone. Be your normal self and use your normal conversational tone. Don't shout to reach to the audience. Speak at moderate speed and bring pauses in between. Approximately placed pauses will make your speech effective and you will get the attention of your audience. Whether you are speaking to a small group or a large group, your voice is the most important tool. When your voice matches the ideas, emotions, feelings and concepts, you attract your audience and create a connection with them. They will be more attentive listeners boosting your self-confidence.

The following terms define vocal qualities:

1. Volume. Make sure your voice is loud enough to be heard by everyone in the room. You can take a feedback from your audience if your voice is audible. Adjust your volume accordingly. Use varying volumes for emphasis. Always remember to adjust your volume to the size of the room you are speaking in.

2. Tone. Tone represents the characteristic of a sound. The tone of your voice will tell the audience the level of your confidence. The tone or quality of your voice says a lot to your audience words can never convey. Try to adjust the tone of your voice with your ideas and emotions. Proper tone of your voice would connect you better.

3. Pitch. The pitch of your voice is at its highness or lowness. Try to put variation in your pitch. This would give emphasis to your speech and make it more interesting and exciting. Nervousness, and fear may result in an unintentional higher pitch. Relax and do breathing exercises. This would bring self-confidence.

4. Pace. Varied pace helps to maintain the audience's interest. Do not go so fast that people may miss something or too slow that your speech becomes monotonous and your audience stop paying attention. Use strategic pauses such as pausing before an important point to lay emphasis. Fill up the gaps of long silence when you are about to use the audio visual aids to explain what you are doing. You can also fill the gap of long silence with a small joke. The pace of your speech should correspond with the mental level of your audience. Some audience may be more comfortable with a fast pace.

Listening Skills

Listening is one of the most powerful presentation skills. You can make your presentation interactive by listening to others. This will also help you to know whether you are getting the positive response from your audience and whether they are taking the information the same way you expected them to understand. Be an active listener. Use your active listening skill to gain information, to determine the level of understanding of your audience. Listen with a purpose.

You should keep in mind the following points to achieve active listening skills.

1. Maintain eye contact with the speaker. It helps you keep involved in the speech.
2. Focus on content, not delivery.
3. Move your face towards the channel of information. Lean slightly forward. Use body to show your concern.
4. Do not answer questions with questions.
5. Avoid emotional involvement. Be open minded, positive and objective.
6. Let your audience talk. Do not dominate the conversation.
7. Avoid distractions. Do not let your mind wander or be distracted. Maintain concentration.
8. Do not finish the sentence of others. This will annoy your audience.
9. Listen with empathy. See the situation from speaker's point of view.
10. Make certain that everyone involved gets an opportunity to speak. Do not interrupt. You cannot hear if you do all the talking.

Active listening creates positive feelings like love, affection, concern, interest, joy, fearlessness, strength which would boost the self-confidence of the speaker.

Inactive listening creates the negative feelings like distrust, hurt, depression, fear, anxiety, criticism, inadequacy, anger which would affect the presentation of a speaker.

Types of Effective Listening

1. Paraphrasing. Restating what another person has said in your own words for example, a speaker says, "It was not right for her to join that company". Listener repeats, "You think she should not have joined that company."

2. Open questions. Open questions help a person to think more about an issue. For example, the speaker says, "I did not like the picture". An open question would enquire, "What did you not like about it"?

3. Emotional Listening. To listen actively what is being felt. To understand what a speaker is feeling, you must listen to his words, his tone of voice and his body language.

EXERCISE

1. What do you understand by presentation?
2. How can a well planned and prepared presentation help you in your organisation?
3. How will you organise a presentation?
4. Discuss the importance of gestures, postures and body movements in a presentation.
5. How can listening skill help you?
6. What do you know about voice modulation?
7. Plan and prepare a presentation on the topic "Regulation of traffic in metros in India".

❑❑❑

Chapter 5

DEMONSTRATION

"Success is going from failure to failure without a loss of enthusiasm."

—Winston Churchill

DEMONSTRATION

A demonstration is a form of explaining or presenting an information with examples. A demonstration can illustrate an activity or a skill and should include some audio-visual aids. The simplest demonstration is where a presenter shows his audience how to do something on explain his point of view through demonstrating examples.

Demonstration gives the participants an opportunity to share what they have learned. It makes the presentation interactive and educational. The presenter can organize the ideas logically and present them in a systematic order. He can express himself more clearly and convincingly. Demonstration would require a detailed research of the topic so the audience would get better information. The major points are emphasized through the use of different aids.

Demonstration requires the demonstrator to be competent and confident in showing and communicating all aspects of the topic. Demonstration is practical and can provide hands on experience. It incites a feeling of gathering more information. If demonstration is exciting, the audience will take interest, involve themselves and try to learn more.

Tips to Make Demonstration Exciting

1. Be well groomed with formal dress.

2. Introduce yourself and briefly explain your interest in the area of demonstration.

3. Demonstrations should be largely memorized. Use the aids as your guides.

4. Be relaxed, confident and try not to talk too fast.

5. Make sure that visual aids are visible to all the audience and audio aids are audible.

6. Make sure that you do not use aids for too long for example, flashing slides too quickly or keep them showing too long.

7. Always remember that the purpose of demonstration is to present information and not to confuse the audience. The aids you use are only a tool to help you during the process of demonstration. Make them simple, purposeful and consistent.

8. Match design to purpose. Tailor your demonstration according to the level of your audience.

9. Be aware that unexpected can happen. The power may go out. You may forget or get distracted. The audience may confuse you. Take a deep breath if unexpected happens. Maintain your level of confidence. A small pause will help you in regaining confidence.

10. If your demonstration is being judged, try to obtain a score card to know what the judges will be looking for. You can focus on the areas you in are afraid of.

11. The demonstrations are composed of three parts the Introduction, the Body and the Conclusion. In the introduction, introduce yourself and your topic in the way to arouse interest. Expand your ideas in the time available in the body. Explain the information clearly by giving and showing examples. In the conclusion, remind the audience of the things you want them to remember the most. Sum up the main ideas in few short sentences. Ask for questions and then thank the audience.

12. Keep a damp towel located near your work area so that you can wipe your hands and table top when you have finished.

13. Clear away your work area and present the final product. Make sure your exit is smooth. Gather and remove all materials quickly and neatly. Watch your steps so that you don't slip or drop anything.

AUDIO-VISUAL AIDS

An audio-visual aid is something the audience can see and hear that helps the speaker send his message across to the audience. The use of audio-visual aids helps in communicating the message effectively to the audience. Their attention can be focused. The receiver retains the message for a longer period since the message is presented both aurally and visually. Audio-visual aids are used to support your presentation. They are not a substitute for your presentation but an aid to communicate your message effectively to your audience. The purpose is to facilitate understanding. All audio-visual aids require a little imagination to make them truly effective. They should be arranged in such a manner that they make presentation interesting and not distracting. There are a variety of audio-visual aids that can be used to make a presentation more productive. They can help you with your presentation.

The audio-visual aids make you more persuasive by adding variety and emphasis to your presentation. For the speaker, they act as a 'trigger' for memory and keep the presentation focused. For the audience, they add interest and provide an additional way of receiving the message. There are many types of audio-visual aids that can be used. But you should not be carried away with technology and use them just because they exist. Use them sparingly, and intelligently and carefully so that your presentation gets an enhanced effect.

Choosing Audio-Visual Aids

1. Keep in mind the shape, size, lighting arrangements and equipment available in the place of presentation.

2. Selection of aids should be made according to the seating arrangement. Use those aids which will be visible and audible to everyone.

3. Look for the electrical points for the equipment you plan to use.

4. Time factor is very important. The basic activity is your presentation. Audio-visual equipments are going to provide help to you. So while choosing audio-visual aids, keep in mind the time allotted and distribute accordingly. If a short time frame is allowded, then fewer aids requiring less explanation should be used.

5. Use only those aids with which you are comfortable. It is important to practice using aids in exactly the same way you plan to use them during your presentation. Do not underestimate the difficulties that may arise.

6. The aids should fit naturally into the presentation. Main focus should be on the presentation and not on aids.

Handouts

Handouts should be used to cover fine details. Be careful not to disturb your audience with reading material. They should be listening to you. Handouts are not meant to be read while you are speaking—they are meant to be taken away. So, handouts should be given either after the show or much before it has started. Make sure to have the extra copies for unexpected guests.

Handouts are simple and easy to use. There is no audibility or visibility problem in their use. They can depict lots of information. They are inexpensive to use and can last for long. But handouts can create distraction and don't help in enhancing the quality of actual presentation.

Flashcards

They have limited use. They may not be of much help when addressing large audience because they are not big enough to be clearly visible from a distance. Make them bright enough to catch attention.

Flipcharts/Posters

They are very effective for summarizing information. Make them simple and large. They are also a good medium for providing responses to the questions. But flipchart is effective with small group as it is relatively small in size. Title each page with a short topic or heading. Do not fill the page to the bottom. People in the back will be unable to see. Highlight key points. Allow time for reading, retention and note taking.

Chalkboard

The chalkboard is a popular, accessible and simple aid. It is available almost everywhere. It is a flexible aid and modification can be done immediately. The speaker should not address the audience while writing on the board. Write neatly and large enough to be read by the entire audience. The main drawback of using a chalkboard is the lack of any permanent record of what has been written, unless an electronic chalkboard is used.

Overhead Projector

Overhead projector is used to deliver images to audience. It is a simple and all round device that does not require high-tech skills. It provides variety, transparencies can be made by writing, drawing, painting, photocopying and printing. Number your transparencies. Keep the screen in full view of the audience. Do not block the view when presenting. Darken the room appropriately by blocking out sunshine.

Overhead projector is a common equipment which can be prepared quickly. It enables effective interaction with the audience. It can be used both in large and small gathering as well as formal and informal presentation.

Slide Shows

Slides represent an easily manageable visual format. They bring realism into your presentation. You can make excellent slides using a computer graphic program.

They are good at getting attention, help in maintaining interest and can have high impact. Sometimes technical failures may bring disastrous effects.

Video Tapes

Video is an extellent means of delivery, especially where movement is required. Be sure the video tape is rewound and at the starting point. Check the audio level and visual images. Use high quality tapes to avoid the last minute disappointment. Always carry a back up tape.

Video/Data Projector

If it is connected to a video player, it will project video image onto a screen or wall. Image can be enlarged in the process. If it is connected to a computer, the display will be seen on the monitor screen. All forms of projectors have fixed light output. The larger an image is, the dimmer it will be.

Computer

Presentation software application can be used to deliver all kinds of data in a visually pleasing way. Data from other application such as spreadsheets, databases, drawings, photographs, text documents etc., can be used to present information. Laptop presentation with data projector is a popular aid. The visuals can be sophisticated and modified. The presenter can check the visuals by looking at the laptop.

Audio Tapes

Audio is an effective aid and can be easily used. Materials are commonly available. Be sure the tape is rewound and at its starting point. Use a quality player for effective results. Adjust the volume so that it is audible to all the audience. Give an idea about what you are playing and introduce the speaker to the audience. Always carry a backup tape.

EXERCISE

1. What is demonstration?
2. Name the three parts Demonstration is composed of.
3. Mention the points a demonstrator should focus on while demonstrating.
4. Why are audio-visual aids supposed to have a long impact on the audience?
5. What factors should be kept is mind while choosing audio-visual aids?
6. What are the merits and demerits of handouts?
7. When should the handouts be given to the audience?
8. What points should be kept in mind while making flipcharts?
9. What is the drawback of using a chalkboard?
10. What is the difference between slideshows and overhead projector?
11. What are the problems a slideshow can face?
12. What is a video/data projector?
13. What points should be taken care of in the presentation using audio/video tapes?

❑❑❑

Chapter 6
CONVERSATION

"A special kind of beauty exists which is born in language, of language and, for language."
—**Gaston Bachelard**

INTRODUCTION

Conversation is a social activity. It is a spoken exchange of thoughts, opinions and feelings. It is an interactive process which involves both the speaker and the listener. Thus conversation is communication by two or more people, often on a particular topic. To talk with others, we must think about their feelings, thoughts and their needs. In return, we expect them to think about us also. Thus if two or more people are to communicate, they must co-operate and give others the chance to talk. In other words, conversation is a reciprocal process.

Conversation involves an immediate response. There is no time lapse between what you say and the response you get from your listener. For example, if you say something which is not approved by your listener, you will immediately get the feedback. To make the flow of conversation a smooth process, you have to be tolerant and receptive.

Conversation is a complex and difficult activity. You must be clear about what is to be said and what is not to be said, you must use your words carefully and your movement, gestures, posture, gaze should be appropriate since your body language supplements your words. If you are not careful about the selection of your words, and you do not follow the proper etiquettes during conversation, you may not be socially popular. To ensure an efficient and effective conversation, you should have the ability to adjust to other people. You can improve your conversation skill by observing etiquettes, patience, tolerance and some control. In short you should learn to listen as well as to speak.

USES OF TELEPHONE MEDIA

Telephone media is the most readily available and the fastest channel for communication. The extensive worldwide telephone network has made direct communication between two people anywhere in the world quick and easy. Good telephone skills can turn your calls into relationship builders. While poor telephone skills can cause customer dissatisfaction or loss of customers, damage the organisational image and threaten caller's goodwill.

Use of the telephone is increasing day by day because it provides an easy and quick way to communicate. Successful business use of the telephone requires a good understanding of the telephone as a communication channel. Because telephone only has the auditory element, your voice becomes the only channel of communication. Speak clearly and listen attentively to achieve effective results.

Avoid placing or receiving calls when you are doing other things. Plan your outgoing call and receive your incoming calls when you are appropriately prepared. A telephone call is a purposeful activity. You need to develop your questioning technique in order to receive the intended information. Your caller calls you with some purpose; your skill would help you to elicit that purpose as quickly and as clearly as possible.

Appropriate greetings and endings to calls would help you establish a good rapport. When you end the call, you should be certain that the caller is satisfied with your answers. Telephone etiquettes demand that the caller puts down the receiver first.

To use your telephone effectively, you need to manage its use. Outgoing calls should be adjusted according to your schedule as well as the schedule of the receiver. Incoming calls should be screened to avoid the interruptions in the middle of the work. By scheduling your calls, you will be able to give full attention to all the calls you receive or make.

Disadvantages of Telephone

1. Casual Approach. Most of us have grown up with telephones. We have learned to use telephone much the same way as we learned other forms of oral communication. We are often more casual with its use. Our casual approach to telephone calls may sometimes bring disastrous results.

2. No record of the agreement. Because it is oral communication, agreements reached on telephone do not have the written evidence. In future disputes may arise and lack of written evidence would put one at a loss. It does not provide any record for legal purposes.

3. Different time zones. Different time zones around the world complicate long distance conversation. Suppliers, customers clients can virtually be anywhere and if they are not considerate about the different time zones, the telephones calls may cause inconvenience.

4. Awkward timing. It would be proper if prior arrangements are made to converse at a specific time. Otherwise telephone calls become inconvenient for the receivers who may be doing something important when their phones ring.

5. Wrong numbers. Since telephone is not a visual means of communication, you may not know if you are speaking to the right person. You may connect to a wrong number and leave a message to a wrong person.

How to Use Telephone Effectively?

1. Introduce yourself. State your name clearly. If it is your first call and a formal one, introduce yourself with your last name. You may also spell it.

2. Give the name of your organisation. If the speaker is not already familiar with you and your organisation, speak slowly and clearly while giving the name of your organisation. If the name of the organisation is complicated, spell the name for better understanding.

3. Be Patient. Even if you do not understand something, even if you do not approve of what the speaker says, observe patience and try to understand his point of view. Stay calm even if the call is a heated one and try to be helpful. Avoid providing an answer or a conclusion before the speaker has conveyed his opinion.

4. Be direct and brief. Do not go in details. Be concise and direct.

5. Ask for approval. Ask if it is an appropriate time for him to receive the call. After taking his approval go ahead, otherwise ask for the suitable time to call.

6. Follow up calls. Conduct follow up calls to show your loyalty to the customer. This way you can win the confidence of your client.

7. Devote your full attention. Remember that you are transmitting a message even if you are not visible. Your distraction would be apparent in your tone. Put off making calls when you are distracted or tired.

8. Be polite. Be helpful to the caller. If the issue does not relate you, try to find someone who can help now or who can ring him back later. Do not put the caller on hold for indefinite period.

9. Listen Properly. Be active listener. Ask questions or use prompts to ensure that the caller gives precise information so that the message received is accurate.

10. Be interested. Let your caller feel that you are genuinely interested in his talk. Try to use the name of the caller in between to give a personalized effect to the call.

11. Smile. Although you are not visible to the caller, your smile on the face would reflect in your voice.

12. Speak with confidence. Be firm and definite while talking an telephone. You should be so certain that the listener believes in what you say.

13. Be composed. If you are stressed up or not in pleasant mood, let the voice mail pick the call until you are completely composed and can handle the caller.

14. Be sincere. People call to have a problem answered. Give importance to the needs of the caller and try to solve with sincerity. He will remember how sincere and attentive you were to his needs.

15. Let the phone ring twice. It will give you a moment to change your frame of mind. You will get time to shift your attention from what you are currently doing. Give the caller your undivided attention.

Taking down Notes. Before you make a call, write the name and title of the person you are calling. Write down the name of his organisation as well as the purpose of the call. Write down your queries and the points you want to put forth. Otherwise you may forget something. A business call is not a casual conversation. You will appear unprofessional if you place a second call to say something which should have been communicated in the original call. Your notes of the telephone conversation may be the only record of what you discussed. Be careful while noting down the information. If you handle a number of calls each day, then it is essential to take notes with date and time. Do not wait for the call to end to take notes. Taking notes on telephone calls should occur during the call.

EXERCISE

1. How can telephone help you in your organisation?
2. Discuss the advantages and disadvantages of telephone media.
3. What etiquettes should you follow while using telephone?
4. What will you do if you get a call during your work?
5. Write down five important characteristics essential for the effective use of telephone.

❑❑❑

Chapter 7

SOCIALISING AND PUBLIC RELATION DEPARTMENT

"I know you believe you understand what you think I said, but I am not sure you realize that what you heard is not what I meant."—**Richard M. Nixon**

IMPORTANCE OF SOCIALISING

Workplace socialising has a positive and important role in the growth of a career. In today's fast paced global society, etiquette and protocol skills are necessary to ensure success and gain respect and recognition.

Socialising with colleagues can help in building your professional support network. You need to practice politeness and decorum to understand what it means to be socially acceptable. Etiquette and protocol are the outer expressions of your character and play a vital role in projecting the right image. Getting along with the people you work will help you produce effective and productive results.

1. Take interest in everyone. Do not form groups or have biased attitude.

2. Attend company activities such as sporting events, staff parties, lunches.

3. Organise group activities like celebrating festival together, celebrating important occasions, wishing greetings, after-work trips.

4. Present opportunities to develop relations with your co-workers.

5. Avoid gossiping, talking behind someone's back or taking sides in internal conflicts.

6. Accept co-workers as they are and avoid passing judgement on their lifestyle or their choices.

7. Planning socialising get togethers once a month will make you know your co-workers. You can develop rich relationships that can actually help improve your career.

8. Volunteering your time for a good cause like charity events will bind you with your co-workers and help in improving professional relationships and your career.

9. Pick up games you are interested in. Play games and spend time with your co-workers in a fun way. This way you can release your work stress too.

10. Car pooling is a great way to help protect the environment and socialize with co-workers at the same time.

Public Relations Department

The successful growth of an organisation largely depends on its positive and active interaction with external as well as internal members. It is not an easy job as the members are hetrogeneous and the nature of interaction is diverse. In order to manage this difficult task, a professional department known as the Public Relation Department is established by various organisations.

Public Relation involves supervision and assessment of public attitudes in addition to maintaining mutual relations and understanding between an organisation and its public.

An organisation needs to interact at constant rate. As the channels of communication have multiplied drastically, its main function is to improve those channels and find out new ways of setting up a two way flow of information and understanding. Public Relations open the channels of communication between an organisation and its various stakeholders, whether they are the investors, the community, employers, government or users. It involves

1. Evaluation of public attitudes and opinions.
2. Formation and implementation of an organisation's procedure and policy regarding communication with its public.
3. Co-ordination of communication programme.
4. Fostering a positive relationship between an organisation and its public constituent.

Duties of a Public Relation Officer

1. Relationship with Mass Media. He ensures a permanent link with the local and regional media by supplying information. He arranges the presence of media at the most important events. He organises press-conferences. He edits official statement and press-briefings. He keeps the media update. He suggest events or activities with a media impact in order to support the image of his organisation. The duties of a Public Relation Officer include maintaining cordial relations with media correspondents. He ensures that the organisation gets a positive and favourable image in the press. Press has to be provided with information and handouts.

2. Communication. It is the duty of a Public Relation Officer to apprise the customers, suppliers, employers, dealers and others, of the latest happenings in the organisation. They have the right to know about their future plans, their strategies, the present working conditions, the growth etc. Otherwise misunderstanding may arise which may affect the business in the long run. A smart and intelligent public relation officer would present the positive picture of his organisation which would go in its favour.

3. Lobbying. Effective Public Relation Officer can influence public policy. An important function of a Public Relation Officer will be to maintain close relations and convince influential people in various walks of life.

4. Counselling. Doubts have to be removed from the minds of the people through meetings and counselling which will help keep a direct contact and not let doubts remain which may have an adverse impact on the organisation.

5. Internal Communication to Support Public Image. Internal set-up consists of those people connected with the organisation like employees, shareholders, suppliers, distributors, bankers, advisors etc. A Public Relation Officer will maintain the relationships and help in clarifying doubts and misunderstanding.

6. Organising Meetings. He organises regular Inhouse meetings between the board and the employees in which both the parties can interact and put forth their ideas and complaints.

All organisations need Public Relation Department. A Public Relation Officers' job is a difficult job which involves endless press releases, an invitation for press-conferences, follow-up programmes, maintaining internal and external relationships, organising lectures, exhibitions, events. So a Public Relation Officer must have an extrovert outgoing personality. He should have excellent communication skill, both written as well as spoken. He should have the ability to work under pressure.

EXERCISE

1. Discuss the importance of socialising in an organisation.
2. Does socialising improve the quality of work in an organisation?
3. As a manager of a company, what would you do to improve your relationships with your junior staff?
4. Discuss the duties of a Public Relation Officer.
5. Discuss the importance of celebrating cultural events and functions in an organisation.

❑❑❑

Chapter **8**

DEBATES/SPEECHES

"Use soft words and hard arguments."

DEBATES

A debates is a discussion between two sides with different views. Participants speak for the topic or against the topic. Debates are means of encouraging critical thinking, personal expression and tolerance of others' opinions. Debates are conducted in governing assemblies held in lecture halls or public arenas, presented in schools and colleges, written in newspapers and magazine columns, heard on radio or watched on television.

Delivery

Speak with energy, enthusiasm and variety. Use your voice and gestures to emphasize and highlight the important arguments and the important words in your evidence. You will not sound confident if you speak in an unconcerned, monotonous and plain tone. Be confident about your arguments. Pronunciation and articulation are important to ensure the speaker is understood.

Be natural. Be yourself, Do not try to be fake. You want others to believe you. Your natural characteristic will present you in true self.

Voice Modulation and Body Movements

A monotonous tone bores the audience and the speech may lose impact. Change your voice for emphasis but do not speak too loudly or too softly. Change the tone of your speech according to your expressions but keep it natural. Use volume, pitch and speed to emphasise important points. Your facial expression should match the points you are speaking. Use your hand gestures with confidence. Right movements of arms, body, face and hands can add dramatically to the presentation but meaningless, nervous and repititive gestures should be avoided.

Choose Your Side to Debate

There are always two ideas in a debate to argue. You must select one viewpoint and stick to it. If you are little confused or shaky about your opinion, it will appear in your debate. Believe firmly what you say. You must commit to your viewpoint in order to create a strong debate.

Research both Sides

Even if you have chosen your side, it is important to research both pros and cons of the topic. This will help you in understanding your opponent's point of view and will give directions for your preparation. Researching both the sides will prepare you for the expected questions which may crop up from your opponents. You can frame answers, accordingly. When you have understood both the directions, you are prepared to contradict the other side.

Plan the Structure

Like speech, debate has a structure too. It has an introduction, body and a conclusion. The main difference is that you have to prove your point of view through evidence. Debates have to be oral and sometimes you are expected to speak extemporarily when you are asked a question by your opponent. You can start the debate with a general thought or anecdote but do not deviate from the subject matter. You should have sufficient information. In case you forget a point you should have another for substitution. Conclude your debate by disproving the opponent's point. Use reasoning to make logical connections between ideas and evidence.

Maintain Your Confidence

Your presentation, speech and appearance matter almost as much as your delivery and content. Dress appropriately. Have notes prepared. But do not read from the script. Practice speaking in front of the mirror or in front of your friends or family members. This will boost your confidence.

PRESENTATION

Believe in what you say and whatever you say is right and your opponent is always wrong. After you make each point, link it back to your team case. This will make you appear more prepared. Never insult the opponent. No matter, how much you want to, don't ever humiliate your opponent. Do not use personal attacks. Have patience as well as passion while presenting your debate. The speech should not be too fully prepared or it will be difficult to respond to the opposing arguements. The object of the debate is to persuade the audience that your own stand is more valid. Timing is very important. Conclude with strong arguements within the time allotted is that your own.

Team Work

Because debating is a team work, it is important to establish unity and logic. Each member of the team needs to reinforce the team line and be consistent with what has already been said and what will be said by other members of the team. When you are presenting a particular arguement make sure that the arguement is logical and that you make clear links between your team line and the arguement.

Persuasion

Both material and method combine to influence an audience. Appearance, enthusiasm, humour, personality and sincerity all contribute to the persuasiveness of a speaker. The speaker needs to be fully understood throughout the entire presentation to achieve a persuasive result. Anecdotes, emphasis and repetition all combine to get the message across.

Planning your Speech

Planning of speech involves not only the selection of thoughts but selection of relevant thoughts. What to say is important but what not to say is equally important. Irrelevant ideas even remotely hurting the audience should be excluded. After having carefully drafted the final ideas, arrange them in logical sequence. A well prepared speech is already nine tenth delivered. Hence preparation should be given enough time. It requires concentration, lot of spade work. It should come from heart and touch other's heart too. Remember "Pen is mightier than sword".

The Occasion

Prepare your speech according to the occasion. The occasion will dictate not only the content of your speech but also the duration, the tone and the expectation of your audience. For example, jokes or humour may not be appropriate for a business presentation while they may enhance the quality of a wedding speech or a social speech.

The Audience

Speech should be always targeted at your audience. Prepare the speech according to the mental, financial, social level of the audience whether the audience are familiar or not. If you are speaking to unfamiliar audience, you try to build a degree of trust with the audience.

The Purpose of Your Speech

Before you start writing the speech, keep in mind the clear goal. When you know the purpose, the writing will flow naturally.

Writing the Speech

A good speech should have a structure. Provide the speech with a beginning, middle and an end.

The opening. In the first thirty to forty seconds, you can grab the attention of the audience. If you fail to do so, you will not have the interested and attentive audience. You can open your speech by asking a thought provoking question or make an interesting or controversial statement or tell a joke or recite a relevant quotation. If you are successful in achieving the attention of the audience, you will feel more confident and your speech would move effortlessly to the middle.

The Middle (Body)

The body is the longest part of speech. Plan a series of points and discuss them one by one. The points should be well organised so that smooth transition takes place from one point to the next point. This will give a logical progression to your speech and the listener will establish the relation with different points. Be concise. Do not confuse the audience with countless points. It is better to have well explained fewer points than to have poorly explained more points.

The Closing

The closing of the speech should summarise the main points. The closing should be inspirational and thought provoking. Close with pleasant gratitude leaving an impact on the minds of the audience.

Delivery of the Speech

Scripts-Notes. Even if you are not using notes, keeping them with you will take away the nervousness.

Reading from a Script. Reading from a script may give you confidence but it is undesirable. You will not see your audience if you are engrossed in reading the speech and the audience may not get involved. When you are reading your script, you are not delivering a speech, you are just reading it aloud to the audience creating less impact.

Using Notes. Your notes should consist of the key words or points of your speech. You may refer to your notes occasionally just to look at the point.

Recite from Memory. Reciting from memory needs a lot of prior preparation. You may have prepared an excellent speech, your delivery is superb but if you forget in between, it will be disastrous. Keeping notes with you may save you from disappointment.

Speech Delivery Tips

1. Personal Appearance. Your appearance should be simple, straight, attractive and must depict your personality.

2. Speak clearly and adjust your voice so that everyone can hear you. Don't shout. Shouting will present an unpleasant sound.

3. Do not speak too fast. Take a deep breath if you are nervous and give appropriate pauses in between.

4. Use pauses effectively to emphasise a point or to give audience time to react.

5. Make proper eye contact to build a relationship with your audience.

6. Use gestures to enhance the effect. Avoid nervous gestures like cracking fingers, shaking leg. Do not put your hands in your pockets.

7. Be your natural self. Do not act or copy others. Your originality would attract the audience.

Difference between Debate and Group Discussion

1. In a debate, the speaker assumes that there is a right answer and only the speaker has it while in a group discussion, it is assumed that many people have pieces of the answers and together they can come to a solution.

2. Debate is about winning while in group discussion, participants explore common problem and try to find a solution.

3. In debates, participants try to find flaws with the other side, while participants work together towards common understanding in group discussions.

4. In debates opponents listen to find flaws and make counter-arguments while in group discussions participants listen to understand and find meaning and agreement.

5. Participants defend their own views against those of others in debates and in group discussions participants believe and admit that others' opinions can improve their thinking. Participants are defensive in debates and in group discussions participants are receptive.

6. Participants are in search of weaknesses in debates and participants are in search of strengths and values in group discussions.

7. Debates seek closure and a conclusion while group discussions discover new options and open grounds for new discussions.

EXERCISE

1. Discuss the important elements required for an effective speech delivery.
2. What is the difference between a debate and a speech?
3. How is a debate different from group discussion?
4. Write a debate on the topic: "Women should get 33% reservation".
5. Prepare a speech on the following topic: "IT Growth in India."

❑❑❑

Unit V
Value Based Text Readings

Chapter 1

THE AIMS OF SCIENCE AND THE HUMANITIES

—*MOODY E. PRIOR*

1. There are certain differences between the methods and aims of science and the character of its distinctive products compared to those of the humanities. It is important to insist upon them because the tendency in much of the present-day discussion of these matters has been to obliterate or obscure these differences.
2. Among these differences, one of the most conspicuous is that, unlike the sciences, the humanities are concerned with emotional responses to experience and they evoke these responses. And this is true of all the arts and in varying degree of most humanistic writing. Another difference is that the humanities address themselves to an understanding and an evaluation of human goals, and this, while less apparent with the most abstract arts like music, is especially apparent in all forms of humanistic discourse. By comparison, a scientific generalization, whether a mathematical formulation, or a theory, or a concept, carries no implication within itself of its relevance to any human uses to which it may be put, to the human choices which may be governed by it, or to the inherent human striving for happiness or self-fulfilment in action except as it points to further scientific activity. The creations of science—its mathematical syntheses, its proven generalization, its fruitful concepts and theories—are neutral with reference to their moral and social implications. But with the humanities, the involvement in both the human meaning and response to the experiences and observation dealt with is inescapable and is inherent in all typical humanistic products. They could not, in fact, be described or defined without reference to these.
3. Science and the humanities share in common the capacity to arouse a particular form of aesthetic responses—the pleasure which is induced by those products of creative effort in which discrete elements of matter or experience are brought together in a meaningful organization, even in connection with this aspect, however,

there is a difference: it is possible to define a product of scientific activity without reference to this aesthetic aspect, but it is hardly possible to do so for a work of music or a poem.

4. There is a further difference. Though both attempt to discern and express order and unity in the variety of experience, their generalizing powers tend in different directions. Science attempts to subdue a multitude of incidents to a grand generalization which, until challenged by new events is universal in its application. Scientific generalization is capable of accurate prediction with reference to all future events that belong to the category of incidents with which it deals. Humanistic works, on the contrary, are concerned rather with the individual experience, and they relate it to general principles not in order to have it lose its identity within them but in order to reveal its special meaning. Humanistic works therefore tend toward uniqueness, and in their totality call attention to the diversity and plenitude of human experience. All sunsets can mean only one thing in any given statement about them in the science of physics. But to a painter each sunset is a distinct phenomenon to be given a special personal meaning in the whole range of sunsets and is capable of many emotional evocations.

5. Lastly, there is also a parallel difference in the resultant products of the two forms of creative activity. Whereas the products of scientific genius are in their final form impersonal, the products of artistic genius are unique and inseparable from the special power of the one mind which produced them.

Moody E. Prior, Science and the Humanities (Northwestern University Press, 1962)

GLOSSARY

1. **Obliterate** (verb)—destroy, annihilate.

   Antonyms—build, construct, create.

   Related forms:

   Obliterable—(adjective)

   Obliterator—(noun)

2. **Obscure** (adjective)—not clear or plain, ambiguous, vague, uncertain.

   Antonyms—certain, clear, noted.

   Related forms:

   obscuredly, obscurely —(adverb)

   obscureness—(noun).

3. **Inherent** (adjective)—elemental, genetic, inborn, inmate, natural, hereditary, basic.

   Related forms:

   inherently—(adverb).

   Antonyms—acquired, external, learned.

4. **Aesthetic** (adjective)—artistic, pertaining to a sense of the beautiful or the science of aesthetics, artful, creative, refined, cultivated.

   Related forms:

   aesthetics—(noun).

   aesthetically—(adverb).

   Antonyms—displeasing, ugly, unattractive.

5. **Discern** (verb)—discover, descry, espy, detect, differentiate.

   Related forms:

   discerner—(noun).

   Antonyms—disregard, neglect, overlook.

6. **Plentitude** (noun)—abundance, a full supply.

7. **Evocation** (noun)—invocation, summons, an act or instance of evoking; a calling forth.

8. **Induced** (adjective)—convinced, actuate, prompt, incite,

   Antonyms—dissuade, hindered.

   Related forms:

   inducible—(adjective)

   induce—(verb)

9. **Conspicuous** (adjective)—prominent, easily seen or noticed, manifest

   Related forms:

   Conspicuously—(adverb)

   Conspicuousness
Conspicuity]—(noun)

   Antonyms—concealed, hidden, inconspicuous, unnoticeable

10. **Discrete** (adjective)—apart or detached from others, discontinuous

    Related forms:

    discretely—(adverb)

    discreteness—(noun)

    Antonyms—attached, combined, joined.

EXERCISE

A. Which of the following statements are true?

(*a*) One of the most conspicuous difference between science and humanities is

1. The humanities are indifferent towards emotions.
2. Science is concerned with emotional responses to experience.
3. The humanities are concerned with emotional responses to experience.
4. None of them is concerned with emotional responses to experience.

(*b*) Humanistic works tend towards
1. Capability
2. Practicality
3. Theory
4. Diversity

(*c*) Scientific generalisation focuses on
1. Universality
2. Accuracy
3. Variety
4. Diversity

B. Answer the following questions:

(*a*) How are the aesthetic responses different for a scientist to a humanist?

(*b*) Write down the differences between Science and Humanities as explained by M.E. Prior in "The Aims of Science and Humanities." Do you agree with him?

(*c*) Both Science and Humanities find unity in a variety of experiences. How do they make generalisation from their experiences?

(*d*) What is the common thread between Science and Humanities? Are the end results same?

(*e*) How can the study of Humanities understand human emotions?

(*f*) Which appeals you the most—Science or Humanities? Why?

C. Which of the following statements are not correct? Rewrite the incorrect statements in correct form.

(*a*) Both Science and Humanities are concerned with human emotions.

(*b*) Music can understand and evaluate human goals to the maximum.

(*c*) All scientific activities are centered around the inherent human striving for happiness or self-fulfilment.

(*d*) The scientific theories and concepts are indifferent towards their moral and social implications.

(*e*) Both Science and Humanities contribute equally in evoking aesthetic responses.

(*f*) Scientific works are concerned with the general experience while Humanistic works are concerned with individual experiences.

(*g*) Scientific approaches are unique, aesthetic, distinct and emotional.

(*h*) Scientific creativity is impersonal while humanistic creativity is personal.

D. Pair each word in column I with a suitable word in column II to form compound words.

Example:

Self fulfilment = Selffulfilment

Column I	Column II
Common	Bye
Green	Hand
First	Life
Lay	House
Good	Man
Wild	Sense

(*b*) **Write down ten compound words other than the above columns.**

E. We add suffixes or prefixes to bring changes in the root word. Separate the root word from the following words and indicate suffix/prefix used. Explain the change in meaning also.

1. detachment
2. endearment
3. impersonal
4. diversity
5. imperceptibly
6. awesome
7. inexorable
8. handful
9. impartially
10. methodological

F. Composition

Write down a composition on the "Power of Music in the treatment of diseases."

❑❑❑

Chapter 2

The Language of Literature and Science

—*Aldous Huxley*

1. As a medium of literary expression, the common language is *inadequate*. It is no less inadequate as a medium of scientific expression. Like the man of letters, the scientist finds it necessary to 'give a purer sense to the words of the tribe.' But the purity of scientific language is not the same as the purity of literary language.
2. The aim of the scientist is to say only one thing at a time, and to say it *unambiguously* and with the greatest possible clarity. To achieve this, he simplifies and jargonizes. In other words, he uses the vocabulary and syntax of common speech in such a way that each phrase is susceptible of only one interpretation; and when the vocabulary and syntax of common speech are too imprecise for his purpose, he invents a new technical language, or jargon, specifically, designed to express the limited meaning with which he is professionally concerned. At its most perfectly pure, scientific language ceases to be a matter of words and turns into mathematics.
3. The literary artist purifies the language of the tribe in a radically different way. The scientist's aim, as we have seen, is to say one thing, and only one thing, at a time. This, most *emphatically*, is not the aim of the literary artist. Human life is lived *simultaneously* on many levels and has many meanings. Literature is a device for reporting the multifarious facts and expressing their various significances. When the literary artist undertakes to give a purer sense to the words of his tribe, he does so with the express purpose of creating a language capable of conveying not the single meaning of some particular science, but the multiple significance of human experience, on its most private as well as on its more public levels.
4. What is a rose? A daffodil? A lily? One set of answers to these questions may be given in the highly purified language of bio-chemistry, cytology and genetics.

'A special form of ribonucleic acid (called messenger RNA) carries the genetic message from the gene, which is located in the nucleus of the cell, to the surrounding cytoplasm, where many of the proteins are synthesized.' And so on in endless, fascinating detail. A rose is a rose, is RNA, DNA, polypeptide chains of amino acids.

5. The primary interest of the literary artist is not in cells or genes or chemical compounds, not in the orbicularity of bulbs or the number of stamens, not even in the manufacture of pills or the concoction of herbal emetics. His concern is with his own and other people's more private experience in relation to flowers and with the multiple meanings he finds in them. He is a man, and men must sweat for a living; so he considers the blessed lilies that do not toil. He is often depressed by too much thinking, or bored by too little. But then, daffodils flash upon that inward eye, the bliss of solitude.

Aldous Huxley, Literature and Science (Chatto to and Windus, 1963)

GLOSSARY

1. **Unambiguously** (adverb)—certainly, categorically, decidedly, decisively, positively.

   Antonyms—doubtful, questionable, indefinite.

2. **Jargon** (noun)—the language, esp. the vocabulary, peculiar to a particular trade, profession or group; medical jargon; unintelligible, meaningless talk or writing; gibberish, colloquialism, cliche.

   Related forms:

   jargony / jargonistic —(adjective)

   jargonize — (Verb)

   jargonist / jargoneer —(noun)

   Antonyms—standard

3. **Susceptible** (adjective)—exposed, naive, vulnerable, impressionable, influenced.

   Antonyms—resistant, resisting, unsusceptible.

   Related forms:

   Susceptibleness—(noun)

   Susceptibly—(adverb)

4. **Imprecise** (adjective)—vague, ill-defined, incorrect-blemished, distorted, not working, wrong.

   Related forms:

   imprecisely—(adverb)

   imprecision / impreciseness —(noun)

   Antonym—accurate, correct, strong, working, perfect.

5. **Radically** (adverb)—in a complete or basic manner; thoroughly, fundamentally.
   Related forms:
   radicalness—(noun)
   radical—(adjective)
   Antonym inessentially
6. **Emphatically** (adverb)—positively, energetically, decidedly, definitely, forcibly, assuredly.
   Related forms:
   emphatic —(adjective)
   emphaticalness —(noun)
   Antonyms—hesitantly, indecisively, indistinctly.
7. **Cytoplasm** (noun)—Cell Biology, the cell substance between the cell membrane and the nucleus, containing the cytosol, organelles, cytoskeleton, and various particles; the protoplasm outside the nucleus of a cell.
   Related forms:
   Cytoplasmic—(adjective)
   Cytoplasmically—(adverb)
8. **Cytology** (noun)—the study of the microscopic appearance of cells, esp. for the diagnosis of abnormalities and malignancies
   Related forms:
   cytologic]
   cytological] —(adjective)
   cytologically—(adverb)
   cytologist—(noun)
9. **Syntax** (noun)—the study of the rules for the formation of grammatical sentences in a language; arrangement, pattern, structure, system.
   Notes—Grammar consists of a description of all the elements in a language;
   Syntax—focuses on the relationship between words that determine their oder in sentences—**Grammar** is the entire study and **Syntax** in one part only.
10. **Orbicular** (adjective)—like an orb; circular; ringlike; spherical; rounded.
    Related forms:
    Orbicularity]
    Orbicularness] —(noun)
    Orbicularly—(adverb).
11. **Concoction** (noun)—mixture, medley, blend; the act or process of concocting a delicious concoction of beans, rice, and meat.
    Related forms:
    Concoct—(verb)
    Concoctive—(adjective)

Concocter
Concoctor —(noun)

12. **Solitude** (noun)—the state of being or living alone; seclusion, privacy, isolation, loneliness.

Related forms:

Solitudinous—(adjective)

Antonyms—companionship, friendship, togetherness.

EXERCISE

A. **Answer the following questions in one or two sentences:**

(*a*) What is the main aim of scientific language?

(*b*) What is the aim of literary language?

(*c*) Why does a scientist use a jargon?

(*d*) Write in two sentences the basic difference between scientific and literary language.

B. **Answer the following questions in a paragraph:**

(*a*) Why does the writer compare scientific language, at its purest, to mathematics?

(*b*) "The Primary interest of a literary artist is not in cells or genes". Explain.

(*c*) Why does a literary artist turn to nature?

(*d*) Explain the concluding paragraph of the essay.

C. **Explain:**

(*a*) "Give a purer sense to the words of the tribe"

(*b*) "A rose is a rose is a rose" ....

D. **We add a suffix to convert a verb into an adverb**

Example:

Simultaneous + ly = Simultaneously.

(*a*) Find out more such verbs from the chapter which can be used as adverbs by adding a suffix.

(*b*) Write down ten verbs which can be converted into adverbs by adding a suffix.

E. **Prefix "Un" and 'In' are added to the Root word to change it into negative.**

Example:

In + adequate = Inadequate

Un + ambiguously = Unambiguously

Write down ten such words which can be used as Negatives after adding a prefix 'Un' or 'In'.

F. **Composition**

Write down a composition or a poem on the topic "The Blessed Lilies that do not toil."

❑❑❑

Chapter **3**

MAN AND NATURE

—*J. BRONOWSKI*

1. 'A Machine or a Self?' is a question which is crucial to an enquiry into the identity of man. I take as the starting point for an answer, and for my enquiry, an equally crucial and basic proposition. My fundamental assumption at the outset is that man is a part of nature.
2. This simple proposition seems innocent enough, and neutral. Nearly all educated men accept it now: the Bible readers as well as the agnostics, the Sunday strollers and the earnest haunters of museums. In the latter half of the twentieth century, it seems self-evident to say that man is a part of nature, in the same sense that a stone is, or a cactus, or a camel. How easily, indeed, these three childhood categories rise to our lips from Animal, Vegetable or Mineral to exhaust the universe. Yet this bland proposition contains the explosive charge which in this century has split open the self-assurance of Western man.
3. For to assert that man is a part of nature surely denies (or seems to deny) that he is unique. This is the hidden charge that troubles yet silences us; it is the perpetual heresy, for which men went to the stake at least as long ago as 1,600. Giordano Bruno was asked then to abjure, and would not, his wild belief that the earth we stand on is not the only world, and that we are not the only chosen creatures in the multitude of worlds. This was a piece of Renaissance extravagance that was happy to have man play neither the master nor slave of fate, but simply play in the boundless plenty of nature, and to set both of them free together. But it did not, and still does not, win over the jealous man who wants to guard the sense of his immortal station. He wants to feel that he was cast from birth in a supernatural mould; larger than life, or at least larger than nature.

J. Bronowski, The Identity of Man (Penguin Books, 1967)

GLOSSARY

1. **Outset** (noun)—commencement, onset, beginning, origin, dawn
2. **Agnostic** (noun)—skeptic, doubter freethinker, unbeliever.

   Notes—an **agnostic** is one who believes that it is impossible to know whether there is a God; an **atheist** is one who disbelieves or denies the existence of God.

   Antonym—believer.

   Related forms:

   agnostically—(adverb).
3. **Perpetual** (adjective)—continuing or enduring forever; everlasting, constant, incessant.

   Related forms:

   Perpetuality—(noun)

   Perpetualness—(noun)

   Perpetually—(adverb)

   Antonyms—temporary, discontinuous.
4. **Heresy** (noun)—blasphemy, disbelief, any belief or theory that is strongly at variance with established beliefs, customs, etc.

   Antonym—orthodoxy.
5. **Abjure** (verb)—to renounce or give up under oath; forswear, to avoid or shun, to withdraw.

   Related forms:

   abjuratory—(adjective)

   abjurer—(noun)
6. **Renaissance** (noun)—rebirth, renewal, reawakening, resurgence, revival.
7. **Extravagance** (noun)—superfluousness, lavishness, profusion.

   Antonym—frugality.

   Related forms:

   extravagantly—(adverb)

   extravagancy—(adjective)

   extravagant—(noun)

EXERCISE

A. Answer the following questions:

(*a*) What does the writer want to say in the essay "Man and Nature"?

(*b*) Why was Giordano Bruno burnt at the stake?

(*c*) Why does the writer call man jealous?

(*d*) Explain man's relationship with nature.

B. Find out compound words from the chapter and use them in sentences of your own.

Example: Sunday—Strollers.

C. There are certain words which can be used both as a noun and as a verb.

Example:

(*a*) This is the hidden charge that troubles (verb) yet silences (verb) us.
Trouble and silence have been used as a verb in the above sentence.

(*b*) This is the hidden charge that gives us a trouble (noun) yet puts a silence (noun) on us.

Trouble and silence have been used as a noun here.

(*c*) Find out ten more words that can be used both as verb and as noun.

D. Write down a paragraph using the following five sentences in right order.

(*a*) But man wants to feel important and immortal.

(*b*) Bronowski says—that man is a part of nature.

(*c*) He also wants to feel that he has been, from the beginning, larger than nature.

(*d*) This is the statement which has made western men lose his self-assurance.

(*e*) He lost his self-assurance because the statement means that man is not unique.

E. Form nouns from the adjectives given below:

Example:

educated—Adjective

education—Noun

certain, great, strong, high, wise, complex, able, buoyant, wide.

F. Match the sentences in section A with the correct statements in section B. Ensure that the sentences must correspond with the author's point of view on the subject.

Section A	*Section B*
1. Man is part of Nature.	1. Man should live in harmony with nature.
2. Self-assurance of western man.	2. Giordano Bruno.
3. Renaissance and belief.	3. Larger than life and nature.
4. Earth is not the only world.	4. Man is unique.
5. Modern man.	5. Identify of man.

G. An AGNOSTIC is one who believes that it is impossible to know whether there is a God; An ATHEIST is one who disbelieves or denies the existence of God.

Write down ten more one word substitutions on the same line.

H. Composition

Write a paragraph on the topic

"Can Money Bring Happiness?"

❑❑❑

Chapter 4

THE MOTHER OF THE SCIENCES

—A.J. BAHM

1. In at least three ways, philosophy functions as a comprehensive science. It criticizes the sciences, synthesizes the sciences, and is the mother of the sciences.
2. All sciences, such as biology, psychology, sociology, astronomy, aesthetics, semantics, physics, etc., stand in need of criticism. Such criticism is of two sorts: namely, that directed toward premises and that toward conclusions. Each science makes presuppositions which, if examined carefully enough, may be found to be untenable or at least improvable. To philosophy falls the task of careful examination. Again, each science makes presuppositions of other sciences. Also, each science eventually arrives at results which may appear to conflict with the conclusions of other sciences. To philosophy falls this task of comparing assumptions and conclusions.
3. Synthesis is a second function that philosophy performs for the sciences. Each science dwells on one aspect, or phase, of experience. Each does its part. But wherever there is a part, there is a whole. To know only a part is to have an incomplete or distorted view. The final goals of science should be to understand the whole, to see the picture complete. Philosophy, as a science of sciences, as a supreme science, or as a comprehensive science, seeks constantly to perform this function. 'The object of philosophy,' says Broad, 'is to take over the results of the various sciences, add to them the result of religious and ethical experiences of mankind, and then reflect upon the whole, hoping to be able to reach some general conclusions as to the nature of the universe and as to our positions and prospects in it.'
4. Who has not heard the story of the blind men of Burma who visited the elephant? Upon returning from their venture, they compared views about the nature of the beast. Said one, who had felt the elephant's leg, an elephant is like a tree. Another had grasped the tail, and reported him to be like a rope. The trunk was traced by a third, who insisted it was much like a serpent. A fourth, who had stretched

himself on the elephant's side, likened him to a barn. Whenever a scientist insists that the whole universe is like the part which he investigates, he may be compared with a Burmese blind man. We might have the separate reports of all the sciences and yet not see the whole elephant. In order to comprehend the total scheme, the function of synthesis is necessary.

5. As the mother of the sciences, philosophy has had a long and interesting history. At one time, no distinction was made between philosophy and science. Gradually, as reflections upon problems became increasingly complex and as special techniques were developed, specialists limited the range of their inquiries, and the particular sciences were born. Among the first were mechanics, mathematics and astronomy. Among the latest were psychology and sociology. The romance of the maturing of these offspring of the fecund mother must be left to the history of science. Deeper concern is felt for those yet unborn, especially about the philosophical sciences that have not yet been granted independence. Wonder about these new children given rise to speculation about philosophy's future. Will the philosophical sciences become, one day, sciences in their own right? If so, will philosophy's task be done? Will she become barren? Or will there be new conceptions now unsuspected?

6. But philosophy's future promises more than intellectual pioneering. The job of synthesizing partially *incoherent* sciences will become more and more difficult as greater numbers of sciences develop and demand their places in the larger picture. Each new science presents another challenge to the hope for wholeness and total *coherence*. Thus does philosophy's task become greater rather than smaller. As a comprehensive science, then, philosophy has the functions of, first, giving birth, secondly, settling quarrels, and, finally, harmonising in one house the several somewhat self-centred sciences. And, especially since births and quarrels continue. 'A mother's work is never done.'

Archie J. Bahm, Philosophy: An Introduction (Asia Publishing House, 1964)

GLOSSARY

1. **Comprehensive** (adjective)—broad, wide, extensive, full.

   Related forms:

   comprehensively—(adverb)

   comprehensiveness—(noun)

   Antonyms—exclusive, incomprehensive, selective.

2. **Untenable** (adjective)—that cannot be held, defended, or maintained; incapable of being tenanted; indefensible, unreasonable.

   Related forms:

   Untenability
   Untenableness] —Noun

3. **Fecund** (adjective)—productive, fruitful, prolific, fertile.

   Antonyms—impotent, infertile, unproductive, sterile.

4. **Incoherent** (adjective)—unintelligible, confused, muddled, inarticulate.

   Related forms:

   incoherently—(adverb)

   incoherence—(noun)

   Antonyms—coherent, intelligible, understandable.

5. **Semantics** (noun)—the study of meaning; the study of linguistic development by classifying and examining changes in meaning and form; interpretation, denotation.

   Related forms:

   Semanticist
Semantician } —noun

EXERCISE

A. Answer the following questions:

(*a*) What message does the writer want to convey through the story of blind men of Burma?

(*b*) How can philosophy function as a Mother of the Sciences?

(*c*) Discuss the function of philosophy described in the introductory paragraph and the functions described in the concluding paragraph.

(*d*) How has Broad discussed the "Object of Philosophy"? Write in your own words.

(*e*) Do you agree with A.J. Bahm's views in the "Mother of the Sciences"? Discuss in detail.

B. Answer the following questions in one or two sentences:

(*a*) Which branches of science should be criticised and why?

(*b*) How is philosophy superior to other sciences?

(*c*) What should be the ultimate purpose of science?

(*d*) Which are the initial, latest and dependent sciences?

(*e*) Discuss the functions of philosophy as a comprehensive science.

C. Sum up author's views in his essay "The Mother of the Sciences." Do you agree with his views.

D. Write against each of the following words the part of speech indicated in dictionary :

Example:

Comprehensive—adjective

Comprehend—verb.

Presupposition

Presuppose

Distorted

Distort
Interesting
Interest
Increasingly
Increasing
Maturing
Mature
Speculate
Speculation
Coherent
Coherence

E. **Here are eighteen words of six different families. Each family has three members. Separate the families:**

Awe	Drizzle	Rope
Blot	Fright	Scar
Chilly	Grateful	Shivering
Cool	Indebted	Shower
Cord	Obliged	Strain
Downpower	Panic	String

F. **Write down the antonyms of the following words:**

Comprehensive
Synthesis
Distorted
Complex
Coherent
Speculation.

G. The writer in his essay "The Mother of the Sciences" has discussed the various functions of philosophy. He has used CLASSIFICATIONS as he has divided the functions of philosophy into three—how philosophy "criticizes the science, synthesizes the science and is the mother of the science." He has also used NARRATION when he relates the story of "Blind Men of Burma" to illustrate a point.

Write an essay on the "Functions of any one Science." Draw up an outline, give your essay a title and then write. Mention the dominant mode used. You may use the combination of two or three modes.

❑❑❑

Chapter 5

SCIENCE AND SURVIVAL

—BARRY COMMONER

1. There is considerable scientific disagreement about the medical hazards of the new pollutants; about the effects of DDT now found in human bodies, about the diseases due to smog, or about the long-range effects of fallout. But the crucial point is that the disagreements exist, for they reveal that we have risked these hazards before we knew what harm they might do. Unwittingly we have loaded the air with substances that interfere with the functioning of the blood. Because we wanted to build nuclear bombs and kill mosquitoes; we have burdened our bodies with strontium-90 and DDT, with consequences that no one can now predict. We are, in effect, conducting a huge experiment on ourselves. A generation hence–too late to help–public health statistics may reveal what hazards are associated with these pollutants.
2. To those of us who are concerned with the growing risk of unintended damage to the environment, some would reply that it is the grand purpose of science to move into unknown territory, to explore, and to discover. They would remind us that similar hazards have been risked before, and that science and technology cannot make progress without taking some risks. But the size and persistence of possible errors has also grown with the power of science and the expansion of technology. In the past, the risks taken in the name of technological progress–boiler explosions on the first steam-boats, or the early injuries from radium–were restricted to a small place and a short time. The new hazards are neither local nor brief. Air pollution covers vast areas. Fallout is worldwide. Synthetic chemicals may remain in the soil for years. Radioactive pollutants now on the earth's surface will be found there for generations, and, in the case of carbon-14 for thousands of years. Excess carbon dioxide from fuel combustion eventually might cause floods that could cover much of the earth's present land surface for centuries.
3. At the same time the permissible margin for error has become very much reduced. In the development of steam engines a certain number of boiler explosions was

tolerated as the art was improved. If a single comparable disaster were to occur in a nuclear power plant near a large city, thousands of people might die and a whole region be rendered uninhabitable—a price that the public might be unwilling to pay for nuclear power. Modern science and technology are simply too powerful to permit a trial-and-error approach.

4. It can be argued that the hazards of modern pollutants are small compared to the dangers associated with other human enterprises. For us, today, the fallout hazard is, for example, much smaller than the risks we take on the highway or in the air. But what of the risks we inflict on future generations? No estimate of the actual harm that may be done by fallout, smog, or chemical pollutants can obscure the sober realization that in each case the risk was undertaken before it was fully understood. Science has forgotten that one of its major duties is the prediction and control of human intervention into nature. The true measure of the danger is not represented by the present hazards, but by the disasters that will surely be visited upon us if we dare to enter the new age before us without correcting this basic fault in the scientific enterprise.

   Barry Commoner, Science and Survival (Viking Press, 1966)

GLOSSARY

1. **Pollutant** (noun)—contaminant, hazardous waste, poison, toxic waste.

   Related forms:

   Pollute—(verb)

   Polluted—(adjective)

   Pollutedness—(noun).

2. **Smog** (noun)—air pollution, fog, haze, smoke, soot.

   Related forms:

   Smogless—(adjective).

3. **Strontium** (noun-chemistry)—a bivalent, metallic element whose compounds resemble those of calcium found in nature only in the combined state.

   Related forms:

   Strontic—(adjective).

4. **Persistence** (noun)—perserverance, the continuance of an effect after its cause is removed.

   Antonyms—idleness, indolence, indifference.

5. **Combustion** (noun)—flaming, kindling, turmoil, tumult.

   Related forms:

   Combustive—(adjective).

6. **Radioactive** (adjective)—contaminated, dangerous, irradiated.

7. **Inflict** (verb)—to cause or give, impose, wreak, saddle, dispense.

Related forms:

Inflictable—(adjective)

Inflicter, inflictor—(noun)

Inflictive—(adjective).

8. **Enterprise** (noun)—endeavour, undertaking, venture, plunge, pursuit, zeal, inventiveness.

   Antonyms—idleness, inactivity, apathy.

EXERCISE

A. Answer the following questions briefly:

(*a*) Name the three pollutants which are hazardous for the atmosphere.

(*b*) What would happen if there was an explosion in a nuclear power plant?

(*c*) What does the writer say about the major duties of science?

(*d*) What is the price that the public might not be willing to pay for the nuclear power?

B. Write down a summary of the chapter "Science and Survival". Do you agree with the views of the writer?

C. Fill in the blanks:

(*a*) To build nuclear bombs and kill mosquitoes, we have burdened our bodies with .... and ....

(*b*) In the past the risks taken for technological growth were restricted to ....

(*c*) Excess carbon dioxide from fuel combustion might cause ....

(*d*) A single explosion in a nuclear power plant might ....

(*e*) Synthetic chemicals may remain in the ....

(*f*) One of the major duties of science in the ....

(*g*) DDT and Stronium-90 in the air may interfere ....

D. DIS and UN are common prefixes used to form words which have the opposite meaning.

Example:

1. Agreement — Disagreement
2. Intended — Unintended

Use a prefix with the following words to form a word opposite in meaning:

qualify	integrate
memorable	soluble
obedient	enfranchise
proportion	laden
oblige	pointed

perturbed	intended
favour	registered
	wrap

E. Trial and error is a noun meaning repeated attempts continued until successful. **Write down ten such words and use them in sentences.**

Example:

high and mighty (adjective)—arrogant

F. **Write a paragraph on "How Wealth accumulates and men decay."**

❑❑❑

Chapter 6

Humanistic and Scientific Approaches to Human Activity

—*Moody E. Prior*

1. Some of the essential differences between the two cultures become evident when we compare the humanistic and scientific approaches to human activity. The effect of a scientific ordering is to produce detachment from the individual experiences which are being dealt with; the effect of a humanistic ordering is to encourage involvement.

2. A simple illustration may help to give concreteness to this distinction. In March 1951, the National Safety Council of America predicted that the one millionth traffic fatality since the first recorded automobile death in 1899 would occur on December 22, 1951. And it did the preliminary publicity was aimed at leading up to a solemn response to an awesome national tragedy. The public response was not as to a tragedy; it was the kind proper to a scientific generalization. The lifeless body on the highway was a mere number representing the operation of inexorable impersonal laws and paying tribute to our genius for accurate measurement. One could not expect the response to have been otherwise. The closer an intellectual synthesis approaches the scientific ideal, the more completely will the human act lose its individual significance, and the more fully will we remain detached from its human meaning. Where numerical formulations are involved, this effect becomes especially noticeable.

3. The contrast to this may be seen in literature, for the power of literature lies in its capacity to involve us in its data in a predetermined way, as well as in its capacity never to lose sight of the uniqueness of individual experience. There is a respect in which literature shares with science the capacity to formulate concepts which give us a new outlook and provide a new measure of control over our observations. The world takes on a different aspect after mass and gravity and

evolution have been conceptualized, and in a similar fashion we apprehend experience differently once *Hamlet* on *War and Peace* has been conceptualized.

4. Unlike the creations of science, which are necessity neutral with respect to their human meaning or use, works of literature of necessity involve us in such responses as pity, fear, sorrow, pleasant and bitter choice. We can remain neither detached from nor indifferent to their human meaning. In successful works of literature, our involvement is so complete that they attach our sympathy even where they do not compel our intellectual conviction or belief. Antigone's compulsion to bury her brother, if only with a handful of earth, has its origin in a world of taboos alien to our own, yet her tragedy moves us, at this remove from classical Athens. Because they can do this, works of literature have the capacity to extend the range of our sympathies; they impress upon us the diversity of human experience and direct attention to the values which determine individual choice and through which human actions acquire their meaning.

5. It does not—to state the obvious—follow that a man of letters or a student of literature and the arts and humanistic learning is of necessity more human and wise and perceptive than one who is not a humanist, any more then it follows that a scientist, by virtue of his practice of science, always thinks more logically, clearly, and impartially than the non-scientist. It is reasonable to suppose that continuous involvement in the discipline of science will leave its impression on the ways a man thinks, and that the demands which the practice of science makes upon him will shape his character. By the same token, it is equally reasonable to suppose that the arts and humanistic learning will contribute their share to shaping the attitudes of those who take a serious interest in them. And both, imperceptibly, leave their marks on the age in which they flourish and on the society which gives them support and scope for their activities.

6. There are important functions which the humanities cannot perform, and there are important functions which science cannot perform, if for no other reasons than that they do not ask the same kinds of questions. The humanities cannot take over all the methodological procedures of the sciences nor duplicate the comprehensive inclusiveness of scientific generalizations. And we cannot, therefore, expect that the humanities will provide exact and fully operational solutions to the problems that vex our human conditions. Science lacks the capacity of the arts, especially literature, and of humanistic learning, to become preoccupied with proper human goals and proper human means of attaining them, or to create a concern for the individual experience and to search for its human meaning. And we cannot, therefore, expect its distinctive contributions to lie in the direction of keeping alive and encouraging a sense of our common humanity.

Moody E. Prior, Science and the Humanities (North-western University Press, 1962)

GLOSSARY

1. **Concreteness** (noun)—solid, factual, substantial.

   Antonym—abstract.

   Related forms:

   Concretely—(adverb)

   Con-crete-ness—(noun)

   Con-cre-tive—(adjective)

   Con-cre-tive-ly—(adverb).

2. **Preliminary** (noun)—prefatory, introductory.

   Antonym—concluding.

   Related forms:

   Pre-lim-inari-ly—(adverb).

3. **Solemn** (adjective)—serious, august, devotional.

   Antonyms—Humorous, trivial.

   Related forms:

   Solemn-ly—(adverb)

   Solemn-ness—(noun).

4. **Awesome** (adjective)—inspiring awe, exceptional, outstanding, towering.

   Related forms:

   awe-some-ly—(adverb)

   awe-some-ness—(noun).

5. **Inexorable** (adjective)—unbending, merciless, relentless, die-hard, adamant, implacable.

   Antonyms—flexible, merciful.

   Related forms:

   Inexorability—(noun)

   Inexorableness—(noun)

   Inexorably—(adverb).

6. **Formulate** (verb)—frame, articulate, compose, specify.

   Related forms:

   Formulable—(adjective)

   Formulation—(noun)

   Formulator—(noun).

7. **Predetermined** (adjective)—deliberate, proposed, destined, fixed.

   Antonyms—unarragned, undetermined, unplanned.

8. **Conceptualize** (verb)—develop a thought, visualize mentally.

   Related forms:

   Conceptualization—(Noun)

   Conceptualizer—(Noun).

9. **Apprehend** (verb)—to understand, to be apprehensive, to take into custody.

   Related forms:

   Apprehender—noun.

10. **Perceptive** (adjective)—sensitive, discerning, keen, astute.

    Related forms:

    Perceptive-ly—(adverb)

    Perceptivity—(noun)

    Perceptiveness—(noun).

11. **Vex** (verb)—aggravate, fret, irk, harass, hector, anger.

    Antonym—delight.

    Related forms:

    Vexer—(noun)

    Vexingly—(adverb).

12. **Fatality** (noun)—a disaster resulting in death, casuality, deadliness, mortality.

    Antonyms—birth, entity, existence.

13. **Taboo** (noun)—A ban or prohibition resulting from social custom or emotional aversion, stricture, regulation.

    Antonym—allowance, mentionable.

    Related form:

    Tabooed—(verb).

EXERCISE

A. Answer the following questions in one or two sentences:

(*a*) What is the effect of humanistic approach to human activity?

(*b*) Write down the effect of scientific approach to human activity.

(*c*) How can literature help us in realizing human emotions?

(*d*) Which are the areas where humanities fail?

(*e*) What are the limitations of science?

(*f*) Discuss the role of literature as stated in the chapter.

B. Answer the following questions:

(*a*) What was the prediction of the National Safety Council of America in March 1951?

(*b*) What was the public reaction to the prediction of the National Safety Council of America and why?

(*c*) What is common in both science and literature as stated by the writer in this essay?

(*d*) Where do science and literature differ? Discuss.

(*e*) What are the benefits of reading literature? How does literature extend the range of human emotions?

(*f*) Discuss Moody A. Prior's view on literature. Do you agree with his views?

C. 'Ness' is common suffix used to form nouns from adjectives.

Example:

Unique + ness = Uniqueness

Concrete + ness = Concreteness

Write down ten adjectives which can be used as nouns by adding 'Ness' as a suffix.

D. Write down the antonyms of the following words:

Detachment	Indifferent
Encourage	Diversity
Inexorable	Vex
Apprehend	Distinctive
Methodology	Perceptive

E. Make sentences of your own using the following words in different parts of speech:

Certain	Creation
Distinctive	Involvement
Insist	Capable
Evoke	Totality
Evaluate	Resultant
Generalization	

F. Write your reviews on a book you have studied recently. Maintain the unity, coherence and emphasis while writing the reviews. Introduce variety in your writing.

❑❑❑

Chapter **7**

THE EFFECT OF THE SCIENTIFIC TEMPER ON MAN

—*BERTRAND RUSSELL*

1. The men of the seventeenth century who invented the modern scientific method had an advantage over their *predecessors* in a new mathematical technique. But, in addition to this technical advance, there was another advantage almost more important. Before their time, observation had been *haphazard*, and baseless traditions were accepted as if they were recorded facts. The laws which were invented to account for phenomena were not legitimate *inferences* from observation, but were infected by a belief that nature conformed to human tastes and hopes and fears. The heavenly bodies were supposed to move in circles or complications of circles, because the circle appealed to aesthetic taste as the perfect figure. *Pestilence* and earthquakes were sent to punish sin. Refreshing rain was sent as the reward for virtue. *Comets* foretold the death of princes. Everything on earth and in the heavens had reference to Man or to *aesthetic* tastes which closely resembled those of human beings.
2. The scientific temper *abandoned* this point of view. To find out how nature works, we must forget our own hopes and fears and tastes, and be guided only by careful investigation of fact. Although this may now seem a simple idea, it was, in truth, revolutionary. When *Kepler* discovered that the planets moved in ellipses, not in circles or epicycles, he dealt a death-blow to the interpretation of nature through the medium of human emotions. The essence of the scientific attitude thus inaugurated is this: Nature does what it does, not what we should wish, nor yet what we should fear, but something *blandly* unconscious of our existence.
3. From the realization of this fact, the modern world, for good or evil, has *inexorably*, developed. It is, I repeat, a curious circumstance that most of the men who are thought in the West to be *embodiment* of Western culture are ignorant of this development, which was due, at first, to a tiny minority and is still, in the main,

confined to people whom their literary counterparts regard as narrow and *uncouth* specialists.

4. It is not pure science, however, but scientific technique which represents most xfully the influence of the West upon mankind. The Industrial Revolution, which is still in its infancy, began in a humble way in Lancashire and Yorkshire and on the Clyde. It was hated in the country of its origin by most cultured gentlemen, and was tolerated only because it contributed to the defeat of Napoleon; but its explosive force was so great that, by its own momentum, it spread first to the other countries of the West and, later, to Russia and Asia, which it is completely transforming. It is this, and this alone, that the East is willing to learn from the West. Whether the discovery of this kind of skill is to prove a boon or a disaster is, as yet, an open question. But, whether for good or ill, it is scientific technique that is the main cause of the changes that the world is undergoing.

Bertrand Russell, Fact and Fiction (Allen and Unwin, 1961)

GLOSSARY

1. **Predecessors** (noun)—a person who precedes another in an office, position, etc.; antecedent, ancestor, forerunner.

   Antonyms—Descendant, successor

2. **Haphazard** (adjective)—unplanned, aimless, casual, desulatory, disorganized, unsystematic.

   Antonyms—methodical, systematic, organized.

   Related forms:

   Haphazardness—(noun)

   Haphazardly—(adverb).

3. **Inference** (noun)—conclusion, deduction, assumption, reasoning.

4. **Pestilence** (noun)—a deadly or virulent epidemic disease; something that is considered harmful, destructive or evil.

5. **Abandoned** (adjective)—forsaken or deserted; uninhibited, rejected.

   Related forms:

   Abondonedly—(adverb).

   Antonyms—maintained, supported, defended, cherished.

6. **Bland** (adjective)—pleasantly gentle or agreeable; non-irritating as food or medicine : a bland diet, soft, mild, suave.

   Related forms:

   Blandly—(adverb)

   Blandness—(noun).

   Antonyms—cruel, harsh, irritating, boorish.

7. **Embodiment** (noun)—manifestation, representation, avatar, incarnation.
   Antonym—exclusion.
8. **Uncouth** (adjective)—awkward, clumsy, strange and ungraceful in appearance or form; unusual, discourteous, rude, uncivil.
   Antonym—courteous.
   Related forms:
   Uncouthly—(adverb)
   Uncouthness—(noun).
9. **Temper** (noun)—a particular state of mind or feelings; heat of mind or passion, shown in outbursts of anger, resentment, etc., nature, condition.
   Related forms:
   Temperable–(adjectie)
   Temperamental—(adjective)
   Temperament—(noun)
   Temperer—(noun)
   Temperance—(noun).

EXERCISE

A. Answer the following questions in one or two sentences:

(*a*) What was the essence of the scientific attitude with reference to natural phenomenon?
(*b*) Who are embodiments of western culture?
(*c*) What does the writer mean by "tiny minority"?
(*d*) Why did, according to men of the pre-scientific era, earthquakes occur?
(*e*) Which country was the pioneer in the field of Industrial Revolution?
(*f*) What brought changes that the world is undergoing these days?

B. Answer the following questions in a paragraph:

(*a*) In what ways the beliefs prevalent in the society before 17th century could harm men?
(*b*) How could scientific awareness help mankind?
(*c*) Which point of view was abandoned by the scientific temper and why?
(*d*) Which superstition did prevail in the society before 17th century and how did it influence the people?

C. Which of the following statements are true?

(*a*) Men of the sixteenth century believed that nature acted in accordance with man's tastes and hopes and fears.
(*b*) Men of the seventeenth century accepted baseless traditions as recorded facts.
(*c*) The sixteenth century people believed that comets appeared before the death of a king.

(*d*) The seventeenth century people believed that nature functions without any reference to human hopes, desires and fears.

D. Write down the antonyms of the following words:

Predecessor	Humble
Minority	Inferences
Tolerance	Cultured
Haphazard	Ignorance

E. Write down the synonyms of the following words:

Virtue	Transformation
Reward	Explosive
Realization	Force
Literary	Momentum
Contribute	Tiny

F. Use the following words in sentences of your own in different parts of speech.

Example:

Infect (*v*)—Contaminated water infects thousands of people every year during rainy season.

Infection (N)—Stomach infection is generally caused by the contaminated water.

Infectious (Adj.)—Diarrhoea is an infectious disease caused by the contaminated water.

Advance	Ignore	Accept	Inaugurate
Resemble	Curious	Guide	Transform
Interpret	Contribute		

G. Industrial Revolution—a blessing or curse. Discuss.

H. Write a paragraph on the "Evils of Superstition".

❑❑❑